THE
Crazy Makers

Also by Carol Simontacchi

Your Fat Is Not Your Fault

THE
Crazy Makers

*How the Food Industry
Is Destroying Our Brains and
Harming Our Children*

Carol Simontacchi

JEREMY P. TARCHER/PUTNAM
A MEMBER OF
PENGUIN PUTNAM INC.
NEW YORK

Most Tarcher/Putnam books are available at special quantity discounts for bulk purchases for sales promotions, premiums, fund-raising, and educational needs. Special books or book excerpts also can be created to fit specific needs. For details, write Putnam Special Markets, 375 Hudson Street, New York, NY 10014.

Jeremy P. Tarcher/Putnam
a member of
Penguin Putnam Inc.
375 Hudson Street
New York, NY 10014
www.penguinputnam.com

The Library of Congress catalogued the hardcover edition as follows:

Simontacchi, Carol N.
The crazy makers : how the food industry is destroying our brains and
harming our children / Carol Simontacchi.
p.   cm.
Includes bibliographical references and index.
ISBN 1-58542-035-2
1. Neurotoxicology.   2. Food additives—Toxicology.   I. Title.
RC347.5.S56   2000   99-045188
615.9'54—dc21
ISBN 1-58542-104-9 (paperback edition)
Printed in the United States of America
9   10   8

Book design by Tanya Maiboroda

Acknowledgments

Many people have worked together to bring this book to print. My first "thank you" goes to my family for their patience. Most children look for mom either in the kitchen or the family room. My children look for me in my office. Fortunately, my office is in our home, or they may not have seen me for a long time. Thanks for being there for me.

To my husband, who endured a wife who frequently stared off into space at dinner and who, when innocent bystanders asked about my book, had to listen to the same story over and over again, and seldom interrupted me in my most eloquent moments.

A special note of thanks is extended to Roger Miller, principal, and Marla Lancaster, science teacher, at Vancouver Christian High School, who helped put the research project together. Your enthusiasm, your willingness to help, and your students were terrific. You were good-natured through it all. Well, most of the time . . . Thank you.

Thank you, Karl Riedel of Nature's Life, for providing the breakfast drink and the flax oil for the project. I appreciate your support, and the kids benefited from this great nutrition.

I am grateful to Mead West, N.D., Ian Bier, N.D., Ph.D., and Paula Bickle, Ph.D., who reviewed the manuscript and made several excellent suggestions. Your knowledge of nutrition and medicine was invaluable. Your patients and clients are fortunate to work with such a caring and competent healer.

Thank you, Henry and Carol Kriegel of Kriegel Marketing Group, whose support boosted my morale during the lonely days of writing and researching. Carol, you always made me laugh.

Kerry Stevenson was a wonderful friend to me and her students.

David Groff, my editor, enhanced the quality of the manuscript and made it more understandable. You were wonderful!

And, most of all, thank you to my Heavenly Father, who designed the most wonderful food, perfectly suited to nourishing our brains and our spirits. We have turned aside from Your providence and tried to manufacture our own. How foolish of us.

To mothers and fathers everywhere who are struggling
to understand why their children . . .
can't learn
can't cooperate
can't relax and enjoy life,
Or why their teenagers are . . .
defiant
angry
depressed.

To the men and women who are . . .
unhappy and uncertain
struggling just to maintain their sanity
beset with mental struggles that have appeared
seemingly from nowhere . . .

To the mental health practitioners and educators . . .
frightened at the increase in mental disorders . . .
searching in the wrong places for the answers.

I pray this book will bring some understanding.

Contents

Introduction   1

1
Our Food and Suffering   9

2
Building the Infant Brain   37

3
Nourishing a Baby's Brain   53

4
Feeding Your Child's Brain   87

5
Feeding the Adolescent Brain   135

6
Feeding the Adult Brain   173

7
A Case for Optimism   203

8
A Recipe and Menu Primer   223

Notes   261

Appendix I: Resources   287

Appendix II: Nutritionist Referrals   289

Index   291

THE
Crazy Makers

Introduction

You're making me crazy!" This common phrase is amusing, puzzling. Can one person really make another person crazy? The logical answer is no. Frustrate, anger, humiliate, disturb, inconvenience, or annoy, perhaps.

We use the term so loosely, so frequently, that meaning takes leave. The American Heritage dictionary defines the word as "affected with or suggestive of madness, insane," which conjures up images of insane asylums of long ago, of people staring blankly into the air, or mumbling to themselves as they shuffle down the street. We visualize bizarre behavior or strange movements.

When we say someone makes or drives us crazy we're trying to express frustration, anger, inconvenience. We never actually mean that someone is harming our minds. And anyway, is it really possible for someone to make us lose our sanity? Does anyone possess that power? Bad behavior makes us uncomfortable, but it doesn't damage brain cells.

It may be unlikely that a person could damage our brains, but what about our favorite instant and "fast"-food toys? What about infant formulas and baby foods? These items have become so much a part of the American food culture that we never consider the impact they have on our mental abilities. We've been told over and over that our food choices are contributing to degenerative diseases like cancer, diabetes, and heart disease. Maybe it's time that we explore the possibility that these major American consumer brand "foods" are destroying our brains, too. Cell by cell.

When Rachel Carson wrote the indictment against industrial polluters in *Silent Spring* in the early seventies, environmental rapists were held responsible for their destruction of the world we share. They have been and are being forced to clean up and to undo the damage they've done, either knowingly or unknowingly. They've been held accountable, and rightly so.

What about food industries that wantonly destroy our bodies and our brains, all in the name of profit? We call them "food manufacturing companies," a nomenclature that is chilling. Are they manufacturing food or

1

food artifacts that look, taste, and smell like the real thing? Are they re-defining what we think food to be, while the words "food" and "nutrition" have lost their true meaning in our marketing/advertising-driven world?

Food used to be brilliantly colored fruits and vegetables, rich brown grains, milk and butter, lean game meats, and plump fish wrestled from living rivers and oceans. Food used to be plucked from the garden after a summer of planting, fertilizing, raking, and weeding. It used to have roots deeply embedded in soil that nearly pulsated with life-forms that enriched the earth. Food used to feed on tender green plants and drink out of pristine streams that sparkled with life from the sun.

Food used to be something we ate to give strength to our bodies, to heal us when we were sick, to satisfy an appetite at the end of a day filled with purpose and work. We ate to satisfy a need that arose from deep within. We ate when we were hungry, and savored the food that satisfied that hunger.

Food is different now.

Now, we are sold packages, boxes, artificial flavors, coloring agents, and pseudofoods that strip the body and leave the brain poverty-stricken. The product is colorful and flavorful, but not from natural goodness. The colors come from a chemist's beaker, from FD&C Blue No. 1, Red No. 40, and Yellow No. 5, or from cochineal (from the female insect, coccus cacti from the West Indies). The flavor comes from allyl anthranilate or isopulegol or linalyl benzoate or methyl delta-ionone, while gravies and sauces are thickened with wood fiber and emulsified by dioctyl sodium sulfosuccinate. While some of these agents have been tested for carcinogenic properties, virtually none have been studied to learn their impacts on brain chemistry.

Instead of being eaten when we are physically hungry, food is now consumed to satisfy artificial cravings generated by a brain that isn't working right and whose receptor sites beg for synthetic stimulation from chemicals. We eat, but we're never satisfied. We're full, but we aren't contented.

Looking with a careful eye, there isn't much dissimilarity between environmental rapists and certain food-manufacturing companies. Industrial polluters spill toxic waste into the soil and water. Some food manufacturers slip toxic products into our cereals, our soups, our breads, our beverages, our fish, and call it progress. We carve a culture out of our favorite food icons and we don't link the food artifacts with the depression, the anger, and the heartbreaking assortment of mental illnesses that beset us.

Nutritionists made the initial connection between many of these toxic products and our physical health years ago. Products like margarine can cause heart disease; hormone-injected beef can wreak havoc with our own hormonal systems. We can greatly reduce our risk of certain diseases just by making simple lifestyle and dietary changes.

No one, though, has looked at the rapacious industry that has altered our consumption of basic nutrition so that our brains are deprived of the essential building blocks required by our brains.

The issue of brain health first led me into the health food store and started me on the road to better health through better nutrition when I was in my twenties. I suffered from severe emotional illness in the form of deep depressions, hostility, fatigue, and confusion. Then I read how sugar is a poison, and I greatly reduced my intake. I learned that the B complex is required for enzyme activity in the brain and started eating foods rich in B complex. I learned that I needed amino acids and essential fats to build neurotransmitters and neurohormones, and replaced my nutrient-deficient diet of breads and pastries and cakes and ice cream with wholesome forms of protein and beneficial oils. I started eating vegetables.

I read about brain nutrition and made drastic changes in my diet and became convinced that it was impossible to be contented and emotionally stable while poisoning my brain with the Standard American Diet (SAD).

Consider the common figures we all hear about—how the average American eats over two hundred pounds of sugar and artificial sweeteners per year (over twenty teaspoons per day). The average teenager guzzles twice as much soft drink as milk, but young adults from their twenties to their thirties drink nearly three times more than that.[1] The typical teenage male who drinks soda drinks over forty-two ounces every day, and the habits of girls are only slightly better.

Parents today can't count on school districts to help teach their children good nutritional habits. Many of the people managing the school are in on it, too, earning millions of dollars each year by inviting fast-food chains and soft drink dispensers into schools. They perform a vital function in the marketing scheme of these mega-companies. The schools end up being complicit in "teaching" that it's okay to drink pop instead of water, to eat candy bars instead of fresh fruit, to load the body up on artificial this-and-that—as long as money can be made. Meanwhile, students' test scores are dropping, and the administrations cry out for more funding.

Mind-altering pharmaceutical drugs are one of the leading industries in this country and growing rapidly. Yet no one is making the association between what we are putting into our mouths and the toxic thoughts and feelings that pour out of our brains. Instead, we blame the breakdown of the family, parents, teachers, and political administrations.

In response to public fears about food safety, Congress did seek to regulate the food industry by passing the Delaney Clause, first introduced in 1958. Delaney was considered to be rigorous, forbidding the sale of food containing a substance shown to produce cancer in laboratory animals or humans.

Delaney was amended in the late 1980s as a result of a policy written by the FDA "based on the doctrine of *de minimis,* which holds that the law does not concern itself with trifling matters and that courts should not apply literally the terms of a statute to mandate results. Under this doctrine, if a food additive or any of its metabolites or breakdown products increases the chance of developing cancer over a lifetime by less than one case per million cases of cancer, the threat is considered too small to be of concern." This policy is currently being challenged in court as too lenient to ensure public safety.[2]

As a result of Delaney, the U.S. Food and Drug Administration (FDA) and industry researchers aimed their efforts and money at proving that food additives are benign in terms of producing cancer. When anecdotal and epidemiological reports were delivered to the FDA concerning the neurotoxic effects of some of the top-selling sweetening and flavoring agents, the reports' significance was dismissed by the food industry. Instead of trying to raise the standard, they bolstered efforts to debunk what they were hearing. In some cases, as we will see later, brand-name food manufacturers hired their fiercest critics to work in their legal or public relations departments to silence them.

It is possible that this myopic view was held simply because scientists did not understand much of the biochemical workings of the brain. Not much was known at that time about receptor sites and neurohormones and about the communication link between the endocrine system and the neurological system. Receptors were not isolated until 1972, long after the first neurotoxic chemical hit the food market.[3] In fact, we still don't know as much about these complex systems as we would like.

Receptor sites are embedded in cells all over the body, allowing the endocrine and neurological systems to "talk" to one another. They are activated by bodily produced hormones but are not selective. They also can be activated or shut down by chemicals produced outside the body in doses as low as a few parts per trillion. Such small numbers may be difficult to grasp, but when you understand that infinitesimal amounts of a substance can cause a misfiring of the brain's signals or cause an endocrinological message to be lost, it becomes clear that more research needs to be done if we are to save our minds.

If government regulations were passed requiring food additives and artificial foods to pass the same rigorous standard concerning brain chemistry as was set by the Delaney Clause for cancer prevention, tests would be developed to help us understand how these chemicals influence brain chemistry. But it already costs over $112 million to bring a new substance onto the food or drug market; is the industry willing to ante up more dollars to ensure our safety in terms of brain health? At some point, financial viability is lost. It simply wouldn't be profitable to do it, and when no profit is to be made, it is amazing how quickly the research dollars dry up.

The Crazy Makers will illustrate where the Western world has gone astray in the most fundamental of life issues: the quality of its food supply. During the past century, food-processing companies and their creative marketers have changed the definition and composition of our food. Marketing efforts have been so successful that we no longer think it strange or even unhealthy to drink a liter of Coca-Cola per day instead of water, or that our lunch consists of a bagel with cream cheese, a meal so stripped of nutrition that laboratory rats perish on it.

Many of us think of people who lobby for pure water and pure food as food faddists or health nuts. We call a section in our local supermarket the "Health Food Section." What is the rest of the store called, the "Death and Disease Section"? Food that has been robbed of its beneficial oils is called "heart healthy," while we regulate the amount and types of fats consumed, as if we could convince Mother Nature to change her mind about the importance of balancing essential fatty acids in the sustenance that she bestows.

When I warn lecture attendees that virtually everything written about nutrition in the mainstream press is wrong and potentially harmful, they stare at me in disbelief. Learn about the architecture of the brain, though, and you'll discover what it requires for optimum health. We can start over and learn from nature instead of trying to teach it.

This book will shatter so many popular myths about health and nutrition. When I began the process of pulling research data together, it quickly became clear that I would have to limit the contents of the book to address nutritional issues alone. This one topic could not be covered adequately in these pages, along with a responsible discussion of all the other influences that are contributing to making a deterioration in our brain structure and chemistry.

The information covered here does not include environmental toxins, genetically modified organisms, the influence of recreational or pharmaceutical drugs on the brain, or family or social issues that affect learning and emotions. I write only about food, but how very important it is.

One of the most famous Gallup polls was conducted in September 1989 when pollsters called up a cross section of Americans one evening to ask them what they were eating for dinner. Fifty percent of those people replied that they were having "frozen, packaged, or take-out meals." The next time you start to phone a delivery service, stop by the supermarket, or visit a favorite take-out spot on your way home from work, it would make sense to change this habit—for one simple reason.

Our food is, quite literally, driving us crazy.

1

Our Food and Suffering

Foods of the future will be different from foods currently consumed. They may have different shapes, colors, flavors, nutritional and pharmacologic profiles, and longer shelf-lives. Foods of the future may appear to be unusual and will probably be more intense in flavor and be natural or nature identical . . . They will have extended shelf-lives, primarily due to irradiation. The only limitation may be the imagination of the food technologist.

—Practical Handbook of Nutrition
in Clinical Practice[1]

P ublicly the tales of our mental lives are told in the accounts that splash across the front pages of our newspapers about school shootings or violence in the workplace. We read about them when the latest test scores of students are released, or when a politician or panel of experts holds a town hall discussion or conducts a study about the safety of our neighborhoods and the societal issues plaguing America. They are apparent, too, when a new psychoactive medication achieves FDA approval, and a marketing campaign begins with advertisements in magazines and commercials on televisions that include an ever-present roll of side effects.

More often, though, the most poignant stories of our mental lives are told in conversations along the sidelines of soccer and baseball fields and over backyard fences, as mothers compare stories of their teenagers or whisper the secrets of their own fears and depressions. These are the stories of the men and women, teenagers, and children who struggle to maintain an emotional balance but often succumb to feelings of despair. They struggle with their schoolwork because they can't remember or focus. They fight anger that bubbles up from nowhere and scalds the people they love most dearly. They find themselves fighting irrational fears that hinder them in relationships, schools, and on the job.

Millions of people can't get their mental lives together. Sometimes they resort to violence and seem driven to live a life on the edge of destruction, but most often they suffer in silence. They are the "walking wounded" who seem destined to fail or fall short in life because their minds cannot think properly.

They include Heather, a teenage girl who spent several months in a juvenile facility because of drug addiction. After returning to her home and school, clean and focused on the future, she started dabbling in drugs again, driven by an internal need over which she felt little control. They include Sandra, a middle-aged, well-educated woman who has used antidepressant medications for years in an attempt to control her overwhelming depression. They include Barbara, a mother of five children and wife of a successful businessman who can't shop in her local supermarket because of her intense fear of open spaces. They include Heidi, a beautiful teenage girl who is doing fourth-grade work in school. She isn't learning-disabled. She simply can't concentrate and, as a result of her educational handicap, has turned to drugs and alcohol. They include Jack, a young man who comes from a "good family" but has spent several years in jail because he can't control his impulses. And they include me, thirty years ago, beset by depression and mental confusion so severe that at times I was barely functional.

As part of my research for this book and my desire to understand the walking wounded more clearly, I applied for and received the approval of an Investigational Review Board (IRB). The approval was to conduct a basic study on the influence of diet on cognition and mood states in a local private high school. The study imposed no huge dietary restrictions or changes on the students. They were simply required to arrive at school early each morning for four weeks to consume a nutrient-dense breakfast drink and take tests prior to and after the testing period.

The breakfast drink, supplied by Nature's Life, a California-based supplement manufacturer, was an over-the-counter blend of protein, carbohydrates, vitamins, and minerals specifically designed as a meal replacement. To the drink was added flaxseed oil, a rich source of Omega-3 and Omega-6 fatty acids, both of which are essential to brain function and the production of energy. While the calorie count of the drink was low (less than one-third the daily requirement for calories in adolescents), most of the kids either skipped breakfast altogether or ate such a poor-quality breakfast that the added nutrition could only benefit them.

After obtaining the informed consent of the parents of the students, we gathered the small student body together to explain their part in the project. "You've been chosen to participate in a formal research project that will be published in a book and submitted to peer-reviewed magazines," I explained, searching their faces for some sign of enthusiasm or, at the very least, compliance. I could see none. My reputation as a nutritionist had preceded me. I knew what they were thinking. I saw trepidation and just a little annoyance.

"You'll be asked to take a cognition test and a mood states test. You'll also be divided into two groups: control and test. The control group will continue to eat what they usually eat. The test group will be given a chocolate or vanilla drink every morning just before school starts for four weeks. At the end of the four weeks, both groups will be given the same tests, and we'll learn if the drink has made any difference in how you think and feel."

Despair swept over their faces. I tried to make it sound as attractive as possible, appealing to their adolescent self-interests, but my salesmanship failed. They weren't buying. Reluctant compliance appeared in their eyes, and hands started waving, seeking recognition. "Can I be part of control, please? Let me be control."

Every morning I arrived at the school early to prepare the drink in the blender, pour it into paper cups, and watch the students drink it. I instructed them on filling out food diaries. Flaunting their adolescent independence, several of the test-group kids brought cans of soft drinks every morning to wash down the nutrient-dense breakfast drink, casting a rebellious eye in my direction.

When the final morning rolled around, the student body gathered in the auditorium to retake the tests. First, the principal had a message to deliver. The students' participation in Spirit Week wasn't up to his expectations, and he threatened to curtail planned activities if they didn't put more heart into it. For ten minutes, he lectured. As I listened to the speech and watched the faces of the kids, my heart sank. I could see anger and frustration written all over their faces. This wasn't part of the protocol. No one, test or control, would be in a good mood after this.

After compiling the stats, though, I was astounded by the results. Even after being thoroughly scolded, the kids who had faithfully used the nutrient-dense breakfast drink showed a clear improvement in mood. In fact, the results were so good that we reran the statistics to verify the findings.

The mood test (Profile of Mood States, or POMS) measures six identifiable affects or expression of emotional states, including:

- Tension-Anxiety
- Depression-Dejection
- Anger-Hostility
- Vigor-Activity
- Fatigue-Inertia
- Confusion-Bewilderment

Each of these affective states is rated from 0 to 5, "0" meaning "Not at all," and "5" meaning "Extremely." Being a positive mood, "Vigor-Activity" is calculated as a positive score, while the other states are negative scores. The "Vigor" scores are therefore subtracted from the totals of the other moods. (To obtain a copy of the formal results of the study project, see the resource section on page 289.)

The drink made a significant difference in how these teenagers felt emotionally. It also made a small difference in the cognitive ability of the students, following the pattern of previous studies. The results that we obtained from this study have been replicated in private counseling sessions with nutritionally minded physicians and clinical nutritionists, and in other studies around the world. Food wields a powerful influence over mood, both to our advantage and to our disadvantage.

This study highlighted many questions that need further exploration. In the case of our small study population, would their mood and cognition have improved even more dramatically if they had eaten several daily servings of vegetables and fruits, and limited the amount of sugars and other processed foods? What if they had supplemented their diets with essential fatty acids and good sources of protein?

Why did the breakfast drink make such a powerful difference in their emotional state? Did it normalize their blood sugar (blood sugar provides energy to the energy-hungry brain)? Did the proteins in the drink stimulate the production and activity of neurotransmitters and neurohormones? Did the vitamins and minerals fuel enzymatic reactions? Or all of the above?

I think it is fair to say that if we all simply ate better (if we ate real food) instead of waiting for scientists and studies and the advice of the "professionals," the answers to these questions would be moot. Our obsessive need to check with the experts before we sit down to a meal is unique to this century. Until the past few decades (since man started tampering with the food supply), we ate what nature provided, grew healthy brains, and never gave it another thought.

THE AMERICAN FOOD CULTURE

Over the past century, the American food culture has gone through a transformation so pervasive and enormous that we have almost completely lost sight of what constitutes a normal diet. In our quest for convenience and a shift in culture and priorities, we have pushed aside the notion that the purpose of eating is to provide energy for our day-to-day activities and to maintain the structure of our changing bodies and brains.

Our new foods have changed our bodies and our brains. We look very much the same as our ancestors looked, although, statistically speaking, we are taller and heavier. Our babies are fatter when they are born, and our girls reach puberty several years earlier than their mothers and grandmothers.

Our new foods, however, are altering the ability of our brains to think. They are altering both the structure and function of our physical brains, leaving us less able to cope with stress and more susceptible to the forms of mental illness I outline in the second half of this chapter.

Food has always played an important role beyond that of just providing nutrition. Our ancestors who were farmers and hunters had a kind of spiritual relationship with their food because they watched it grow. They handled it and tended it in the field and sought it out in the forest. When these people served food, they knew that it was the stuff that built strong, vibrant children. A heavily laden table was the sign of a good provider, a sign that God and nature had been good to them.

While the food was simmering on the stove or baking in the oven, the aroma prepared the family to receive the meal. Salivary glands pumped out digestive juices well ahead of the first bite. The stomach, liver, pancreas, and other organs of digestion anticipated the meal's arrival. The mind and the body participated in the preparation, intake, and metabolization of the food. Eating was a fundamentally holistic experience, and as such, nourished the body and the mind.

Shifts in the way we procure our food and in the types and quality we are consuming, however, have left our brains and bodies deficient in the building materials that the brain needs in the first two years of life when it is undergoing its most critical period of development. Food has been stripped of the nutrients needed to remodel the brain later in life. We've been robbed of the very materials needed to create the neurohormones and neurotransmitters that comprise our body's communication system.

How did we let this happen?

Beginning in the 1800s, agriculture yielded to technology. In the latter part of that century the rolling mill brought white flour to the masses. Earlier mills were inefficient in removing all the bran and germ from the grain; however, the grain was still relatively rich in vitamins and minerals, more nutritious than it is today.

In her book *The Food Factor*, Barbara Griggs explains how "until the

The fictitious person named Betty Crocker was first created in 1921 as a pen name for General Mills' consumer response department and, under her well-recognized image, turned several generations of Americans away from their traditional foods and toward highly processed, less-nutritious foods.

Excerpts from the promotional materials of General Mills explain how this happened: "We are on safari in Africa. How the women who live on remote farms in Kenya find the time and energy to devote to the finer points of baking while dealing with lions, leopards and locust plagues is remarkable. . . . The flour used here is simply ground wheat, not so fine nor white as General Mills Softasilk cake flour. Could you possibly tell us . . . what might be done to improve the quality of the Kenya flour?" (Letter from Mrs. Ernest Hemingway, 1954.)

The response of General Mills: "There isn't much your friends can do in their own kitchens to improve their flour, but they might refine the flour some by putting it through a sifter, fine strainer or through loosely woven silk cloth . . ."

By 1940, nine out of ten American homemakers knew Betty Crocker. She was the second-best-known woman in America, following First Lady Eleanor Roosevelt.[2]

invention of roller milling, wheat and other grains had been ground in stone mills to produce a whole-wheat, creamy-colored flour. For the fine white bread of the rich—which the poor also hankered for hopelessly—this flour was sifted through finer and finer cloths to get rid of the bran and produce a flour of perhaps eighty-five or ninety percent extraction, as we would say today. What was removed in this sifting was the coarse outer covering of the wheat, its bran—which we now know to be rich both in minerals and the roughage of which constipated modern man is so sorely in need. But even the most dedicated sifting never removed all of the germ of the wheat; and this, we now know, is rich in the B-complex vitamins, in an oil containing vitamin E, and in essential fatty acids. Thus what was considered fine white flour at the beginning of the nineteenth century was still relatively nutritious and vitamin-rich.

"The new roller mills revolutionized man's most basic foodstuff. They split the wheat grain into a thousand fragments; with mechanical thoroughness they sifted it into a dozen different streams, so that at the touch of a button, the miller could now select for his customers only the fine starchy endosperm, to give them a flour white as never before."[3]

Poor people could enjoy soft, fluffy bread instead of the heavy, dark bread that was so inexpensive. This event heralded the beginning of the food-processing industry, an industry that exploded with new technology in the twentieth century. Side by side with food technology came changes in agriculture that denuded the soil of nutrients. The soil itself, and the foods grown in it, became impoverished.

Sugar consumption was about ten pounds per year in 1821, but after the turn of the century, sugar intake began to soar, rising decade by decade to over 147 pounds per person in 1993, with noncaloric sweeteners adding another fifty pounds per person in the United States. In 1942, the American Medical Association issued a warning about sugar consumption, reporting, "The consumption of sugar and of other relatively pure carbohydrates has become so great during recent years that it presents a serious obstacle to the improved nutrition of the general public."[4] Nobody listened then, and the AMA has since become nearly silent on the subject.

Consider these nutritional stats:

- From 1986 through 1996, sugar intake has grown by 20 percent, now accounting for over 20 percent of teenagers' calories.[5] Rancid, processed fats account for another 50 percent of all calories consumed by teenagers.

- At the birth of a new century and millennium, more than one-third of all meals are eaten away from home, with the vast majority of these meals taken at fast-food restaurants. Sales in restaurants and bars have nearly tripled just since 1980, with nearly $60 billion in annual sales.

- Consumption of fresh produce has plummeted, with fresh apples down 75 percent, fresh cabbage down 65 percent, fresh potatoes down 74 percent, and fresh melons down 50 percent. The average American eats less than two servings of both fruits and vegetables per day, with a quarter of servings in the form of greasy, nutrient-dead french fries.

- Consumption of processed fruits has increased 913 percent, processed vegetables are up 306 percent, and processed fats and oils are up 139 percent. Just between 1960 and 1981, soft drink consumption increased 182 percent, food color consumption increased 1,006 percent, and corn syrup is up 291 percent.[6]

There has been a long chain of concerned doctors and nutritionists who tried to awaken America's conscience about the way they were eating, starting around the turn of the century. Dr. Max Bircher-Benner, Dr. Robert McCarrison, Dr. William Howard Hay, Dr. Henry Bieler, Dr. John Tilden, Gaylord Hauser, E. V. McColum (writer for *McCall Magazine*), Paul Bragg, and hundreds of other lesser-known teachers traveled around the world, wrote books, taught to huge audiences, and tried to open the eyes of the medical community about the hazards of eating highly processed foods. They were often censored by their fellow doctors, but they never softened their message.

During the earlier part of the century, periods of food shortages provided doctors with a unique opportunity to study the influence of processed foods on the health of entire nations. During World War I and World War II, when people often couldn't afford such luxuries as sugar and white flour, or these foods were restricted by the government, they resorted to eating fresh vegetables, whole grains, and limited amounts of beef. Researchers found that the incidence of chronic disease and death dropped during these periods of deprivation.

The Danes enjoyed a diet rich in pork and dairy products. During the Allied blockade, Professor Mikkel Hindhede was appointed Food Adviser to the Danish Government, and following his instructions, eighty percent of the pigs and one-sixth of the cattle were slaughtered to save grain. To further save grain, the distillation of spirits was banned, causing shortages of hard liquor as well as beef and pork.

The Danes were forced to eat their traditional black rugbrød made from whole rye, enriched with extra wheat bran and barley meal. The bread wasn't light and fluffy; it was dark and hard, but they ate it with lots of greens, potatoes and root vegetables, oatmeal, butter, milk, a little cheese, and fruit, with little or no meat. They didn't have access to liquor at all.

During the lean years, the Danish death rate fell to the lowest ever recorded in a European country. Hindhede concluded, "It would seem, then, that the principal cause of death lies in food and drink."[7]

McCarrison carried out rat studies, comparing the typical rat diet with the typical British diet of white bread and margarine, sweetened tea, boiled vegetables, and tinned meat. In her book *The Food Factor*, author Barbara Griggs wrote, "Stunted and nervous, with lacklustre coats, they snapped at the attendant and took to cannibalism after three days; after they'd killed and eaten three of their number, they were segregated, to die of pneumonia and a variety of gastro-intestinal disorders."[8]

Dr. Theron Randolph, a Chicago allergist, found a similar link with food and mental states when he discovered that both environmental toxins and food could provoke cerebral allergies. Griggs wrote: "The sickness such chemicals could cause affected 'man in his totality': not merely physical symptoms such as colitis, migraine, arthritis, and the classic asthma and rhinitis, vague joint pains, and general malaise, but many of the mental problems then considered the exclusive province of the psychiatrist—depression, panic attacks, nervous irritability." Austrian psychiatrist Francis Hare continued to explore this topic in his book *The Food Factor in Disease,* observing that the difficulty lies in the inability to metabolize sugars and starches.[9]

Joseph Beasley, author of *The Kellogg Report,* wrote: "Sugar's amazing rise has been paralleled by the dramatic rise in arterial disease and other chronic conditions during this century, leading some experts to wonder about the physiological (and psychological) impact of consuming enormous quantities of what is very nearly pure blood sugar. Indeed, few realize today just how relatively new sugar is to the human diet. It was the inscrutable Jesuits, in 1751, who introduced the United States to sugar—bringing cane plants to New Orleans from Haiti—and by 1791 commercial production of this new delicacy was humming."[10]

Sugar consumption began to rise steeply in the early 1900s, but when these people were teaching, it was a mere fraction of what it is today. The same holds true with white flour and other processed foods.

Our great-grandparents mostly drank water out of the well or the swift-flowing stream. We don't drink much water anymore. Alcohol and soft drink sales are skyrocketing, nearly doubling in the past twenty years. Americans drink more than thirty-seven gallons of alcoholic beverages per year, and soft drinks account for another fifty gallons per year. According to the McDonald's Nutrition Facts, the child's soft-drink portion is twelve ounces, and the small size is sixteen ounces. The child's serving of Coca-Cola Classic contains nearly ten teaspoons of sugar. The large serving is thirty-two fluid ounces, providing nearly twenty-nine teaspoons of sugar.

The *Nutrition Action Healthletter,* published by the Center for Science in the Public Interest, states that Americans drank twice as many soft drinks in 1997 as they did in 1973, and forty-three percent more than in 1985. Americans gulp twice as much soda as milk and nearly six times more soda than fruit juice. Manufacturers produce enough pop to provide every American with fifty-four gallons per year. The average teenage boy who drinks soda drinks three and one-half cans per day, and girls drink nearly that much.[11]

Even so, the soft drink industry is using ever more aggressive marketing techniques to reach a larger and larger constituency. Coca-Cola alone spent $277 million in advertising in 1997; Pepsi spent close to $200 million. Pepsi hopes to take an even larger share of the forty-seven billion beverage servings sold around the world. As the *Nutrition Action Healthletter* laments, "We are drowning in liquid candy."

You aren't off the hook if you eat the typical American breakfast of a bowl of dry cereal and a cup of coffee. Breakfast cereals marketed to very young children contain more sugar, ounce per ounce, than soft drinks. Where Pepsi contains 1.2 teaspoons of sugar per ounce, Lucky Charms cereal contains 2.8 teaspoons per ounce, Froot Loops contains 3.3 teaspoons per ounce, and Quaker Instant Oatmeal, Cinnamon and Spice–flavored, contains 4.3 teaspoons per ounce. And a jar of Heinz Custard Pudding (baby food) contains nearly four teaspoons of sugar, roughly the same amount as can be found in the same portion size of any soft drink.

No one wants to admit that their eating habits are less than optimum, especially parents who work hard to put food on the table and keep their kids healthy. Even though the typical American eats two hundred pounds of sugar and artificial sweeteners per year (many who are health conscious eat a mere fraction of that amount, so the average person actually consumes more than the averages), we can't imagine ourselves eating this much sugar.

Examining the food diaries of real teenagers and adults helps us understand the magnitude of our dietary problem. I distributed food diaries to fifty-five students in a low- to middle-class high school and asked them to complete the diaries every day for one week. What follows is a diet diary of a very honest teenager:

	Day 1	Day 2	Day 3
Breakfast	Orange juice Ham and cheese sandwich	Cereal and milk	Biscuits and eggs
Lunch	Water	Ham sandwich	Chicken noodle soup

Dinner	2 hot dogs	Chicken potpie	Hot dogs
Beverages	Water (1 cup)	Apple juice Water	Punch Water
Snacks	Cheese and crackers	Banana	Orange
	Day 4	*Day 5*	*Day 6*
Breakfast	Bread	Cornflakes and milk	Grits and eggs
Lunch	Double cheeseburger with pickles	Tuna sandwich	Applesauce
Dinner	Burrito with beef and beans	Sirloin burger with country vegetables	Steak and potatoes
Beverages	Water	Water	Water
Snacks		Applesauce	Fruit

This diary was picked at random out of a stack of more than one hundred diaries and is better than most. At least this kid drank water and ate an occasional fruit, which is unusual for a high-schooler.

What about kids attending an upper- to middle-class private school? Surely their diets would be much better?

	Day 1	*Day 2*	*Day 3*
Breakfast	Pepperoni pizza (2 slices)	Cinnamon roll	Nothing
Lunch	Pepperoni pizza (2 slices)	Pepperoni pizza (2 slices)	Peanut-butter-and-jelly sandwich Popcorn cake Kumquat
Dinner	Cheeseburger with ketchup, mustard, and mayonnaise	Chicken with carrots, broccoli stir-fry with noodles and white rice Crescent rolls	Leftovers from the night before

Snacks	White popcorn Cheddar popcorn	Doritos	
Beverages	Water (2 cups) Mountain Dew (1 can) Milk (2 cups)	Milk (1 cup) Water (2 cups) 7UP (1 cup)	Milk (1 cup) Apple juice (½ cup) Water (3 cups) Coke (2 cups)

	Day 4	Day 5
Breakfast	Nothing	Brownie
Lunch	Teriyaki chicken frozen dinner	Teriyaki chicken frozen dinner Brownie
Dinner	Tacos with cheese and lettuce on soft tortilla	Chicken with rice Small baked potato
Snacks	Brownie Marshmallows	Brownie
Beverages	Milk (3½ cups) Mountain Dew (½ can) Water (1 cup)	Chocolate milk (1 cup) Raspberry pop (2½ cups) Tetley Tea (1½ cups)

It is easy to see why our teenagers are overweight and have trouble getting up in the morning.

Adults don't eat any better than kids, according to national statistics and my client records. It is not uncommon to see a seven-day food diary containing twenty-one meals with almost no vegetables, no fruit, no protein, and no water.

In addition to our own habits, the health industry has taken us further afield from food in its natural form and is creatively trying to manipulate the genetic structure of foods to make them more nutritious. Food technologists manufacture products in an attempt to raise the level of nutrition, but it isn't working. The level of nutrition in the Western culture, upper or lower class, is appalling.

Witness the explosion of fat-free foods and the emergence of fat substitutes marketed to us. Walk the aisles of the frozen-food section in your supermarket and count how many entrées are offered to busy parents. Healthy Choice? Lean Cuisine? Heat it in your microwave and offer it to a European or African or Asian or Latin ancestor, and see them turn away in disgust.

THE CURRENT STATE OF OUR MINDS

Despair about our mental health seems to be closing in on us.

While nearly one in two adults experiences a mental disorder at some point in his life, each year one in four people will be victimized by a mental disorder. Depression seems to be the most common, although milder forms of mental angst, such as panic disorders and social phobias, don't necessarily show up in the figures and may affect more people than clinical depression:

- Since World War II, annual prevalence rates of depression have been soaring, becoming increasingly common in young men.[12]

- More than 10 percent of the population has been diagnosed with some form of mental illness (schizophrenia, phobias, depression, and anxiety disorders).

- Up to 24 percent of adults experience a mental health crisis in any given year.[13]

- Five to six million Americans suffer from obsessive-compulsive disorder (OCD), yet fewer than 20 percent seek help.[14]

- Seven to 14 percent of children will experience an episode of major depression before the age of 15.[15]

Within our current mental health epidemic are smaller epidemics of different forms of mental illness, some of which have been with us for a long time, some that are new forms of mental illness. Eating disorders were relatively uncommon among children in the past, for example, but now are common in the very young. Others, like social phobias, are relatively unknown in the lay community but are becoming widely recognized in the professional community. Are these smaller epidemics simply a matter of semantics, labeling conditions that are not true "conditions" but simply an expression of individuality? Or are we developing new expressions of mental illness?

Mental health professionals attempt to deal with this onslaught of mentally ill patients by prescribing drugs. Other than "talk therapy," they have few options. To help put this all into perspective before we move on to another alternative, what follows is a summary of the most widespread battles we are fighting in a mental health war that is exacting its toll on all of us.

THE LEGAL DRUG CULTURE

A trend among the very young is the increased use of drugs like Ritalin and Prozac, prescribed by their doctors and approved, out of desperation, by their parents. Ostensibly, the drugs are used to help kids settle down in class and concentrate on their schoolwork. In some cases, medication may be necessary to achieve that, but questions remain about the numbers of kids on stimulants and the long-term effects of these powerful psychotrophics. Consider these statistics:

- Prozac ranks fifth in the top-ten pharmaceuticals, up 144 percent since it breezed into the marketplace in 1991. In the year 1996–97, prescriptions for Prozac increased over 100 percent, from 111,905 to 273,531.

- Over $7 billion is spent on antidepressants per year.

- Children ages thirteen to eighteen used 148,000 prescriptions for Prozac in 1995, 217,000 prescriptions in 1996 (up 47 percent). Children ages six to twelve used 51,000 prescriptions in 1995, 203,000 prescriptions in 1996 (up 209 percent).

- Children ages thirteen to eighteen used 155,000 Zoloft prescriptions in 1995, 199,000 prescriptions in 1996 (up 28 percent). Children ages six to twelve used 33,000 Zoloft prescriptions in 1995, 46,000 prescriptions in 1996 (up 39 percent).

- Paxil showed the same alarming increases, up 48 percent in children ages 13 to 18, and up 113 percent in children ages 6 to 12.[16]

- The most popular form of antidepressants, serotonin reuptake inhibitors (SSRIs), account for over 40,133,000 prescriptions each year, costing consumers over $3 billion annually, a gain of some 35 percent per year.[17]

According to an article in the *Seattle Times*, antidepressant sales to adults have slowed and companies are looking for new customers. "Formal FDA clearance of antidepressants for children would mean companies could directly market them for use by children. 'It would be a positive,' said Barbara Ryan, managing director of Alex, Brown & Sons, which analyzes the pharmaceutical industry. 'The companies are looking for expanded markets.'" Some manufacturers are preparing the drug in mint- and orange-flavored versions to make them more accessible to younger and younger children.[18]

In her book *Natural Treatments for ADD and Hyperactivity*, Dr. Skye Weintraub, N.D., writes, "One child out of every five suffers from a varying degree of behavior problems . . . ADD is quickly becoming one of the most common health disorders today. It may now affect up to twenty percent of children in the American school."[19] Conservative estimates of the number of children diagnosed with ADD/ADHD range from three to six percent of the school-age population (elementary through high school).[20]

According to *The New York Times*, educators agree that there is a marked increase in the number of children in school on medication, yet the numbers are difficult to document because school districts don't track how many children are being medicated for mental disorders. Unless the medicine is administered within the schoolday (as Ritalin often is) by a school nurse, there is no way for the school to know how many of their students are on medication.[21]

The Drug Illusion

It would seem that with the increased use of pharmaceutical agents prescribed to control depression and aggression, violence would be (should be) decreasing. The illusion is that if we can just prescribe enough pills, if we can just do enough psychotherapy, if we can just control the mind through whatever means are available to us, we should be able to create a well-functioning individual and society. The opposite is happening. We're trying to screw the lid down more tightly, but rage keeps exploding out from different sources.

The Springfield, Oregon, newspaper printed these figures after school shootings there in 1998:

- Number of industrialized countries in the world with worse crime rates than the United States': 0
- Percent increase in the last decade in the arrest rate for juveniles for murder: 93
- Percent of high school students who now carry a firearm, knife, razor, or club on a regular basis: 20

- Percent of public elementary and secondary schools reporting one or more incidents of violence that needed to be reported to law enforcement officials: 57
- Percent of Oregon high school students in 1997 who said they have been physically or sexually abused: 33
- Percent who reported having been in a fight on school property: 13[22]

Rates of violence are higher in the United States than anywhere else in the industrialized world.[23] The childhood homicide rate is five times higher in the United States than in all other countries combined, with eighty-six percent of all firearm-related childhood deaths occurring in the United States. This rate is almost twelve times higher than in all other countries combined. While the overall death rate for children in the United States declined from 1950 to 1993, childhood homicide rates tripled and suicide rates quadrupled.[24]

- U.S. teen suicide rates increased nearly 30 percent from 1980 to 1992.

- Black youth are particularly likely to commit suicide when depressed. From 1980 to 1995, the suicide rate for black youths ages 10 to 19 years more than doubled, becoming the third-leading cause of death among blacks.[25]

- Psychiatric hospitals increased inpatient admissions from 46.2 per 100,000 population in 1969, to over 156 per 100,000 population in 1988, and during the same period of time outpatient additions increased from 12.8 per 100,000 to 51.2 per 100,000.[26]

- In 1990, suicide was the fifth-leading cause of years of potential life lost before the age of sixty-five.[27]

- Seventy-three percent of all deaths among young people result from four causes: motor vehicle crashes, unintentional injuries, homicide, and suicide.

- Over 20 percent of students have seriously considered suicide during the preceding twelve months.[28]

The Drug Reality

The U.S. government spends billions of dollars on the war against drugs each year, a war that we are losing faster and faster and faster. On top of the street drugs is alcohol abuse. In the past few years, there has been an explosion in the amount of hard liquor consumed, a substantial portion in the form of premixed spirit-based drinks. Young people have been targeted for the sale of these types of drinks. The consumer profile for mixed drinks used to be older men. It is now becoming the drink of choice for younger people, especially teenage girls:[29]

- From the year 1991 to 1996, there was a 24 percent increase in "drug episodes" brought to the attention of emergency rooms in hospitals, from suicide attempts, overdoses, unexpected reactions, and other reasons.

- Heroin-related episodes have been increasing steadily since the early 1980s, with a 108 percent increase (from 33,000 to 70,500) between 1990 and 1996.

- Marijuana- and hashish-related episodes rose 219 percent since 1990.[30]

For every single category of illicit drug use (alcohol, nicotine, and street drugs), usage is increasing, year by year, not just in raw numbers but in percentages. While the population as a whole is growing, the rate of drug use is growing faster, outdistancing population statistics.

More Than a Bad Day at Work

The fear of violence in the workplace is increasing to the point that more and more companies are hiring consultants to help them deal with that very possibility. The threat of violence now ranks as the number-one security threat to workers, according to Pinkerton, Inc.

In 1993, there were 1,063 work-related homicides in the United States, with homicide becoming the second-leading cause of fatal occupational injuries.[31] The majority of workplace homicides occurred during robberies; however, there is a growing trend toward revenge killings as well, where alcohol, drugs, or mental illness is involved:[32]

- 3.5 million personal crime victimizations occur annually in the workplace, including 900,000 aggravated and simple assaults and 100,000 rapes and robberies.[33]

- Murder is the leading cause of death for women in the workplace and the second-leading cause of death for men, according to the U.S. Department of Labor, Bureau of Statistics, 1995.

THE SILENT SUFFERING

Although one in every four Americans (about forty-one million people) suffer from mental disorders each year, many of these individuals never see a doctor for their symptoms. They suffer in silence rather than bare their souls to the professionals. They struggle with what one author calls "shadow syndromes" of mental illness.[34]

In their book *Shadow Syndromes*, authors John Ratey and Catherine

Johnson explain that these people do not fit the clinical profile of a full-blown bipolar disorder, schizophrenia, or other mental disorders. Enough of the symptoms are present to cause some measure of dysfunction, but not enough to drive them to seek help.

Mental illness is not black-and-white; you either have it or you don't. There are shades and degrees of psychotherapy. We all have our quirks and peculiarities. We can all see ourselves when someone recites a list of symptoms. Most people do not seek the counsel of a health care professional when they experience episodes of depression or anxiety. Most people wait until they are referred by a loved one or until they can no longer cope with the symptoms before they ask for help.

These people do not appear anywhere in the statistics for mental illness. If we could count the numbers of us who suffer from subclinical forms of mental illness and add them into the figures, it may well include someone in your family.

Social Anxiety

Social interaction is a fundamental human need that is stimulating and gratifying for most of us, but what about individuals with an irrational fear of other people or of social activity? Psychologists call this new category of mental illness "social anxiety disorder" or "social phobia," a biological brain disorder that causes people to dread and avoid everyday social situations so severely that the individual's social, family, and professional life is disrupted.[35] Up to ten million Americans suffer with this condition.

Children Who Hurt Themselves

Self-mutilation is a form of psychological distress of which no one knows the cause or the treatment. When a client of mine, Cassie, came back from her summerlong mission trip, her mother was shocked. Etched deeply into the skin in Cassie's upper arm were the words "Help Me," and numerous other gashes were evident, from her wrist to her shoulder. "What did you do to yourself?" her mother gasped. "Oh, that . . ." Cassie appeared to shrug it off, but her mother could see the pain in her eyes. "I did it to relieve tension. It didn't really hurt much."

Several months later during a stressful time, Cassie burned deep holes into her arm with cigarettes. When her mother saw the wounds, she gasped in horror. "It makes me feel better . . ." Cassie explained. The scar goes all the way into the deep tissue; it will never fade.

It is known that self-mutilation (also called self-mutilation behaviors, or SMB) has been on the rise since the 1960s. The problem with obtaining accurate statistics on this condition is that mutilators frequently commit their acts in private, knowing that their acts are socially stigmatizing. They conceal their wounds from their doctors. When their wounds are revealed to medical personnel, they often recite tales of accidents or blame attacks from other people.[36]

Some studies indicate that about one percent of Americans injure themselves, but these figures are hopelessly inadequate. According to the book *Self-Mutilation,* the problem is taking on major proportions, affecting possibly over one million people in America, and is growing.[37]

Eating Disorders

Growing numbers of children struggle with eating disorders and associated mental problems. Young women are at greater risk than young men. Over the past ten to twenty years, women ages fifteen to twenty-five have seen the largest increases. Over one percent of women have been diagnosed with anorexia nervosa and nearly four percent with bulimia, the statistical rates having doubled over the past twenty years.

However, subclinical levels of eating disorders are now estimated to be as high as ten percent of the population and rising. Hand in hand with eating disorders is an increase in disturbed or negative body-image attitudes, which may afflict nearly every teenager, especially young girls.[38]

The profile of the eating-disordered patient sounds like the typical American girl. Anorexics are preoccupied with diets and dieting and with the shape of their bodies. They tend to be meticulous, compulsive, intelligent, and driven to achieve. They often hoard, conceal, and waste food, even while they prepare delicious meals for the rest of the family. Bulimia, another growing form of eating disorders, presents a different clinical picture. Bulimics engage in episodes of binge eating, during which they lose control of their eating, then either vomit the food, use laxatives and/or diuretics to get rid of the excess amounts of food, or overexercise to burn the calories. Bulimics tend not to be emaciated and are prone to impulsive behavior and depression.

Girls with eating disorders struggle with a distorted sense of true body size, seeing their thin bodies as fat or disproportioned. Several years ago, I counseled a young woman who was working through a number of mental challenges. We stood in front of a full-length mirror. She was dressed in shorts; her ten-year-old figure was well shaped. As she looked at herself in the mirror, she jiggled her thighs and sighed, "I'm really fat, aren't I?"

I jiggled my thighs and asked, "Am I fat?"

She giggled. "Of course not."

"You aren't fat, either. Thighs jiggle as the muscle moves around." But she couldn't see it. Her mind contradicted the mirror.

Because these young girls misperceive themselves as overweight, they fight food and they fight their own negative body image, some even going so far as to try to harm themselves.

Cognitive Disorders

In his book *The Kellogg Report: The Impact of Nutrition, Environment & Lifestyle on the Health of Americans*, Joseph Beasley, M.D., cites study after study showing a downward trend in cognitive ability, or our ability to think and reason. According to Beasley, SAT scores have declined every year for sixteen years and were, as of 1980, the lowest in the fifty-year history of the test.[39] SAT scores of college-bound seniors were lower in 1994 than they were in the counterculture sixties.[40]

What has since happened is nearly impossible to tell; educators disagree on how to assess how kids are learning. But the feeling is that schools are not doing well, that students are not learning as well as they should, that something is amiss in the classroom.

> - Forty percent of fourth-graders can't read at a basic level.[41]
> - Forty percent of the 52,000 fourth-graders performed at the "partially proficient" or "unsatisfactory" level in reading, and in writing, forty-three percent were partially proficient and twenty-two percent were unsatisfactory.
> - Three elementary schools out of seventy-nine in the Denver school district had no fourth-graders score at the proficient or advanced level in writing.[42]

According to *Teacher Magazine,* by the time American kids reach the twelfth grade, only Lithuania, Cyprus, and South Africa fare worse out of twenty-one nations.[43]

It is difficult to assess how our kids are really doing in school, because the tests have been progressively "dumbed down." Because children score so poorly on such national tests as the California Achievement Test—thereby showing what a poor job the schools are doing—they changed the tests. They lowered the standards—and still the scores keep dropping.

Jane Healy, Ph.D., wrote in her book *Endangered Minds,* ". . . because administrators tend to shun tests that make their children look stupid (and themselves incompetent), publishers are naturally pressured to produce tests to make kids look good. When I compared the 1964, 1972, and 1982 forms on a typical, widely used reading test, I was shocked to observe the differences. Each successive edition was so much easier than the previous one that it was hard to believe they were actually given to children of the same grade level! . . . The most scary of all is a new 'Advanced' form, designed for ninth-graders and published in 1988 which calls on such complex skills as reading a menu in a fast-food restaurant."[44]

THE SEARCH FOR AN ANSWER

Fingers are pointed at inadequate schools, inadequate parenting, and an inadequate social structure. Parents blame the schools for not controlling the classrooms so their kids can learn, or they blame the school district for cutting back on teaching staff. Schools blame parents for not spending more time with their kids or for lax discipline.

Parents blame the government for not providing more and better jobs, for social inequalities, and for unsafe streets. The government tries to do all things for all people, so it raises the taxes—so parents have to spend more time at work just to pay their rising tax bills, thus giving them less time with their kids. The media and society in general focus blame on parents and everyone else.

Meanwhile, we're spending more money on education than we've ever spent and the SAT scores continue to drop. While inequality still exists in our society, inequality is a greater problem in some of the less developed countries, and their crime rate and rates of mental illness are lower than here in the United States.

When we discuss the psyche, we tend to think in mystical terms. We can't see the mind; we can't touch the mind; we can't taste the mind. The mind seems to float somewhere outside and separate from our flesh and blood. It is nontangible, ethereal.

When a loved one suffers from a mental illness, the symptoms frighten us because we can't see the illness. It seems to mimic the qualities of the mind—separate, nonphysical, and imposed upon us. Physical illnesses, although equally serious, don't seem as frightening unless our lives are in danger.

Family and friends often say, "Pull yourself together. Stop feeling sorry for yourself. You shouldn't worry so much," as if one could will the disease away.

Physically ill people are not chastened for their illnesses, but mentally ill people are often chided for expressing theirs. If they are not chastised, they are avoided, ostracized, as if the disease were catching. We are uncomfortable in their presence.

The brain is often pictured as different from the mind. When we think of the brain, we think in tangible terms because we can visualize the wrinkles and folds of the gray matter that occupies the space inside our cranium. We understand that the physical brain requires physical matter (oxygen and blood sugar) to quench its incessant appetite for fuel. We have recently begun to understand that the brain sends messages via neurotransmitters and neurohormones between ten trillion nerve cells.

With all that we know about the brain, we still don't think of our brains or our minds as a product of our mother's breakfast, lunch, and dinner. We don't associate the architecture of the nerve cell with our seafood and salad—or our Twinkies and Pepsis. We seldom investigate if we are supplying our gray matter with the essential building blocks that form the structure of that neuronal network. When the brain malfunctions, sending bizarre messages to our mouths or limbs, we never wonder if the toxic thought is the product of a toxic lunch.

We've been told that our brains are formed within the first two years of our lives, and from then until death, little change can be expected. We have forgotten that within those critical first two years of life, from conception through the breast-feeding period, the brain will not develop properly if the maternal diet doesn't supply the building blocks to build it.

We don't realize that within those intricate nerve cells, every day of our teenage and adult lives, blocks are quietly removed and replaced with new material. New fats. New proteins. New minerals. New vitamins. Where do those blocks come from? From our food. From our water.

But if the blocks have been removed from the food (if our food is, instead, made of materials for which the brain has no use), the brain cannot remodel itself. It has nothing to build with. It cannot make neurotransmitters and hormones from nothing.

In order to achieve vibrant brain health, we must study brain nutrition, because it is in our diets that we will find many of the answers for which we've been looking. The diet must supply the blocks to build and maintain the brain. The diet is the one major change in our culture over the past century that has altered the physical state of our brains and, therefore, altered the state of our minds. We must feed our brains if we want them to be healthy.

How does nutrition affect brain structure and chemistry? The subject of brain chemistry may be extremely complex, much too difficult for most of us to understand. But the subject of brain nutrition is much simpler.

Let's begin with our babies.

2

Building the Infant Brain

It is now recognized by leading workers in the field that behavior is determined by the functioning of the brain, and that the functioning of the brain is dependent on its composition and its structure.

—LINUS PAULING[1]

A human egg drops out of the ovarian sac and slowly floats down the fallopian tube, its core pulsating with life. Containing over 300,000 mitochondria, or tiny energy-production factories, it harbors enough energy to fuel explosive growth, should fertilization occur.

As the egg meanders down the passage, it encounters millions of microscopic sperm swimming in the opposite direction—up the fallopian tube. Though infinitesimally smaller, the sperm also pulsate with life. At the moment they meet, the egg is surrounded by flagellating sperm bodies, each trying to penetrate the shell of the egg.

Usually, only one succeeds. The sperm pushes through the membrane of the egg and deposits its DNA in the single nucleus of the egg. The DNAs join and a new life is born. Within days of implantation, what was a simple blend of egg and sperm has divided into hundreds of thousands of cells. The cells begin migrating into what will become the head and brain of the growing child and begin the process of specializing into neurons, or nerve cells.

Newly developing nerve cells will scatter throughout the embryo's body, and some will migrate through the cranial area until they have found permanent residence, developing such areas of the brain as the cerebrum, the thalamus and the hypothalamus, the midbrain, the pons, the cerebellum, the medulla oblongata, and organs with endocrine or messenger functions. Each one of these sections or structures will perform a unique aspect of thinking, of emotion, of management over the rest of the new child's body.

From the moment of conception through just the first nine months of life in the womb, the simple egg/sperm combination will have divided into scores of trillions of cells, with over ten trillion cells in the brain matter alone.

The most critical period of brain development in human life, according to some research, is from the third trimester of pregnancy through the twenty-fourth month of postnatal life. It is during this time (at twenty-six weeks and just prior to birth) that critical peaks in DNA synthesis occur and when neuronal and other types of brain cell division are proceeding at their highest rate.[2]

The brain grows in stages, in sequence. At first, the numbers of neurons or nerve cells are increasing. Active cell division is forming new cells, each one a duplicate, and, at the same time, a variation that allows them to perform different functions. The size of the cell bodies themselves doesn't increase until just before and after birth as the added nutrition of breast milk supplies large amounts of fat and other nutrients that go into laying down more tissue.

At this point, because of environmental and other stimuli, the axons and dendrites sprout new growth, reaching out to neighboring neurons, creating new opportunities for data input and signal transmission. The ways in which cells communicate with each other are numerous. Chemical messengers in the form of neurotransmitters flick between the gaps between the dendrites and axons. Hormones (messenger proteins synthesized in the organs of the endocrine system) transmit signals to cells, docking onto receptor sites on the wall of the cell to download their chemical signals. Receptor sites or receptor molecules embedded in the fatty substance of the cell wall are sensitive or receptive to a single type of hormone. Nerve cells contain receptor sites for hormones, but receptor sites are also located on cell walls in the endocrine system, intestinal wall, and other parts of the body.

Hormones like thyroid-stimulating hormone, estrogen or testosterone, insulin, and scores of other hormones stimulate specific activities within the cell. As the hormones are swept along in the bloodstream, they locate the portal into which they will dock and fit like a key fits into a lock, sending their signals to the interior of the cell. When hormones lock onto a receptor site, an intense vibration occurs or, as author Candace Pert calls it, a "humming dance."[3] The dance or electrical impulse stimulates the cell into action.

There are about as many neurons in the human brain as there are stars in the galaxy. Several trillion cells are in the skull, and yet none of them actually touch. The space between them is called the synaptic gap, across which trillions of messages are sent and received by neurotransmitters and neurohormones.

Axons and dendrites communicate with neighboring axons and dendrites across the synaptic gap. Each neuron may sprout 1,000 to 10,000 synapses, creating a staggering complexity of transmittal capabilities. If the brain contains approximately ten trillion neurons, and each neuron supports up to 10,000 synapses, the most sophisticated computer system on earth pales in comparison with the simplest human brain on earth.

The solid matter of the brain is constantly bathed in fluids rich in chemicals that supply nutrition, neurotransmitters, neurohormones, and other proteins. This watery mass is a stew of protein bodies and sugars, feeding the voracious appetite of the energy-hungry master organ. While the brain is energized by glucose and blood, physical structure is maintained by replenishing proteins and fats. Minerals and vitamins stimulate the enzymes within the neuronal mitochondria, the energy factories of the cells.

The "fluid structure" of the brain is just as important as the "solid structure," and while it may not be as Daedelian in nature, it must unvaryingly provide a rich environment so the brain's daily tasks can be performed without interruption. The fluids of the cranial cavity are composed of proteins and sugars, as well as vitamins and minerals that activate the proteins and sugars. We will learn something of the balance of these nutrients later.

This labyrinthine structure of nerve cells is composed of proteins, carbohydrates, fatty acids, minerals, vitamins, and water, supplied by the maternal diet. The outer membrane is made of protein and minerals, with fatty acids embedded in the protein matrix to act as receptor sites for incoming nutrients and hormones, and to provide strength and flexibility to

When this exquisite arrangement of cells (their microanatomy, or morphology) is taken together with the number of cells in an object the size of your brain, and when one considers the chemical reactions going on inside, one is talking about the most complicated material object in the known universe.
—Gerald M. Edelman,
Bright Air, Brilliant Fire[4]

the cell wall. The dendrites and axons are encased in a layer of insulation known as myelin that is primarily composed of fatty acids. Fats dominate the brain structure. In fact, some eighty percent of the dry weight of the brain is fat, some saturated and some unsaturated. The fats are electrically active but also act as insulation, helping to speed the signal transmission from cell to cell.

The neurohormones and neurotransmitters also are composed of fatty acids, proteins, and minerals, and are activated by enzymes that are driven by minerals and vitamins. Water is often overlooked as a functional part of the brain but is essential for chemical reactivity. Enzymes, for example, function only in the presence of water. Fluids help move materials from site to site within the brain.

Because such a delicate structure must be constructed correctly from the very outset, from the moment of conception, the diets of the mother and the growing infant are of fundamental importance to the mental health of the child throughout his or her life.

Lacking optimum nutrition during this period may mean that the child will never reach his or her genetic potential, that the brain or certain portions of the brain may not develop adequately.[5] Genetics is an important factor in mental competency, but in the face of undernutrition or malnutrition, genetics is handcuffed.

BUILDING A COMPETENT BRAIN

One critical period of neuronal growth is the first three months after conception, when each building block or nutrient must be present when the DNA/RNA blueprint calls for it. Much like a contractor working round the clock, when materials are coded for, they must be present at the instant of synthesis. If they are not there, synthesis stops and the process must start all over again.

When a mother consumes a diet that undersupplies fats, proteins, carbohydrates, vitamins, minerals, and water for both her and the baby, some part of the baby's brain development will be curtailed. Some structure will go unbuilt; some function will not be performed.

While the body may have a system of prioritizing its needs and making maximum use of limited resources, this sensitive period of brain development is the time when every nutrient should be present at the correct moment for optimal growth to occur.

If a period of malnutrition occurs anytime from week ten through week twenty-three (prenatally), a time when the numbers of cells are increasing, it is possible that irreversible damage has occurred. Fewer or less optimum numbers of brain cells will be produced. If malnutrition occurs later, at a time when the size of the cells is increasing, the damage may not be as severe. It should be noted that it is possible that some recovery can occur, but only if the diet is made adequate.[6]

During this period of fetal development, large amounts of fats are deposited into the brain tissue from Omega-3, Omega-6, and other fatty acids. The types and quantities of these fatty acids differ, depending on the period of development and the needs of the brain at that point in development. At various times, more arachidonic acids (AA) are required; at others, docosahexaenoic acid (DHA) is called upon, and so on.

Scientific literature seems to indicate that during periods of malnutrition, both prenatally and postnatally, the brain's needs take precedence over the rest of the body, at the expense of other organs.[7] We can take small comfort from this in knowing that even if we are deprived of some of those essential nutrients that are so needed for brain growth, we'll get them

---

Arachidonic acid (AA): a polyunsaturated twenty-carbon-chain fatty acid occurring in animal fats, also formed from dietary linoleic acid. It is a precursor in the biosynthesis of leukotrienes, prostaglandins, and thromboxanes. While arachidonic acid is required in human nutrition, large amounts are highly pro-inflammatory.

Docosahexaenoic acid (DHA): an Omega-3 twenty-two-carbon-chain fatty acid, found in fish and marine animal oils. Contributes to the structure and function of the nervous system.

Eicosapentaenoic acid (EPA): an Omega-3 twenty-carbon-chain fatty acid found in fish and marine animal oils. Contributes to the structure and function of the nervous system.

somehow—if they are obtainable from the liver or other organs. It is, however, the biological equivalent of robbing Peter to pay Paul.

It is also clear that if the period of malnutrition or undernutrition occurs at critical junctures during brain development, the myelin does not develop properly,[8] and when the myelin is underdeveloped, nerve transmission is hindered. Myelin tissue (the fatty tissue that encases the dendrite of the neuron) is particularly susceptible to deficiencies in fatty acids during their extensive growth period.[9] Undermyelinated nerve tissue causes alterations in the nerve signals.[10]

It is important to remember that the physical structure is built from physical nutrients. If those nutrients are not there when needed, the structure is not built properly. After birth, the requirements for fatty acids remain high until about two years of age, when brain growth is essentially finished.[11]

Protein requirements during this period are also high, as are the needs for vitamins and minerals. The requirements are high and are constant, starting at the moment of conception and continuing all the way through the period of formation. These needs are met only through an adequate diet.

Considering how important nutrition is for proper brain and central nervous system development, how are we doing? Do our diets supply what we need? How have our foods changed over the years and how have these changes influenced brain development?

The History of Mothers' Diets

The diet we enjoy in the twenty-first century differs markedly from the diet enjoyed by past generations, both in quality and in quantity. Ancestral diets were rich in essential fatty acids found in wild game, seafoods, nuts and seeds, and vegetables. The fat content of the diet of the average island dweller or Greek, for example, may have been as high as forty percent or more—with none of the detrimental effects alleged to be caused by this amount of dietary fat in modern society.

In the 1930s, an enterprising dentist, Dr. Weston Price, set off on a world tour with his wife to study the effects of the modern diet on dental health. Because in many parts of the world people eating the traditional diet lived beside family members and neighbors who had adopted a more Western diet, he was able to study, firsthand, the effects of diet on both dental health and mental health. Dr. Price took thousands of pictures of the teeth and facial structures of Eskimos, Aborigine tribesmen, island dwellers, residents of the Hebrides Islands, and other people.

Certainly, the lipid content of the average Eskimo diet was far in excess of forty percent, from highly saturated fats from the blubber of whales and seals. For example, researchers compared the amounts and types of fats eaten by Alaskan Eskimos and found that the residents of villages close to the ocean ate high amounts of Omega-3 fatty acids—and enjoyed superior health as a result![12] These fats provided their babies with optimum levels of fatty acids from which to construct brain tissue, nerve tissue, and other complexes throughout the body.

The North American Indians ate wild game (moose and caribou). During the summer months, vegetables were added to the menu. Residents of the archipelagos of the South Pacific and the islands north of Australia lived on shellfish and scale fish, accompanied by plant roots and fruits.

Central and Eastern African tribespeople enjoyed sweet potatoes, beans, and some cereal, with freshwater fish. Some tribes ate goat meat and domesticated beef, while others depended more on wild animals. They also collected insects (locusts and ants) to eat. Price laments that "one of the great luxuries was an ant pie but unfortunately they were not able to supply us with this delicacy."[13] Africans enjoyed cereals like maize, millet, and Kaffir corn, along with legumes, all ground just before cooking.

This incredible diversity of food traditions is all part of our cultural tradition, too. Our ancestors may have adopted the Western world for their new home, but their genetic and ancestral codes are deeply embedded in our own DNA. None of these cultural traditions favored low-fat meals.

While we might have something to say about the culinary desirability of this diet, we might envy the way this type of nutriture affected fetal and infant brain development. Unfortunately, our modern database contains no nutrient breakdown for ant pie, dried-fish eggs, or baked cods' heads stuffed with oats and cod liver, delicacies from other cultures! We can't compare Kraft Macaroni and Cheese with roasted caribou and a few vegetables soaked in seal fat. Our diet of highly processed foods and artificial beverages might, according to our sensitivities, taste better—but it doesn't build better babies. It doesn't build better brains.

The differences between people who had eaten their ancestral diet from birth and people who had feasted on sugar, white flour products, and soft drinks are astonishing. The traditional wholesome diet produced wide faces with jaws wide enough to accommodate all thirty-two teeth with proper spacing, high cheekbones, few to no cavitations, and wide foreheads to house their brains. They are beautiful people with bright, shiny eyes that sparkle with intelligence and good humor.

The facial structures of the people who enjoyed a more "civilized" diet are not so beautiful. Their jaws are narrow with so little room that the teeth crowd together in two crooked rows. Cavities are common, and in cultures where dental care is inadequate, the pain and suffering are intolerable. Their foreheads are also narrow, or misshapen, with scarcely enough room for a growing brain.

Dr. Price described his findings and the dietary traditions that differ radically from each other, depending on climate, accessibility to the ocean, terrain, tradition, and so on. Traditional diets are often high in fats, much higher than current recommendations by many health care professionals. Some are extremely high in protein; others less so. But the one commonality they have is that the traditional diets are nutrient-rich in proteins, essential fats, unrefined carbohydrates (in the form of brightly colored vegetables and limited grains and fruit), and micronutrients (vitamins, minerals, and enzymes).

Dr. Price's work becomes even more interesting in his observations of the emotional, mental, and spiritual health of the people he studied. He was not hopeful that this overall congeniality would continue, though. He introduced the topic by saying, "Although the causes of physical degeneration that can be seen easily have been hard to trace, the defects in the development of the brain, causes of mental degeneration are exceedingly difficult to trace. Much that formerly has been left to the psychiatrist to explain is now rapidly shifting to the realm of the anatomist and physiologist. . . . Many of our modern writers have recognized and have emphasized the seriousness of mental and moral degeneration. . . . The problem of lowered mentality and its place in our modern conception of bodily diseases has not been placed on a physical basis as have the better understood degenerative processes, with their direct relationship to a disease organ, but has generally been assigned to a realm entirely outside the domain of disease or injury of a special organ or tissue. Edward Lee Thorndike, of Columbia University, says that 'thinking is as biological as digestion.' This implies that a disturbance in the capacity to think is directly related to a defect in the brain."

Dr. Price concluded that this "defect in the brain" was primarily the result of poor nutrition. In comparing the "native diet" with modern diets, Price estimated that the ancient diet contains many times more vitamins and minerals than the diets in the 1930s and 1940s. The following table summarizes some nutrients and how many times more of them were included in the typical primitive diet than the diets of the late twentieth century:[14]

	Eskimo	Indian	Swiss	Gaelic	Aborigine
Calcium	5.4	5.8	3.7	2.1	4.6
Phosphorus	5	5	3.7	2.3	6.2
Iron	1.5	2.7	3.1	1	50.6
Iodine	49	8.8	?	?	?
Magnesium	7.9	4.3	2.5	1.3	17
Fat-soluble vitamins	10	10	10	10	10

Price's list is incomplete; there are scores of other nutrients that are critically important to the development and long-term health of the fetus and baby that are not listed here and were unknown in Price's time. It is safe to assume, however, that as these nutrients were supplied more abundantly in ancient diets than in our foods today, it is true for other nutrients as well.

Vitamins and minerals aren't the only nutrients lacking in the early twenty-first century. We are eating less Omega-3 fatty acids now than ever before, and these levels are continuing to fall.[15] Ancestral diets contained Omega-3 and Omega-6 fatty acids (both of which are important in balanced ratios), in a ratio of approximately 1:1. Today's ratios stand between 1:10 and 1:20–25 (Omega-3:Omega-6).[16]

We simply aren't getting nearly enough Omega-3 fatty acids to grow a healthy brain. Corn and safflower oils provide most of our Omega-6 fatty acids, but it is Omega-3 fatty acids from docosahexaenoic acid (DHA) and eicosapentaenoic acid (EPA) that are critical in the development of brain tissue, forming the very membrane that encases each of the ten trillion neurons in the brain and the myelin sheath that protects the dendrite and axon, and hastens nerve transmission.

We could manufacture DHA in the liver if we consumed large amounts of the Omega-3 fatty acids from plants like olives and flaxseed, but we don't eat much of those oils either, certainly not enough to provide the growing brain with huge amounts of DHA.[17]

We aren't making the grade when it comes to dietary fats that create healthy brains in our babies. Mass-produced animals don't contain the same amount of Omega-3 fatty acids that wild-raised animals contain. For example, farm-raised fish like salmon have a different balance of Omega-3 fatty acids from salmon that jump the waterfalls in icy-cold rivers and feast on natural foods. The alpha-linolenic acid in grass is used to produce EFA; fish make DHA and EPA from plankton. Grazing animals produce higher amounts of Omega-3, while animals fattened on grains are deficient in Omega-3.[18]

Many pregnant and nursing moms in the Orient eat twelve eggs per day—just to get long-chain fatty acids for their babies. The Orientals know that eggs, rich in saturated fats, are a brain food. A story has been told about a woman in Japan whose husband died while her son was still young, throwing the family into poverty. To provide her child with just one egg per day, she sold off all her possessions, one by one, so he could be intelligent. Her son went on to college. It may be wise if you want your children to go to college to give them eggs, cod liver oil, and butter.

Can our modern-day dietary fats be converted in our bodies to the types of fat that build brain tissue? Not according to fatty acid expert Dr. Michael Schmidt. His position is that "people who eat conventional foods along with oils like flax seed oil don't convert them into DHA and EPA. Flax oil is not adequate to do that. Without a balance of Omega-3 fatty acids, DHA, and EPA, the brain will be inadequately developed."[19]

It is estimated that the essential fatty acid content of our current diet differs from our ancestral diet by as much as several hundred percent. The possible implications of this dietary shift are enormous.

An Imbalance of Other Nutrients = Diminished Brain Function

The altered balance of essential fatty acids isn't the only difference we see in our current eating patterns compared to our great-grandparents' diets. The delicate balance between proteins and carbohydrates has also changed. Part of the problem is with the increased consumption of sugar and other refined carbohydrates.

The other part of the problem is that we don't eat enough quality protein. While we are still arguing over how much protein the average American eats, we certainly eat far less seafood, far less wild game, far fewer legumes and whole grains, far fewer greens, far less of anything our ancestors ate. Unless pregnant moms are supplementing their diets with high-quality protein, consuming at least twenty percent more protein than before they became pregnant, they may not be able to provide their baby with the amino acid building blocks for a healthy brain.

The minerals calcium, potassium, zinc, and magnesium are needed in a growing brain to activate hundreds of brain enzymes, take part in the manufacturing of adenosine triphosphate (ATP) or cellular energy, aid in the transfer of nerve signals, help regulate enzymes, and increase the passage of nutrients in and out of cell walls. They take part in the Krebs cycle (to produce cellular energy), help maintain the critical acid-alkaline balance throughout the body and brain, help rid the brain of toxic metabolic waste products, ensure optimum cell replication through DNA promotion, and strengthen cell membranes. They also regulate the amount of sugar (the fuel or food of the brain) flowing to the brain.

Do we get enough minerals in the diet? Unfortunately, no.[20] The foods we enjoy don't contain enough minerals or vitamins to satisfy the ravenous requirements of the brain and nervous system, let alone the rest of the body.

The B complex vitamins, for example, are needed to metabolize the vast quantities of sugars we are eating, but our current diet provides only a fraction of the vitamins needed just to handle the onslaught of sugars, leaving very little of this precious cofactor for the work of the brain. Vitamins are used as enzyme cofactors, along with minerals to energize the solid and fluid structures of the brain. Minerals are also needed to metabolize sugars; we eat precious few minerals either, leaving the brain's work undersupplied with zinc, magnesium, and others.

With the millions of dollars spent on nutrition research that attempts to discover precise amounts of nutrients necessary to prevent deficiency diseases like rickets and scurvy and the billions of dollars spent synthesizing products to match research findings, we are more poorly nourished than our ancestors who had no electronic gadgets or research budgets. Medical research has made sure that more babies and mothers have a better physical chance of surviving, but in the mental arena, the opposite is happening today.

We eat nutrient-dead food, food that is devoid of the structural materials needed to develop into the brains of our growing babies, and then wonder why our babies cry so much or seem so restless. We wonder why they can't sleep soundly or bond to their mothers. We can stop blaming our parenting skills. We should blame our food and the foods that our children eat.

What makes this dauntingly difficult to prove is that deficiencies (and the damage caused by deficiencies) may be so subtle, so minute, that our instruments are inadequate to measure the damage done at the molecular and cellular levels, long before it becomes obvious at the organ level. We can do liver biopsies; we can't do brain biopsies. The brain is so delicate, so fragile that we can't take it apart to examine it like the heart or the lungs.

Who is to know if tiny pieces of myelin are missing because there weren't enough Omega-3 fatty acids in mother's diet? Who can tell if important neurotransmitters are not being constructed because the amino acids tryptophan or tyrosine were not available when they were needed?

Besides, we are all biologically unique. No tests have been devised to measure how many neurotransmitters we need or have, or if our neurotransmitter docking systems are in place and functional. Can we say, for absolute certainty, that our poor diets are a contributing factor in our craziness? No, we have to make inferences, based on our understanding of biology.

When you set out to build a house, you hire an architect and a general contractor. The architect draws the building plans; the contractor puts it together according to plan. If, when the builder seeks to purchase materials to build the house, he finds that a critical shortage has occurred and he can obtain only ninety percent of the materials he needs, he may continue to build. The resulting structure may look fine to the unpracticed eye. What he omitted from the architectural drawing may be as small as electrical wiring or windowpanes. Some nails or screws may be missing. We may not immediately see what is not there—but days or weeks or years down the road, we discover the loss when something falls apart prematurely or when the electrical system short-circuits when too much stress is placed on the wiring.

So it is when constructing a brain. When nutritional deficiencies occur at critical moments of construction, the brain may look identical under the microscope or in a PET scan. The child will certainly appear normal. We don't categorize some types of abnormalities as "birth defects." Although nearsightedness or astigmatism or crooked, crowded teeth or bad skin are now considered "normal," they are, in fact, a sign that imperfections have occurred at the genetic or molecular or cellular levels. What about tiny imperfections in the brain? The differences may be subtle, "hidden defects"—defects that are behavioral or attitudinal, or in the lack of ability to remember details or stay focused in class.

Subclinical deficiencies occurring during the process of development may diminish the child's ability to reason or consider consequences of bad behavior, or be cheerful—or a hundred other "defects of character." When we see those behaviors in children, we don't think of the diet. We naturally blame parents for bad parenting. Is it possible that some of the tissue that was supposed to create logical thinking or a happy temperament wasn't laid properly into the brain structure at the beginning?

Instead of doing the research needed to manufacture products that mimic nature, that nourish our brains and provide those essential building blocks, food manufacturers are cranking out millions of pounds of toxic food artifacts that are stripped bare of the nutrients that feed our brains. We are being systematically starved, and the result is that we are being robbed of our sanity, of our ability to reason and be happy. Artificial food products inflict permanent structural and functional damage to the brain.

In order to save our own brains and the brains of our children and grandchildren, we're going to have to look at what lies behind the advertising glitz. We're going to have to stop buying the products described in this book. Because if we don't, if we continue to eat the pseudofood being offered, we may destroy our brain trust, forever.

3

Nourishing a Baby's Brain

To my mind, one of the greatest offenses against a man is to deprive him of the normal supply of nourishment during infancy. It gives a bad start. He is shorn of his natural rights . . . The present abundance of nursing bottles and infants' foods in the drug stores is evidence of degeneration . . . Shall our children be sacrificed?

—EPHRAIM CUTTER,
February 1881

You would have been breast-fed if you were born sometime between the dawn of man and the early decades of the twentieth century. No other options were available. In generations past, if the postpartum mother could not breast-feed her baby, a wet-nurse was called in to perform this vital task. In some cultures, this practice is still carried out.

In the early part of the century, doctors recognized the difficulties some mothers had after birth and enlisted the support of the community in feeding the young. Across the country, communal milk banks were established to share the milk of mothers who had an extra supply. Difficulties arose with this system, though, as sanitation was not well controlled and supplies were often unstable.

To meet the need in the 1930s, American pharmaceutical companies began producing and marketing infant formulas. Competition eventually reduced the number of companies that produced the infant products to the three giants: Abbott (Ross), Bristol-Myers (Mead-Johnson), and American Home Products (Wyeth). Nestlé (Carnation) and Gerber were already producing baby foods from before the turn of the century.

World War II saw huge cultural changes as more and more women entered the workforce and Ross Laboratories, Mead-Johnson, or Wyeth took over feeding Rosie the Riveter's babies as she worked in wartime factories. After weaning, Gerber baby foods took over the task. World War II ended in the middle of this cultural upheaval as soldiers returned home and the baby boom was born, ushering millions of babies into the marketplace. While mothers experienced a new freedom in the workforce away from their children, advertising agencies saw a huge economic potential for their clients and began targeting formula advertisements at the readers of both medical and consumer magazines.

As a result, the numbers of breast-feeding mothers halved between 1946 and 1956, dropping to twenty-five percent at hospital discharge in 1967. By then, the birthrate had begun to fall. To maintain profitability, infant-formula manufacturers sought new markets in developing countries,

and as sales to industrialized countries decreased, sales to developing countries increased
with only occasional protests from health professionals and consumer groups.[1]

The shift from breast-feeding to bottle
feeding as a cultural norm was a huge deviation
in feeding practices, a dramatic about-face from
natural to unnatural. Suddenly, for the first time
in human history, we were fed from a laboratory
instead of mother's breast.

In the sixties, militant groups of women
worked to increase nursing practices, and for a
short time, breast-feeding rates increased. Soon,
however, breast-feeding rates started falling
again, and from 1985 to 1990, only about fifty percent of new mothers were
nursing when they took baby home from the hospital. When baby's first
birthday rolled around, only about six percent were still feeding at
mother's breast.[2]

THE MARKETING OF INFANT FORMULAS

To understand more clearly just how formulas were allowed to become
so entrenched in our American culture, it helps to take a look into marketing history, back in the early 1930s when baby food companies started
to mass-market infant formulas.

According to those companies' promotional literature, they went into
the market to fill a need; with more and more mothers entering the workplace, someone had to feed the babies. Doctors filled the gap, for a while,
by establishing the milk banks. Mothers who produced more milk than
they needed for their own children sold their milk to the banks; some
women made their living this way, but milk banks were, at best, only a
temporary solution.

Advertising dollars of the 1930s and 1940s were aimed at two targets:

mainstream magazines with a predominantly female readership, and trade publications written for doctors. Advertising in the form of articles and news clips that look like endorsements by the magazine were scattered throughout the professional articles in the medical journals. For example, in 1930, *JAMA* (*Journal of the American Medical Association*), published an excerpt from an article from *Northwest Medicine, Seattle,* as follows:

"Olmstead [the author of the original article] recommends the use of unsweetened evaporated milk in infant feeding because: It is entirely adequate from a nutritional standpoint when fed in conjunction with other foods and vitamins; it can be given in a concentrated state equivalent to whole cow's milk; it is easily digested; it is palatable, from the infant's standpoint; it is cheap and easily procurable."[3]

In fact, the Committee on Foods of the Council on Pharmacy and Chemistry of the American Medical Association fully endorsed commercial products on a regular basis, mimicking the information supplied by the manufacturers. Their statement reads: "The following products have been accepted as conforming to the rules of the Committee on Foods of the Council on Pharmacy and Chemistry of the American Medical Association. These products are approved for advertising in the publications of the American Medical Association, and for general promulgation to the public. They will be included in the book of accepted foods to be published by the American Medical Association."[4]

The endorsements don't look like advertisements; they carry the full weight of approval by doctors—something a mother would find difficult to disagree with. In the professional articles and advertisements, nothing is said about the superiority of human milk over infant formula. For example, in 1931, an excerpt from an article from *JAMA* reads:

One of the unmistakable characteristics of present-day infant feeding is the use of a large variety of food products to replace or supplement human milk or the simpler modifications of cow's milk that were formerly depended on almost universally. The number of brands of proprietary products is bewildering; their respective virtues are extolled in terms of the latest discoveries in the science of nutrition. The commercially prepared infant foods on the market today include several distinct types. The group represented by powdered, evaporated and condensed milks is also self-explanatory. The unsweetened milks may be ordinary whole milk without any modification other than the removal of water or they may have been partially skimmed. . . . Of greater novelty are the so-called reconstructed baby foods. A recent technical bulletin describes them as especially compounded for babies under one year of age and to be used to augment, or in place of, breast milk. They are known as reconstructed infant foods because, when redissolved in the proportion designated by the attending physician, they have many of the diet qualities of milk but contain additional easily digested ingredients. These ingredients are alleged to be desirable for the baby's growth and development and are added to meet certain definite digestive and nutritive requirements.[5]

Later that same month, *JAMA* wrote that "after the first quarter of the first year, artificially fed infants show a significantly greater mean rate of gain, and this superiority becomes progressively greater up to the time of weaning."

Though they lamented that the number of infections in the bottle-fed babies was considerably higher than in the breast-fed babies, they were not dissuaded from writing, "There is no evidence in this series of cases of increased resistance to infection from breast feeding, but rather evidence of either greater susceptibility or greater exposure or of both. Weaning after the third month is not per se to be feared, provided artificial feeding under good conditions is available."[6]

It is not so hard to understand how formula companies were able to exert their financial power over medical professionals to ensure their endorsement, and then, as today, the word of the doctor went a long way in the minds of most people. Did doctors actually think, though, that smart brains could be built from the food designed for dumb animals? That highly processed foods are the same as raw, natural foods? Hadn't they considered that even if the babies appeared to thrive (indeed, they grew big and fast like calves), small defects might occur, defects so small as to be invisible to the naked eye but devastating in the long run?

Knowing that breast-feeding offers the baby the best chance of being healthy and intelligent, even today AMA does not take a strong stand for breast-feeding.

"The American Medical Association," the Web site statement begins, "and other professional groups concerned with the care of newborns advocate breast-feeding." Then the message is watered down. "The decision to breast-feed or bottle-feed your baby should be based on your feelings as well as your lifestyle. If you prefer to bottle-feed your baby a commercially prepared formula, you can be assured that both your baby's nutritional and emotional needs will be met. Commercially prepared infant formulas supply the appropriate combinations of proteins, sugars, fats, and vitamins to meet your baby's nutritional requirements. Talk to your pediatrician about which formula would be best for your baby."

The information "you can be assured . . . nutritional and emotional needs will be met" isn't accurate, as we will see.

AMA then spends nearly the rest of the Web page discussing the breast-feeding negatives, followed by three paragraphs on the negatives of bottle-feeding. The uncertain mother who is seeking to find the best answer for her baby would find it difficult to find a strong breast-feeding message in this information.

Concerned organizations have tried to balance the marketing strategies of these companies with the best interest of mothers and babies, particularly in Third World countries where nutrition is marginal.

According to the organization Voluntary Service Overseas (VSO), the 1981 World Health Assembly adopted the International Code of Marketing of Breastmilk Substitutes in order to "ensure that women's decisions about how to feed their infants are informed by the knowledge that breast-feeding is the healthiest method of infant feeding, and that women are protected from the promotional activities of manufacturers and distributors of breast-milk substitutes."[7]

The International Baby Food Action Network (IBFAN) has spent the past two decades monitoring the advertising and promotional activities of these baby food marketers over two decades. They have found evidence, as recently as 1996, of violations of the code by some of the largest manufacturers of infant formulas.

Violations included "information associated with a company name which either promoted bottle feeding and/or discouraged breast-feeding, and in the countries surveyed, free samples of the company's products, unrequested visits from company personnel to give product information to mothers, incentives to health workers to promote products, and product promotion outside facilities through retailers and the media."

The research was carried out in Poland, Bangladesh, Thailand, and South Africa. As the organization stated, "Breastfeeding continues to be threatened by the marketing activities of companies. There is strong evidence that companies are systematically breaking the code on marketing and putting the health of babies in the developing world at risk."[8]

According to the Nestlé (Carnation) Web site, Nestlé supports the recommendations of the World Health Organization (WHO) International Code of Marketing of Breast-Milk Substitutes in developing countries, and writes: "Breastfeeding provides the best nutrition and protection from illness for your baby."

Instead of encouraging mothers to exclusively breast-feed their babies for at least one year, as is recommended by nutritionally trained physicians, they dilute the message and promote the use of their products. They state that "for most infants, breast milk is all that is needed for the first 4 to 6 months. Many mothers continue to breastfeed after 6 months and then give other foods as well."

Ross Laboratories conducted their own survey of breast-feeding practices a few years ago, and according to their numbers, minor improvements in baby-feeding practices have been made. Nearly sixty percent of babies now start out on mother's milk, up from fifty-two percent. There was a nineteen percent increase in the rate of breast-feeding at six months of age; about twenty-one percent are still nursing at six months.[9]

Twenty-one percent may be a little better—but not much better, particularly when you consider the studies showing that the real benefits in cognition and mood are gained when breast-feeding is continued through the first birthday and longer. According to one paper, "The number of U.S. babies who receive breast milk as part of their diet through one year of age, as recommended by the American Academy of Pediatrics, or through two years of age, as recommended by the World Health Organization, is so small as to be almost statistically insignificant."[10]

Virtually no one breast-feeds their babies past the first birthday. It takes a strong woman to stand up to the pressures heaped upon her by public opinion and continue to breast-feed her child after he has grown teeth and started walking. Instead of seeing her offering a gift of love only she can give, we see her as a social misfit, maybe even a little exhibitionistic.

In addition, if Nestlé (and other companies) were truly committed to the promotion of breast-feeding, why did they bombard nearly half of the mothers in South Africa with promotional material for their company?[11] This is part of the reason why the Church of England may again boycott some of the largest American formula manufacturers for aggressively marketing their products in Third World countries.

According to *Nutrition Week*, "These manufacturers routinely violate the 1981 World Health Organization Code which forbids aggressive formula marketing in developing nations."[12]

The World Health Organization passed a code forbidding aggressive marketing of formula in a country even where the food supply was in jeopardy and nutrition was not optimum, because only mother's milk provides adequate nutrition for a growing baby.

By marketing their formula to developing countries, formulators may also jeopardize one of nature's methods of birth control: breast-feeding. If mothers do not breast-feed and have dried up their milk, they again become fertile—thereby increasing birth rates.

Community milk banks still exist in some parts of the country. For more information about how to start a milk bank in your community or to inquire about an existing bank, check the Internet. There are several Web sites devoted to milk banks, including the Human Milk Banking Association of North America and the Texas Breastfeeding Initiative.

Quite possibly, it is here, in these numbers, that we truly see what is happening to our culture's brain trust. Our brain trust is drying up in the dried-up breasts of mothers who were never encouraged or taught to breast-feed by their mothers or their doctors.

WHAT IS SPECIAL ABOUT MOTHER'S MILK?

Science is now validating what mothers have known since the beginning of time: Human breast milk was designed for human babies, and cow's milk was designed for calves. The balance of nutrients in bovine milk is designed to grow a hundred-pound newborn calf to several hundred pounds within twenty-four months.

When the untrained eye reads the ingredient listing on the back of the baby bottle or the advertisements from the baby food companies, it is difficult to see that there is a problem at all. Formulas seem similar to mother's milk; nutrients are measured in a few milligrams or grams. When we look closely at the fine print and compare the composition of artificial formulas with mother's milk, however, we see that the differences are great and can, in some cases, translate into tangible, permanent physical deficits.

From the moment of birth when colostrum is delivered to the breast, through the lactational period to weaning, breast milk differs substantially from even the best of the commercial baby formulas. The two milks appear different. Mother's milk looks thinner, almost blue in color, lightly translucent. Formula looks rich, creamy, heavy in texture. It is tempting to believe that such a rich substance must be superior in nutrition.

Depending on the time of day or how long the baby nurses, the composition of mother's milk changes significantly, from colostrum to true milk that varies in fatty acid content, protein content, and so on. Colostrum is higher in protein and minerals than fat, but as true milk replaces colostrum, the fat content increases to reflect the greater needs of the child.

Other bioactive substances in human milk include friendly bacteria, immunoglobulins, enzymes that destroy unfriendly bacteria and aid digestion, growth factors, hormones, and nonessential amino acids that aid in the growth and healing of the intestinal tract. Formula contains none of these additional factors.[13] In fact, there are about one hundred elements found in breast milk that are missing from infant formula. The absence of any of these biofactors has the potential for long-term damage to the vulnerable child.

The composition of mother's milk changes from moment to moment during a single meal and from hour to hour during the day to reflect the varying needs of the child. The fore milk, or first milk, nursed in a single meal contains less fatty acids than hind milk, or the milk nursed in the later part of the meal. The midmorning meal typically contains the most fat. If both breasts are used in a feeding, hind milk and fore milk will mix in the second breast, resulting in milk that is higher in calorie and fat content.[14]

The protein composition is different. For example, the whey-to-casein ratio of mother's milk is approximately 70:30; the whey-to-casein ratios in infant formulas range from 18:82 (Similac and Gerber) to 60:40 (Enfamil, SMA), to 100:0 (Good Start). The amino acid balance in mother's milk gives preference to amino acids that aid in the growth of the brain, as opposed to an amino acid content of cow's milk that spurs the growth of muscle and fat tissue.

Mother's milk contains active enzymes that facilitate the digestion of the milk; infant formulas lack these enzymes, forcing the baby to produce its own enzymes to do the work of digestion. Mother's milk contains

The nutritional content of breast milk is only one aspect of the superiority of breast-feeding. When mother holds her child to the breast and baby is allowed to gaze into his mother's face while he nurses, changes in brain activity take place.

The hypothalamic, limbic, and other brain stem structures are activated, which regulates the sleep-wake cycle and increases attention and vigilance through cortical activity.[15] The emotional bonding between infant and mother is increased. The increased feeding time and the physical closeness of the partners are more satisfying emotionally to both mother and child,[16] causing measurable changes in motivation.

A mother feeds her baby a rich psychological meal when she nurses him.

growth factors that promote the development of the GI tract; these growth factors are missing in infant formula. Mother's milk is rich in immune bodies that help prevent infection in the baby; infant formulas lack these immune protective agents.

Fatty acids that are used to construct the brain and nervous system of the growing child (Omega-3 and Omega-6 long-chain fatty acids) are present in mother's milk but are either missing altogether or are in very short supply in infant formulas.

Where cow's milk averages about 3.5 percent fat, mother's milk, as thin as it looks, contains about 4.4 percent fat, or about 1.4 grams per ounce of fat (a little more than 50 percent of its calories),[17] a valuable contribution to the growing structure and size of the brain. While fat composition can vary drastically, depending on the diet of the mother, how long the child has nursed, and other factors, the ratio between the types of essential fats remains fairly constant but can change to meet the dynamic needs of the baby. Unless the mother's diet is seriously deficient, her milk provides her baby with the structural elements needed to build the structure of his brain.

Human milk also contains types of fatty acids not found in any other species, animal or plant, such as GLA (gamma-linolenic acid), one of the critical precursors of the anti-inflammatory prostaglandin 1 (PGE1) variety. One of these fats, called DGLA, or dihomogammalinolenic acid, is converted in the body to arachidonic acid, from which the prostaglandin 2 (PGE2) hormones and other brain structures are made.[18]

Human milk is high in cholesterol, with about four mg per fluid ounce. The cholesterol in breast milk is used to provide structural strength to the neurons so that they do not collapse in upon themselves from the pressure of the surrounding cells and fluid. Cholesterol is particularly important in the myelin sheath, which surrounds the axon of the neuron. Although several types of fatty acids comprise the insulating myelin sheath, it contains more than twice as much cholesterol as any other fat.

Nearly eighty percent of the dry weight of the human brain is fat. Each one of those fat molecules that form the cell membrane and the myelin sheath, and perform many of the other functions needed for the brain, is derived from either the maternal or the infant diet. Where will the

Infant formulas don't contain DHA, a deficiency that can alter not only neuron development but development of the retina in the eyes as well. An article in *Pediatric Research* stated that "the addi- tion of long-chain omega-3 fatty acids such as DHA to infant formulas may be necessary for adequate neural DHA accretion and optimal neural develop- ment."[19]

baby get these essential fats to construct her brain if they are missing from her infant formula?

INFANT FORMULAS DON'T MEASURE UP

Cow's milk–based formulas do not contain cholesterol, a fatty acid that is used to myelinate the nerve cell sheath and provide a solid structure to the cell membrane. The structurally and functionally important Omega-3 fatty acids, used to enhance the conductivity of the nerve signal, are also essentially absent.

In *Essential Fatty Acids in Growth and Development*, Sheila Innis wrote that the fats provided in artificial formulas, usually from a vegetable source like coconut, corn, safflower, or soybean oil, differ substantially from the oils found in human milk in that they provide only minuscule amounts of the Omega-3 and Omega-6 fatty acids. She is particularly critical of the use of corn oils in formulas because they "may not support normal biochemi- cal development of the [central nervous system] when present as the only polyunsaturated oil in the diet."[20]

It has been speculated that the body can make its own fatty acids from vegetable oils, but Innis goes on to say that whether or not an infant can manufacture his own is dependent on a number of variables, including the vitamin and mineral content of the formula. We certainly can't depend on it, especially since infants may be deficient from birth in some of the nu- trients needed to complete the metabolic transformation.

Animal studies indicate that when they are deprived of adequate amounts of essential fatty acids, the weights of their brains are up to thirty- three percent less than those of animals that received adequate amounts of

In a recent assay of infant formula, I had the amount of fatty acids and individual amino acids measured in a one-ounce serving. The following chart compares mother's milk to two infant formulas, one cow's milk–based and the other soy-based:

	Enfamil Low Iron	Isomil Soy Formula	Mother's Milk
Saturated Fat	0.032	0.013	0.0128
Monounsaturated Fat	0.029	0.014	1.370
Omega-9 Fats	0.029	0.0140	1.310
Polyunsaturated Fat	0.014	0.007	0.450
Omega-3 Fats	0.002	0.001	0.040
Omega-6 Fats	0.012	0.006	0.410
DHA	0.00	0.00	NA
TOTAL FAT	0.075	0.034	0.031
BCAAs*	0.561%	0.297%	0.205%
Tryptophan	0.01523%	0.0012%	0.0184%
TOTAL PROTEIN	2.45%	1.59%	0.987%

Note: Independent laboratory analysis was performed on two infant formulas and on human breast milk, for the nutrients listed above.
*Branched chain amino acids

dietary fats. Even when the deficiency was corrected later, while they were still young, they never recovered beyond a thirty-percent loss in brain weight. Rehabilitation could not reverse the changes in brain composition.[21]

Other studies show that while human infants may, in fact, be able to convert some of the fatty acids found in formula to the essential fats for the construction of the brain, the amount they are able to produce is inadequate to meet the developmental requirements of the infant.[22] When infants are fed synthetic formula instead of breast milk, they have less of the important brain-modeling DHA and other Omega-3 fatty acids and arachidonic acids in their blood, thereby making them susceptible to a form of brain damage—the building blocks for brain material are missing.[23]

THE SUGARS, MINERALS, AND PROTEIN ARE WRONG

The sugars in the infant formulas are different from the sugars found in mother's milk. The mineral content differs in some formulas by as much as 500 percent. But it really is in the balance of essential amino acids (EAAs) where the news is bad.

The proteins and the ratio of amino acids in human milk are designed to grow both a healthy human body and a healthy human brain. When proteins are digested into individual amino acids in the human diet, they circulate throughout the body and are pulled into cells to provide the building blocks of the hundreds of thousands of protein bodies synthesized there. When they approach the brain, however, the blood-brain barrier presents a challenge to amino acids as they try to cross the barrier.

Amino acids compete for entry through the blood-brain barrier into the brain tissue. To get nutrients up into the brain, a type of "shuttle service" ferries nutrients through the barrier to the other side into the blood brain system. A limited number of "seats on the shuttle" are available for amino acid transport; amino acids compete for a place on the transport system.

Branched-chain amino acids (BCAAs) are used primarily in the construction of muscle tissue. Cow's milk is rich in branched chain and other amino acids; human milk contains relatively few BCAAs. When too many branched amino acids seek entry through the blood-brain barrier, for example, they take up too many places on the transport system, thereby blocking other amino acids from entering the blood-brain system. There are only so many "seats on the bus," so to speak. One essential amino acid that frequently gets left behind is tryptophan.

Tryptophan is critically important to the brain, as it is metabolized into serotonin, a calming neurotransmitter. Mother's milk is rich in tryptophan; cow's milk is weighted more heavily toward other amino acids. Infant formulas are particularly low in tryptophan. From the previous table, we see that the total protein content of every formula is substantially higher than that of breast milk. We might think that adding protein to the formula only enhances its value. Protein is, after all, an essential nutrient,

The term "essential" in nutrition conveys a different meaning than when defined in common language. When a nutrient is labeled "essential," it means that:

1. It cannot be manufactured by the body but must be obtained through the diet, and
2. It is essential to the synthesis of a structure, or to a function of the body.

used to build strong muscles and a healthy brain. The problem lies, however, not in the total protein (although that in itself may be problematic) but in the ratios of the individual amino acids that make up the long strings of protein. Many of these amino acids play a minor role in lean tissue building and play a major role in building brain tissue. When they are lacking or unavailable to the brain, serious consequences may follow.

When the blood balance of EAAs is tipped toward amino acids that compete with tryptophan, tryptophan is left off the shuttle and out of the brain.

The essential amino acid, L-tryptophan, plays a critical role in the development of the brain. Tryptophan is first converted to niacin, one of the B-complex vitamins important to brain function. It also converts to serotonin, a neurotransmitter associated with lowering hyperactivity, controlling aggression, muting the response to sensory input, enhancing sleep, and improving mood and cognitive performance.[24]

When adequate amounts of tryptophan have reached the brain, serotonin levels are normalized, exerting a calming effect, decreasing aggressive behavior, inducing sleepiness, elevating mood, and so on. For years, physicians have used tryptophan to treat depression, PMS, carbohydrate cravings leading to obesity, insomnia, and other disorders of the brain.[25] Tryptophan is, indeed, very essential for human happiness and self-control.

Compare the tryptophan content of human milk and infant formulas in the chart on page 66. While these differences may appear trivial, what is *not* trivial is the ratio between the amino acids. The amino acid profile of many of the infant formulas is heavily weighted toward the branched-chain (BCAAs) and other amino acids, reducing the amount of tryptophan available to the brain. What we are seeing in reduced sleep in infants and subsequent aggressive behaviors in childhood may be related to tryptophan deficiency in infancy.[26]

An article published in one peer-reviewed magazine found a possible correlation between these amino acid ratios and brain development:

"The ratio of plasma concentrations of tryptophan to the sum of neutral amino acids (valine, isoleucine, leucine, phenylalanine, and tyrosine) was found to be significantly lower in formula-fed infants as compared to breast-fed infants and to newborns at birth. This tryptophan to neutral amino acids ratio in the blood is thought to control the synthesis of serotonin in the brain . . . Serotonin deficiency in the developing brain based on a decreased plasma tryptophan to neutral amino acids ratio may contribute to developmental obesity and/or permanent changes of mental capacity and social adaptability . . ."[27]

Changes in mental capacity and social adaptability? How about sleep disorders? Serotonin regulates sleep. Serotonin deficiency makes it more difficult to fall asleep and sleep soundly through the night. One research paper noted that after feeding tryptophan as opposed to feeding straight Similac, infants ". . . entered active sleep 14.1 minutes sooner than they did after Similac, and entered quiet sleep 20 minutes sooner."[28]

Noting the significant differences between mother's milk and infant formula, one author stated, "Long-term epidemiological studies have demonstrated a number of interesting differences between breast-fed and formula-fed infants. These have included a link between formula feeding and increased risk of infection, Crohn's disease, Type I diabetes, childhood lymphomas, celiac disease, and *altered neurodevelopmental outcome* among preterm infants"[29] (author's emphasis).

One bit of speculation was given concerning possible connection of SIDS (Sudden Infant Death Syndrome) in serotonin-reduced infants. Researchers commented that serotonin levels are reduced in the hypothalamus (the brain organ that controls the onset, maintenance, and timing of sleep) in SIDS infants, as well as other changes in the availability of serotonin and other neurotransmitters.[30]

The absence of these critically important fats and the imbalance of amino acids and minerals have lifelong effects on bottle-fed babies. Studies have shown that bottle-fed babies do worse in school and struggle with more affect disorders than do breast-fed babies. Whether or not a baby is breast-fed or bottle-fed can make a lifelong difference in intelligence. As one study put it, "These effects are 1) pervasive, being reflected in a range of measures including standardized tests, teacher ratings, and academic outcomes in high school; and 2) relatively long-lived, extending throughout childhood into young adulthood."[31]

It is difficult to determine the causative agent. Are there differences in parenting styles? Are breast-feeding mothers typically more highly educated than bottle-feeding mothers? If physical damage is occurring, where and how is it occurring? Researchers have found that infants who were fed artificial formulas had lower plasma levels of the structurally important Omega-6 and Omega-3 fatty acids.[32] They have also found lower levels of essential amino acids like tryptophan.

Breast-feeding improved intelligence by 4.6+ points on some test scores.[33] Human milk promotes cognitive development (or the ability of the child to acquire knowledge), according to a study done at the University of Akron, Ohio.[34] Whether or not these intellectual and emotional differences are a consequence of the amino acid imbalance, the fatty acid balance, or some unknown factor is of little concern to the parent watching her child struggle through school or struggle with his emotional balance.

The baby food companies, Gerber Companies Foundation, Ross Products Division, Abbot Laboratories, and Wyeth-Ayerst International, banded together to research the question "Should infant formulas be supplemented with bioactive components and conditionally essential nutrients present in human milk?" Considering that the formula companies have publicly agreed that artificial formulas should mirror as closely as possible the composition of mother's milk, this is an interesting question and should have led to changes in the composition of their formulas.

However, after the research was completed, author Margit Hamosh concluded, "Supplementation with [essential fats] is probably indicated for preterm infants, although long-term effects are not known and studies to assess toxicity have not been performed . . ."[35]

Research articles sent from Ross Laboratories acknowledge that there is a difference between breast- and bottle-fed babies,[36] yet their position is that infants are fully capable of synthesizing the proper fatty acids in their livers. That may be true, at least to some degree.

However, according to other information they provided, "It may be that AA (arachidonic acid) and DHA (docosahexaenoic acid) synthesis is too slow to meet tissue needs."[37] If mother's milk contains large amounts of substances not found in infant formulas, and the evidence is clear that formula-fed babies don't do as well in school or behavior over the course of their lives, how many questions have to be answered before the experts decide to mimic nature?[38]

THE SOY ALTERNATIVE

Soy formulas, the alternatives to dairy-based formulas, are specially designed for infants who are allergic to dairy products or for parents wishing to avoid giving their children any animal-based product. Are they better than cow's-milk formulas in terms of brain health?

They may, if possible, be even worse than the milk-based products. Soy-based formulas are rich in plant chemicals (phytochemicals) called isoflavones. The isoflavones so highly touted as the answer to menopause symptoms or reducing the risk of certain forms of cancer in the adult are actually plant-based estrogens. Infants on soy formula may receive the equivalent amount of estrogen that is found in five to ten birth control pills each day.

This daily shot of female hormones can have devastating effects on little boys. In the first six months, the normal infant male can produce approximately the same amount of testosterone as an adult male. It is through the influence of testosterone during this period that the little boy is programmed to be a man. Boys are wired differently in the brain than girls, giving them better three-dimensional perception, an advantage in some ways but a trait that makes some cognitive tasks a little dicier.

Boys on soy-based formulas not only are manufacturing large amounts of testosterone but also are ingesting huge amounts of estrogen. Receiving these confusing hormonal messages can wreak havoc with their emotionality. Many women know that imbalances in estrogen cause the quintessential menopause symptoms of depression, hostility, and aggressiveness. What does the excess estrogen do to little boys?

According to Dr. Wade Welshons, Ph.D., a researcher at the University of Missouri–Columbia,[39] little research has been done on the isoflavones (estrogens) in the infant formulas. Fifteen years ago and prior, when soy-based infant formulas had been developed and were being used as a healthy replacement for cow's milk–based formulas or by infants who were allergic to cow's milk, no negative effects could be seen owing to the use of the soy. Infants seemed to thrive. Because no immediate effects were seen, researchers stopped looking. Research dollars are limited, after all. Conversations about the safety of soy-based formulas are only now beginning to take place.

How a plant-based estrogen expresses itself in an immature infant is unclear. Scientists know that androgens and estrogens are essential in males and females in the developmental and mature stages of life. Both androgens and estrogens are responsible for sexual differentiation, and there are critical windows, or time periods, in the fetal period when these hormones influence different systems of the body. Both sexes need both hormones to develop properly, but in the gender ratios determined by nature.

Human studies on this issue are virtually nonexistent. Animal studies have been done, and while conclusions from animal studies cannot always be extrapolated to the human family, a picture of the possible effects on human babies emerges. Excessive estrogens (just fifty to one hundred percent greater than normal) in rodents during the fetal period lead to aggressiveness or problem behaviors, hyperactivity, precocious puberty in females (early menstruation and body development), increases in certain reproductive cancers, increased breast or prostate cancers, reduced sperm count, retention of testes in the body cavity (cryptorchidism), malformation of the male genitalia (hypospadias), increased risks of enlarged prostate gland, and increased risks of prostate cancer.[40]

According to an article published in the *Proceedings of the Society for Experimental Biology and Medicine,* the high content of estrogen in the soy-based formula results in permanent damage to the reproductive system. The authors write:

> It has long been known that modification of the sex steroid milieu in neonatal rodents alters reproductive axis function and sexual behavior and leads to structural changes in specific areas of the brain. The effects of neonatal steroid treatment, although irreversible, are often not manifested until the reproductive system is activated at puberty . . . [R]ecent theories on human sexual differentiation propose that there are several critical periods for development that occur not only prenatally but also during the early postnatal period.[41]

Sally Fallon, author of *Nourishing Traditions,* says the estrogen in the soy formula can inhibit the testosterone from having its effect on the male programming and on the wiring in the brain.[42] Some suggestions have been made concerning developmental delay. Scientists in New Zealand have been looking at the results of feeding high amounts of phytoestrogens and recently reported that when feeding an infant a soy-based formula along with cereal, the amount of estrogen (isoflavone) the baby received was greater than that shown to alter reproductive functions in adults.[43] The implications of this hormone assault on a developing child, whether male or female, are frightening.

How do plant-based estrogens work? The speculation has been that they act as a blocker on the estrogen receptor site, thereby leaving less access of "real" estrogen to the receptor. Others believe that phytoestrogens act as true hormones, thus increasing by exponential amounts the level of estrogens in the blood.

These potential effects occur due to increased levels of estrogen in the prenatal period, when these sex organs and the brain are developing and growing. Prenatal effects don't always correlate to effects later in life. Increased levels of hormones are transitory in the adult (the body has developed regulatory mechanisms that keep hormone levels in check). These regulatory mechanisms are not in place during the fetal and postfetal period, however, and effects are both different and potentially permanent.

When a cluster of syndromes is seen in the human population that can be produced experimentally in rodents, there is cause for concern. While science hasn't empirically proven that soy is a causative agent for behavioral problems in humans, we can make an inference. If excessive estrogen in rodents leads to increased aggressiveness, hyperactivity, and so on, and we are seeing similar characteristics in the human population, there may be a correlation. The excessive estrogens in soy-based formulas may be causing the increased antisocial behaviors later in life.

Soy-based formulas may not lead to increased aggressiveness in every child; it is possible that some humans can protect themselves from supraphysiological doses of phytoestrogens, but it is also likely that not everyone has the same level of built-in protection. Some children may indeed suffer the consequences of too much estrogen at a critical period in their developmental history. At the very least, the necessary research to learn if this is really the case must be done.[44]

Not only are babies getting supraphysiological doses of estrogen with every sip of formula, they also get a dose of pseudo-estrogen from some baby bottles and teething rings, particularly those made from a clear, rigid plastic called polycarbonate.

Consumer Reports states that polycarbonate leaches a chemical called bisphenol-A, which "has produced physiological effects similar to those produced by estrogen. During such 'endocrine disruption,' chemicals interfere with or mimic the action of hormones, possibly upsetting normal development . . . Based on testing with an intact bottle, we calculate that a typical baby who drank formula sterilized by heating in a bottle would be exposed to a bisphenol-A dose of about 4 percent of an amount that has adversely affected test animals . . . Such exposure may sound very low. However, safety limits for infant exposure can be set as low as 0.1 percent of the level that has adversely affected animals."[45]

They warn that babies could be exposed to a dose of the chemical about forty times higher than a conservative estimate of safety and recommend that you dispose of all clear, shiny plastic baby bottles unless you know that they are not made from polycarbonate.

In his article "Soya Infant Formula: The Health Concerns (A Food Commission Briefing Paper)," Dr. Mike Fitzpatrick of New Zealand lists health concerns regarding soy-based infant formulas:

> The potential for biological effects in infants due to the soy isoflavones has been clearly identified and includes changes in the function of sex glands, the central nervous system, the thyroid, and behavioural patterns.
>
> Exposure of infants fed soy-based formulas to isoflavones is high, greater than 1000 times that found for infants fed on breast-milk or cow's-milk based formula.
>
> Isoflavones are readily absorbed by infants and the levels of isoflavones in the blood plasma of infants fed soy-based formulas are comparable to levels that exert significant estrogenic effects in experimental animals.
>
> Like many endocrine disruptors, the soy isoflavones cause thyroid dysfunction in humans . . .
>
> In one UK feeding study involving premenopausal women, 60g of soy protein per day for one month disrupted the menstrual cycle and the effects of isoflavones continued for three months even after cessation of the soy diet. These effects were at dose per body-weight levels at least one order of magnitude lower than levels that soy-based formula-fed infants are exposed to. For infants, high levels of exposure, coupled with frequent and regular feeding throughout the day, results in soy-based formula fed infants having much higher plasma levels of isoflavones than any other population group . . .
>
> The effects of isoflavones on adult women to date are changes to the sex steroid hormone status and nipple fluid secretion . . .
>
> The reproductive and developmental toxicity of isoflavones has been demonstrated in several species of animals.
>
> It was the toxicity of dietary levels of isoflavones in animals that first raised the awareness of the scientific community to the

fact that soy isoflavones were endocrine disruptors. Reproductive effects, infertility, thyroid disease or liver disease due to dietary intake of isoflavones had been observed for several animals including cheetah, quail, mice, rats, sturgeon, and sheep.[46]

Soy Foods Block the Absorption of Brain-Essential Minerals

Unfermented soy products contain another natural protein that makes soy-based formulas hazardous to your baby's health: phytic acid. Phytic acid is classed as an antinutrient because it blocks the absorption of minerals, especially calcium, zinc, and magnesium. All three minerals play a crucial role in brain health. Zinc and magnesium are used in hundreds of brain enzymes, and low levels of these two minerals are associated with symptoms like depression, aggressiveness, emotional instability, easily aroused anger, learning disabilities, blood sugar disorders, and so on. Even if the formula has been supplemented with minerals to more closely reflect the typical profile in human milk, the phytic acid in the soy formula will block the absorption of those minerals. They will simply pass on through the body and be excreted in the stool.

Fermenting soy products to make tofu and other foods eliminates the phytic acid content of the soy product, but baby products are produced from unfermented soybeans.

Zinc and copper are antagonistic essential minerals. The body needs about 8.5 times more zinc than copper, and keeping these minerals in this proportion is critically important to the health of the brain. Phytic acids in soy block the absorption of zinc in the intestine, which increases copper and unbalances these two powerful minerals. High levels of copper increase emotional lability and cause low energy (by pulling down thyroid hormone), depression, emotional hyperactivity, and mood swings mimicking bipolar disorder.[47]

Babies fed on soy formulas are shown to have a "negative zinc balance"—in other words, babies are losing zinc more rapidly than they are taking it in.[48]

Low zinc levels become problematic for a number of reasons, whether or not they were induced by soy-based formulas. Zinc plays a role in the metabolism of essential fatty acids in the brain and is essential in the myelination of the neuron sheath. Low zinc levels can aggravate EFA deficiency and cause a reduction of the fatty acids in the myelin sheath. When a double deficiency in EFA and zinc occurs simultaneously, as when a soy-based formula is given, for example, there may be an even greater impairment in brain development and maturation.[49]

Just to revisit briefly the cholesterol issue in relation to soy-based formulas, there is no cholesterol in soy-based formulas; cholesterol is needed to form the structural base for much of the brain's architecture. The other essential fatty acids are inadequately supplied, as well.

MOM MADE IT HERSELF

Most of us who were born in the thirties, forties, or fifties remember the homemade formula that mothers used when they couldn't afford commercial formulas, but few of us remember where that recipe came from. It took a little digging, but I found the origin of the homemade infant formula. It came from the medical profession. An article published in *JAMA* in 1930 gives the recipe:

> Wright and Geddes assert that it is perfectly safe to feed normal babies during the first year by appetite on lactic acid whole milk 20 ounces (600 cc) with the addition of 2 ounces (60 cc) of 50 per cent corn syrup, at four hour intervals, five feedings in the twenty-four hours, and for exactly twenty minutes at each feeding, boiled water being offered between feedings and the accessory food factors supplied in adequate amounts. Furthermore, they are inclined to believe that some such simplified feeding is safer to place in the hands of the busy general practitioner than one that requires to be modified at regular intervals.[50]

This homemade version of infant formula, promoted by the medical profession, was even worse than the commercially prepared formulas, if possi-

Why isn't your doctor or your child's pediatrician more supportive of breast-feeding? Many women have noticed that their doctors are ambivalent on the subject and may make only passing references to the fact that breast-feeding is important.

A study published in one peer-reviewed magazine noted that "even though supportive of breast feeding the house staff was not knowledgeable about breast feeding management, answering only 53% of the questions correctly. Only 14% of the doctors described themselves as confident or very confident to manage common breast feeding problems. The authors conclude that physicians in training have very limited knowledge of breast feeding management."[51]

If our culture is to receive the support it needs from the medical profession, adequate training must be provided in medical schools regarding the importance of breast milk in the developing child. But perhaps in this male-dominated profession, the first change to be made is a change of attitude in the doctors themselves.

ble. For one thing, there is clear evidence that feeding cow's milk to an infant sets him up for a greater risk of developing juvenile-onset diabetes, either due to a type of protein called bovine serum albumin (BSA) that can be found in cow's milk–based infant formulas or other milk products, or because cow's milk often stimulates the production of other antibodies that may destroy portions of the pancreas.[52]

Canned whole milk is substantially higher in calories, in sugar, in fat, and in protein, creating the potential for juvenile obesity. Throw in some corn syrup, and not only does the allergy potential increase (corn is a highly allergenic food), setting the baby up for a lifelong tendency toward corn and dairy allergies, but the mineral balance is skewed, particularly with respect to sodium and potassium ratios.

Infants fed whole cow's milk formulas are exposed to inadequate intakes of iron, the essential fatty acid linoleic acid, and vitamin E, and excessive intakes of sodium, potassium, and protein.[53] Every one of these nutrient imbalances affects brain development.

A Mother's Diet Supports a Growing Brain

Even though breast-feeding is nearly always better than any type of formula, our traditional American food culture itself may be jeopardizing the quality of breast milk. If the correct proportions of essential fats or essential amino acids will be deposited into the breast milk, they first must be present in the diet. Some of these fundamental building blocks of a healthy brain are disappearing from even the "good foods" mother may be purchasing and eating.

We have seen how important fatty acids are in the structure and functionality of the brain. It is critically important for the prenatal mother's diet to contain adequate levels of Omega-3 and Omega-6 fatty acids, and that the correct proportion of these be given through the first two years of life while the baby's brain is being built. But even in human milk, differences in the EFA balance can occur, depending on the types of foods the mother enjoys.

Because Japanese and Eskimo mothers typically eat more ocean fish, their breast milks are higher in the Omega-3 fatty acids than the milk from mothers in other cultures. A vegetarian mother's milk contains higher amounts of the essential fatty acid linoleic acid (Omega-6) and less of the essential DHA and EPA (Omega-3 fatty acids). But the real issue is not in trivial preferences (I enjoy fish and broccoli; you prefer chicken and asparagus). It is doubtful we can ensure excellent brain structure and function unless we look closely at the maternal diet and make serious alterations.[54]

Women who consume large amounts of trans-fatty acids (as found in margarine and other hydrogenated products, for example) have lower amounts of essential fatty acids in their breast milk. Hydrogenated fats are not adequate for optimum development of brain tissue. If you are pregnant or breast-feeding, now is the time to make those dietary changes away from highly processed fats and oils, and enjoy the beneficial oils provided by nature, like deep-sea fish, butter, olive oil, raw nuts and seeds, and the like. These oils will help construct a healthy brain in your growing child.

Evidence also shows that unless the diet is seriously deficient, the composition of mother's milk is still superior to any man-made substance. Wisdom tells us that if we want our baby's brains to be developed to their full genetic potential, we will eat the very freshest, the very best foods we can. Above all, we will turn our backs on the American food culture and choose to eat traditional foods instead.

THE INFANT NUTRITION PRIMER

Young women who have never thought about nutrition become interested in the topic when a new life begins to form inside their bellies. Most of the time this interest wanes after the baby is born; they want to get back into their normal clothes again and get on with life. Some young mothers who have engaged in destructive behaviors during adolescence get their act together when they find out they are pregnant. They try to eat and live a healthier life, knowing that the life of their baby is at stake.

Ideally, good nutritional habits should become part of both the father and mother's life several months or years before conception. By the time a new mother realizes she is pregnant, several weeks have passed during which the brain of her child has been rapidly developing. Providing good nutrition during those first weeks helps to lay a good foundation for the structure of the brain tissue.

To produce healthy sperm, fathers need to be well nourished from the outset as well. Nutritionally aware doctors often recommend that young couples prepare for birth several months before expecting to conceive. The prenatal period while the child is developing in the womb is when nutrients like Omega-3 fatty acids, Omega-6 fatty acids, minerals, vitamins, and proteins are needed so that the developing brain grows properly.

Over the past few years of counseling clients and giving lectures to younger and older women, I also have become concerned with how many women never really recuperate from the process of giving birth. By the time they have nourished their babies in the womb for nine months, then breast-fed their child for several months, their mineral and vitamin stores are so depleted that fatigue, depression, and a host of other symptoms dog their steps.

Postpartum depression often sets in shortly after mother returns home from the hospital, and it is all she can do to care for the baby, let alone feel the normal maternal love. Deficiencies in certain minerals can trigger these feelings. For example, the hormones estrogen, progesterone, and oxytocin play a role in maternal bonding.[55] Estrogen and progesterone are closely associated with zinc and copper levels. When estrogen is dominant, copper is dominant; when progesterone is dominant or more optimally balanced with estrogen, zinc is dominant (as it should be). High levels of estrogen (in relation to progesterone) with low zinc levels can reduce the bonding instinct in the mother.

Other Minerals in the Maternal Diet

Building strong bones in a growing infant takes a toll on the magnesium and calcium stores of the mother. Over sixty percent of Americans are deficient in magnesium. Many symptoms of magnesium deficiency are emotional or mental in nature: depression, anger, fears and panic attacks, emotional instability, and fatigue. Unless these minerals are made very adequate in the postpartum mother, it is difficult for her to maintain her emotional balance, especially in the face of sleepless nights, a crying infant, and an altered marriage relationship. If these nutrients are in short supply for Mom, her baby will be undersupplied in the breast milk as well.

Continuing to eat processed foods only prolongs the deficiency state, making it increasingly difficult to recover from childbirth. The new mother should spurn the Betty Crocker, General Mills, Kellogg's, Shake 'n Bake, Coca-Cola, and Lay's potato chip aisles of the grocery store and seek out the fresh produce and animal protein departments.

It is particularly difficult for the young mother with several little ones running around her feet to eat healthy meals. Every time she steps foot into the grocery store, little ones in tow, the bombardment starts. "Mommy, can I get this? Huh, huh? Oh, look! I want this! Here, Mommy, let's buy this!" Items slip unnoticed into the grocery cart and magically appear on the checkout belt. Frosted Flakes, Froot Loops, Raisin Bran,

Honey Crunch Corn Flakes, Corn Pops . . . Kool-Aid, Jell-O, Oscar Meyer Lunchables, Kraft Macaroni and Cheese . . . the worst of the junk.

A mother's energy stores are so low from pregnancy and keeping up with her children that she often falls into the junk food rut, snacking on the run. After the kids are tucked into bed for a nap, she sits down to a cup of coffee and a bowl of sugared cereal just to infuse enough energy to get her through the rest of the afternoon. What she should have done is enjoyed a healthy snack, then curled up on the sofa with a pillow and blanket and drifted off to sleep for a few minutes.

Snacking on healthy foods (with natural oils, protein, and unrefined carbohydrates) will help keep her energy levels high and improve the quality of her breast milk. Some healthy snacks might include almond butter stuffed into a celery stalk, hard-boiled eggs, fruit and cottage cheese, fresh fruit, raw vegetables with a favorite dressing, turkey breast on rice cakes, or salad with an olive oil and vinegar dressing. These healthy foods will feed her brain and her body, providing the energy to care for and enjoy her children.

These snack suggestions are good for both the pregnant and the postpartum mother. (See Chapter 8 for more snack recipes.)

What Will My Baby Eat?

You need to decide what you will feed your child before he or she is born. Get as much information as possible about the benefits of breast-feeding and determine in your heart that breast milk is the best food for your baby. Good sources of information include your doctor, midwife, online sources, and books, and Appendix I in the back of this book. Decide how you are going to work breast-feeding into your life and schedule. There is no question that breast-feeding is best for your child nutritionally. Emotionally and spiritually it is best for your child as well. The bonding that takes place while the baby is nursing will last for a lifetime.

Some of my most precious memories are the hours my babies and I spent together cuddling on the bed, rocking them to sleep in the rocker, or finding a quiet spot in a noisy restaurant or the car to feed them. Often, it was only at those times that other people would leave me alone for a few minutes of peace and quiet. I treasured peace and quiet when the children were small.

Settle it in your mind that you will give your child one of the most precious gifts possible—your breast milk—and that you will continue to nurse your baby as long as possible (two years or so). If, after nine months or so, you believe that your child will benefit from supplementary food, start with a little fresh fruit like bananas or peaches, mashed, unsweetened. Under no circumstances give your baby any type of grains other than a little brown rice for the first eighteen months to two years of his or her life, to reduce the possibility of grain allergy. Grain allergies are one of the most common sources of depression and learning disabilities in the adult and the older child. Do not give your child any type of cow's milk products before the age of two.

What Should a Breast-feeding Mother Eat?

Once you've made the decision to breast-feed your baby, don't be dissuaded by those who suddenly profess to know what is best for you and your child. When I was pregnant with my first child, an older woman regaled me with tales about how breast-feeding causes the breasts to sag. Being young and impressionable, and above all, not wanting to grow old before my time, her stories scared me. I finally stopped listening to her and kept my resolve to nurse my child. Sagging breasts are not the worst that can happen to a woman (it doesn't happen from breast-feeding anyway).

What will you feed yourself during the pregnancy and breast-feeding periods? Chapter 8 provides many healthy recipes and menus that you may enjoy, designed to provide good-quality fats, proteins, and carbohydrates. These foods are rich in the essential fats, amino acids, vitamins, and minerals. The high-quality nutrition from these meals will be passed on to your nursing child.

The nutritional quality of breast milk can vary remarkably, depending on the diet of the mother. For example, the milk of women who eat large amounts of trans-fatty acids (margarine, fried foods, shortening, etc.) contains harmful amounts of trans-fatty acids that are passed on to her child. In fact, trans-fatty acids are transmitted through the placenta[56] into the fetus, impairing formation of the brain tissue. Trans-fatty acids block the metabolism of the beneficial oils, reducing their potential in the body. Avoid the trans-fatty acids found in margarine, shortening, and products made with hydrogenated oils. Read the small print on packaged products carefully.

On the other hand, the milk of mothers who include the beneficial Omega-3 and Omega-6 fatty acids, healthy proteins, lots of brightly colored vegetables, and so on, is rich in the essential elements.

It is also important to drink more than ten glasses of pure water each day and, whenever possible, to choose organic meats and produce. Not only are organic foods higher in nutrient content, but they are free from the hormones and other chemicals that influence brain chemistry. We can't avoid chemical exposure, but we can limit exposure, and reducing the toxic burden from foods and the environment is particularly important to growing children.

Having said that, it goes without saying that the breast-feeding mother needs to avoid aspartame, monosodium glutamate, and other chemicals known to induce brain damage. Just as these substances cross the placental barrier, they cross into the breast milk and the blood-brain barrier, passing directly into your baby's brain to inflict its subtle damage.

What if Your Baby Must Be Put on Formula?

Most artificial formulas synthesized in a laboratory will not provide adequate nutrition for your growing baby's brain. They may grow a large, strong body, but physical growth will be achieved at the expense of his brain. Advertising campaigns or simplicity of the purchase should put no weight on this decision, because the mental health of your child is dependent on feeding him the right balance of all essential nutrients. Good food is important if he is going to be well adjusted and intelligent throughout life.

If there really is no alternative and the baby must be put on the bottle, it is of critical importance that care be given to the choice of the formula. The infant formula must provide a nutritional composition similar to breast milk in essential fats, essential amino acids, sugars, minerals, and vitamins. A number of companies are working to put together infant formulas that more closely match the composition of mother's milk. Check Appendix I in the back of this book for more information.

It is unlikely that even the most astute nutritionist can formulate an infant product to exactly match baby's requirements. However, in her book *Nourishing Traditions*, author Sally Fallon gives a recipe for infant formula that will more closely resemble mother's own milk than do the present commercial products. It does require a commitment of time to prepare these formulas. But the essential fatty acids are similar to those in mother's milk, and the amino acid balance is also similar. If you are interested in preparing your own homemade formula using Sally's recipe, please reference her book, *Nourishing Traditions*. For information on how to obtain the book, please call 1-877-707-1776.[57]

Conclusion

Unfortunately, infant formula manufacturers are only the first line of companies to produce products that inadequately support essential brain development. Our children aren't safe once they've been weaned and put on solid foods. How can we ensure that the nutritional needs of their brains and bodies will be met after they have left our arms and reached for a knife and fork?

4

Feeding Your Child's Brain

It's so simple, so simple. If your child has a hard time falling asleep or staying asleep, cannot concentrate in school or at home, has low grades in school, suffers with allergies, is prone to headaches, is hyperactive or listless, is overweight, cannot go for more than four hours without eating, has a hard time keeping friendships, or has colds or bacterial infections more than once a year, I suggest that you remove sugar (all forms) from his or her diet for two weeks . . . Once sugar has been removed from the diet, energy levels increase, concentration levels become stronger, and self-esteem improves.

—NANCY APPLETON, PH.D.[1]

We've seen the results of poor nutrition through the prenatal and infant period of life. It is frightening for mothers to contemplate that they may, unintentionally, share the responsibility for causing this damage by not breast-feeding through that entire period of development. We thought we were doing the right thing by choosing the very best formula.

The problem is, we now have a situation. Our child's brain may not have received adequate nutrition to lay a healthy foundation of essential fatty acids, or it may not have built an adequate supply of receptor sites for serotonin or other calming neurotransmitters. Our son or daughter may look normal, but we know there is a problem. It is subtle, and difficult to describe to a pediatrician. Something is wrong with our child's brain, in his or her demeanor.

Our boy seems hyperactive. He can't sit still in class and can't concentrate on his work. Our girl is too aggressive in play and throws fits of anger that seem disproportionate to the offense. She doesn't sleep soundly and can't follow a simple set of instructions. The teacher has suggested Ritalin or Prozac. Maybe the school counselor has offered to make an appointment with a family counselor because your child doesn't get along with others on the playground.

You've taken your son to the pediatrician, who dutifully measures and examines him and can find nothing wrong. Something isn't right, but you don't know how to explain it. Mothers know their children at a level that reaches deeper than the eye can see. She senses when something is amiss with her child because of the emotional bond that developed when she carried him in her womb and (hopefully) fed him at her breast.

A mother and child know each other at a soul level.

BEYOND THE DEVELOPING BRAIN

From the moment of conception until roughly two years of age, the brain and nervous system form new tissue and lay down networks of dendrites and axons. The brain weaves neurons, dendrites, and axons into a complex that paves the way for future development, when the child is exposed to new learning stimuli.

After the initial growth has occurred, brain development does not cease. Myelin continues to be built around the axons and dendrites, improving the transmission of nerve signals. Neurons no longer develop, but each new learning phase causes the size of the neuron to expand and more dendrites to form, so that enriched learning environments do indeed enhance brain growth and development.

Beginning at the age of two and throughout life, neurons sprout new dendrites and axons to connect different parts of the brain in reaction to the types of stimulation they receive. When an environment is rich in language, with parents engaging their children in meaningful two-way conversation, the area of the brain associated with speech develops at a higher rate than an area not as enriched.

The same is true for tactile stimulation, when a mother and father are physically affectionate or encourage their child to learn by touching objects. This type of development is called plasticity, and it can vastly increase the weight of the brain in specific areas. The research has focused on environmental or learning richness, not nutrient richness. However, brains don't grow from air, even if their learning environment is rich. They grow from nutrients, provided in the diet.

Speaking nutritionally, a child's diet must continue to provide all the materials needed if this growth is to continue throughout childhood. These nutritional needs do not differ significantly from the needs of infancy, except that calorie requirements may increase or decrease, depending on levels of activity and growth rate. From the standpoint of continued need for essential fatty acids, essential amino acids, vitamins, minerals, water, and high-quality carbohydrates, there is little difference.

GROWING A CHILD'S BRAIN

Children grow from the age of weaning through the late teenage years, laying down new tissue at an astonishing rate. They grow from roughly twenty-five pounds to well over one hundred pounds, in muscle mass, bone tissue, and other structures throughout the body. While they are adding new tissue, metabolic needs have to be met. These needs consume calories, and because most kids are a bundle of combustible energy, keeping those arms and legs in motion requires a significant supply of calories.

The calorie requirements for children are high, thirteen hundred to two thousand calories per day. They need thirty or more grams of well-balanced protein (containing all eight essential amino acids). Fats are important, too, for structure and function tasks, and should comprise roughly twenty-five to thirty percent of total calorie intake.

> CRAZY MAKER
> ★
> **AWARD**
>
> CHILDREN'S DIVISION/FIRST PLACE: American baby-food manufacturers for producing foods that contain unsafe levels of insecticides and other potentially toxic chemicals.

All fats are created equal, but they don't remain equal if they've been highly processed. The fats needed to build the structure of the brain and meet energy requirements are the essential fatty acids in the form of linoleic acid, linolenic acid, gamma-linolenic acid, Omega-3 fatty acids, DHA, and others. The remaining dietary energy is obtained from unrefined carbohydrates found in fruits, vegetables, and whole grains.

Children need vitamins and minerals to fuel their enzymes and energy production; essential amino acids to build tissue and synthesize more than three hundred thousand different functional proteins; and water to keep their bodies clean on the inside and provide a moist environment for the enzymes to work. Kids need everything adults need, but in higher amounts in proportion to their body size. We'll look at the typical diet of a child and see what it is comprised of and what its ingredients are.

WHAT GOES INTO A CHILD'S FOOD?

Pesticides

When we see the Gerber baby with wide, innocent eyes on a jar of mashed peas or bananas, we automatically think, *wholesome.* However,

While the Recommended Dietary Allowance (RDA) for nutrients is by no means complete, it will provide a rough sketch of the nutrients needed to prevent frank diseases. The following chart lists the RDA (for children) of a few of the known nutrients:[2]

Recommended Dietary Allowance for Children

Protein

Age (Yrs)	Weight (kg)	(lb)	Height (cm)	(in)	Protein (g)
1–3	13	29	90	35	16
4–6	20	44	112	44	24
7–10	28	62	132	52	28

Fat-Soluble Vitamins

Age (Yrs)	Vitamin A (IU)	Vitamin D (IU)	Vitamin E (IU)	Vitamin K (IU)
1–3	400	10	6	15
4–6	500	10	7	20
7–10	700	10	7	30

Water-Soluble Vitamins

Age (Yrs)	Vitamin C (mg)	Thiamin (mg)	Riboflavin (mg)	Niacin (mg)	Vitamin B_6 (mg)	Folate (mg)	Vitamin B_{12} (mg)
1–3	40	0.7	0.8	9	1.0	50	0.7
4–6	45	0.9	1.1	12	1.1	75	1.0
7–10	45	1.0	1.1	13	1.4	100	1.4

Minerals

Age (Yrs)	Calcium (mg)	Phosphorus (mg)	Magnesium (mg)	Iron (mg)	Zinc (mg)	Iodine (mg)	Selenium (mg)
1–3	800	800	80	10	10	70	20
4–6	800	800	120	10	10	90	20
7–10	800	800	170	10	10	120	30

hidden in some of these jars of mashed peas and carrots, spinach, or peaches may be chemicals that can have a powerful effect on the brain of your baby. According to the Campaign for Food Safety and other sources, high levels of organophosphate insecticide residues that are toxic to the neurological and endocrinological systems are in many of our most popular baby foods.

According to the Environmental Working Group (EWG), a watchdog environmental organization, nine out of ten children under the age of five are exposed to thirteen different neurotoxic insecticides in their baby foods. While these chemicals rarely cause acute illness, they have the potential to cause long-term damage to the brain and nervous system, which are rapidly growing and are extremely vulnerable to injury during this formative period. For infants from six to twelve months of age, commercial baby food is the dominant source of unsafe levels of organophosphate insecticides (OPs).[3]

Studies done on organophosphate residues are inadequate for children and infants, because safe dosage levels are based on adults, never on children. Many of the exposures to these potent substances exceed safe levels by wide margins. OPs on apples, peaches, grapes, and pear baby food cause 85,000 children each day to exceed the federal safety standard by a factor of ten or more.

Gerber is, by far, the biggest player in the market, with a sixty-nine-percent market share. An article in *Nutrition Week* reported that "laboratory tests of 8 baby foods contain residues of 16 different pesticides. These pesticides were found in lower levels than allowed by federal regulators, but the group stressed that pesticide standards are set for adults, not infants."[4]

No one knows for sure if pesticides cause brain damage. Although testing of the effects of food additives on the liver, brain, kidneys, blood-forming organs, and excretory and reproductive systems is required under the Color Additive Amendment of 1960, it is impossible to test every additive, every pesticide, every herbicide, or every other chemical in the environment. It is even more impossible to test the combined effects of these chemicals.

It stands to reason that if the pesticide disrupts the endocrine or nervous system of the insects they are meant to kill, they could have a similar effect on your growing baby. The purpose of a pesticide is, after all, to either kill insect pests or make them sterile so they can't reproduce. We don't want that. We want healthy, good-natured children, and someday, we want to have grandchildren, too.

The USDA monitors and helps regulate the types and amounts of pesti-cides allowable in our food supply and issues reports from time to time on their findings. According to their figures, from 1964 to 1992, pesticide use in agriculture increased almost 2.5 times. In 1964, 232,750,000 pounds of chemical pesticides were used on U.S. crops; in 1992, 573,907,000 pounds were used, even though total cropland barely increased at all. Browsing the USDA Web site (www.usda.gov) for information on pesticide use can be instructive for an interested parent.

In 1992, 63.8 percent of the oranges tested had residues of the fungi-cide thiabendazole, 59.3 percent of the potatoes tested had residues of the pesticide chlorpropham, 56.5 percent of the peaches had residues of Ipro-dione, and so on. The USDA says the risks are "negligible"; however, chil-dren are more vulnerable to physical damage from these toxic chemicals because kids eat more food per pound of body weight and their neurolog-ical systems are still being developed.[5]

According to the EWG laboratory, the following foods produced by Gerber, Heinz, and Beech-Nut were tested, with the results as shown:

Baby Food	Number of Pesticides Found	Health Effects
Pears	5	Neurotoxins Endocrine disruptors
Peaches	4	Carcinogens Neurotoxins
Applesauce	4	Neurotoxins
Plums	3	Carcinogens Neurotoxins
Squash	3	Carcinogens
Green beans	3	Neurotoxins Endocrine disruptors
Sweet potatoes	2	Effect unknown

More than one-half of all samples contained detectable levels of pesticides.[6] Most of the residues were in doses of a few parts per million, but
even these tiny amounts can wreak havoc on the sensitive neuronal and
hormonal systems of the human body. Tiny amounts of chemicals, either
naturally or artificially produced, can have enormous influences on different body systems. Estrogen, for example, is active in nanogram amounts (a
small paper clip weighs about one gram; a nanogram is one-billionth the
weight of a paper clip).

The residues of pesticides found in baby foods are present in much
higher amounts than estrogen and can similarly influence biochemical
pathways, particularly in the brain and endocrine system. Some of the most
common neurotoxic pesticides are organophosphate and carbamate insecticides, which inhibit the normal function of the nervous system enzyme
acetylcholinesterase. Behavioral effects and damage to the nervous system
may result from low-level chronic exposure to these harmful chemicals.

Current safety standards, the National Academy of Sciences observed,
are no guarantee of protection for children:

> The data strongly suggest that exposure to neurotoxic compounds
> at levels believed to be safe for adults could result in permanent
> loss of brain function if it occurred during the prenatal or early
> childhood period of brain development. This information is par-
> ticularly relevant to dietary exposure to pesticides, since policies
> that established safe levels of exposure to neurotoxic pesticides for
> adults could not be assumed to adequately protect a child less
> than four years of age . . . Notably, the Academy committee con-
> cluded that it is the additive effect of simultaneous exposure to
> pesticides causing the same toxic effect that presents the real world
> risk to infants and children. There are no standards to protect in-
> fants, children or anyone else from multiple pesticides in food (or
> from other sources). The EPA has just begun to consider the ad-
> ditive effects of certain groups of pesticides. The special additive
> adverse effects that these combined exposures may have on the
> young, however, are not being studied.[7]

Pesticide use is growing every year. Many of these pesticides are toxic to the nervous system and brain of your young child, but the cumulative effects of these chemicals on the growing child are not being studied—and these pesticides are showing up in your baby's food.

MSG Is a Natural Food?

In addition to pesticide residues, we also have to consider additives that are intentionally supplemented to baby food to make it taste better.

MSG is categorized as an excitoxin, a chemical that causes a brain cell to become overexcited and fire uncontrollably. MSG (and other excitoxins like aspartame) has the potential for inflicting permanent damage on a growing brain and nervous system. It is known that MSG and aspartame readily cross the placental barrier and can overstimulate the growing brain of the fetus.

MSG first appeared when the Japanese added a sea vegetable called kombu to foods to enhance the natural flavors of the food. In the early part of this century, scientists learned that the ingredient that imparted the intense flavors in kombu was monosodium glutamate, or MSG. The Ajinomoto Company started producing MSG and hydrolyzed vegetable protein (which contains MSG) for export around the world.

After World War II, American food-processing companies jumped on the bandwagon and started adding millions of pounds to processed foods, including baby foods. Millions of metric tons of MSG are now produced worldwide and are added to thousands of food products. The Ajinomoto Company still produces most of the world's supply of MSG.

Over the past few decades, scores of research projects have examined MSG to learn what effect it has on the body, and by some accounts, this chemical is perfectly benign. But in 1957, two ophthalmologists, Lucas and Newhouse, tested MSG on infant mice to learn if it could be used to treat retinal dystrophy. To their dismay, they found that MSG destroyed the nerve cells in the inner layers of the animal's retinas. Ten years later researcher John Olney, M.D., found that not only was MSG toxic to the retina but that specialized cells in the hypothalamus were destroyed as well.

The hypothalamus regulates the autonomic nervous system (contraction of smooth muscle and cardiac muscle and secretions of gland, etc.), is associated with feelings of rage and aggression, regulates body temperature, regulates food intake and thirst, and maintains wake and sleep patterns. The hypothalamus is unprotected by the blood-brain barrier and is therefore susceptible to damage from the influx of toxic materials.[8]

In the late 1950s, MSG was routinely being added to baby foods in doses equal to levels that created brain lesions in experimental animals. Dr. Olney testified before a congressional committee and manufacturers were forbidden from adding MSG to baby foods. Even if pure MSG is no longer added to baby food, our children are still not safe, however. One of the active constituents of MSG, glutamate, is embedded in other ingredients commonly added to baby food, and can have the same effect on the baby's brain.

In the place of MSG, manufacturers started adding to baby foods hydrolyzed vegetable protein (HVP), autolyzed yeast, caseinate, and other flavor enhancers that contain large of amounts of glutamate.[9] In a container of Gerber Graduates with Mini Meatballs & Sauce we find the usual ingredients of water, cooked meatballs, and spaghetti, and as we continue through the list, we find torula yeast and autolyzed yeast. Autolyzed yeast is added to baby food to enhance flavors. A representative from the Gerber consumer information division confirmed that the autolyzed yeast "is rich in natural flavor, and enhances other natural flavors."

Russell Blaylock, M.D., author of *Excitotoxins: The Taste That Kills,* believes that autolyzed, or torula, yeast is a rich source of glutamate, a form of MSG, and gives baby food that special taste that keeps him wanting more.[10] According to Dr. Blaylock, a food label boasting "No added MSG" can be accurate according to the FDA standard, but the product can nevertheless contain huge amounts of glutamic acid.

Under certain pH conditions, glutamic acid has the same chemical composition as MSG and produces the same effect on the brain and nervous system. Food-processing companies do not have to state that MSG is in a product unless it is 99.5 percent pure MSG, even if high amounts of glutamate from other sources are added. You may be feeding substantial amounts of this dangerous excitotoxin to your baby and not even be aware of it.

There is no problem with MSG, according to the government. According to the FDA, "FDA believes that MSG is a safe food ingredient for the general population." They regard it among food ingredients that are "generally recognized as safe" and require that it must be declared on the label of food to which it is added.[11]

Dr. Blaylock believes that the neurologic effects might be subtle, such as a slight case of dyslexia, or more severe, such as frequent outbursts of uncontrollable anger. Excitotoxins like MSG could cause conditions such as autism, schizophrenia, seizures, and cerebral palsy; early exposure could cause a tendency for episodic violence and criminal behavior in later years. Experimental evidence in animals shows that such exposure can result in behavioral changes.[12]

In pregnancy, there is evidence that MSG may be concentrated on the fetal side of the placenta so that the child receives a higher dose. In normal brain development, more dendrites and axons are developed than are needed, and eventually are selectively pruned out, using a sudden burst of glutamate. Once glutamate has finished its job of removing the extra dendrites, levels of glutamate drop and the pruning is completed. In a brain that receives excessive amounts of glutamate during this critical period of development, the pruning process is disrupted so that excessive numbers of dendrites are thinned out, causing shrinkage of the dendrites, loss of terminals, and loss of synaptic connections.

Newly formed brain cells migrate after cell division into the section of the brain where they take up permanent residence. In the presence of excessive glutamate, the migration of the cells is altered, causing the development of abnormal brain tissue.

Children who have been deprived of adequate amounts of essential fatty acids may be particularly vulnerable. There is strong evidence showing that if the brain has not received adequate fats during the developmental stage, it cannot handle later exposure to glutamate. DHA and other lipids are required in the building of the brain cells, but unless a mother is particularly careful with her diet during pregnancy, each child born to the same woman receives less and less DHA, so that the last child receives the lowest amount.

In a study where MSG was fed to infant mice, one single dose increased free-radical damage to the brain by sixty percent, an effect that lasted all the way to adolescence. This one dose also produced damage to the liver, endothelial cells, the circulatory system, and cells throughout the body.

The mice exposed to MSG during pregnancy and early childhood did fine, but later in life they had more difficulty performing mental tasks requiring logical thinking or memory. Scientists also found lowered levels of acetylcholine, a neurotransmitter that plays a large role in memory and learning, and of norepinephrine, a neurotransmitter that plays a role in attention.

There is a strong association between excitotoxin exposure and receptor sites in the brain, particularly dopamine receptor sites. Exposure to excitotoxins during early brain development affects dopamine receptors that may produce schizophrenic behavior later in life, and also addictive be-

As a mom trying to get kids to eat nutritious foods, I have fought many times the addictive-type reactions to processed foods. Why would a child opt for nutrient-poor "junk food" when the body actually prefers "real food"?

I asked Dr. Blaylock if MSG or other excitotoxins are addictive. He wrote me, "They are not strictly addictive, but when food tastes very good, it becomes addictive in the sense that food preferences are altered. A child or teenager will prefer junk food enhanced with MSG over more nutritionally dense foods with unaltered tastes. MSG encourages the consumption of junk food."[13]

MSG or other artificial flavor enhancers give food a greater-than-nature, "better-than-good" taste, blunting the taste for the natural flavors found in real food. By contrast, real food tastes bland, setting children up to permanently dislike natural food.

haviors, violence, attention deficit hyperactivity disorder (ADHD), and other problems of the brain. This type of damage may express itself in different ways, depending on when exposure took place, if adequate DHA was present during the brain developmental period, the level of antioxidants, and so on, plus the genetic influence.

Research results have not shown a clear picture, because the damage is not always readily apparent; subtle forms of damage may take years to express. Our children can appear perfectly normal. They can get by in elementary school, but when they enter high school and are required to engage in difficult cognitive functions, they may have a more difficult time with logic, or they may be reading-impaired.

Flavor enhancers like MSG, autolyzed yeast, and HVP are added to many processed foods especially designed for the growing kid market. A cursory glance through the supermarket shelves reveals that many well-known kids' foods are laced with the stuff. A partial list of foods to which straight MSG has been added includes:

- Doritos
- Cheetos
- Land O'Frost and Taste Escapes packaged entrées for kids
- Oscar Mayer Lunchables
- Salad dressings like ranch dressing
- Hamburger Helper, Tuna Helper, Chicken Helper, and others
- Nabisco flavored crackers
- Sunshine Cheez-Its
- Pepperidge Farm crackers
- Most flavored chips or crackers

In a sense this list is incomplete, however, because flavor enhancers that contain glutamate are not listed on the ingredients panel. They are "hidden ingredients."

REAL KIDS AND FAKE FOOD

Several months ago I took a day trip with my daughter's third-grade class and spent several joyful hours touring the Bonneville Dam with them. Lunchtime came, and as the children piled into the picnic area and pulled their lunches out of their backpacks, my mouth dropped open. Many of the kids watched my reaction with amusement, giggling in secret conspiracy as they unwrapped each new treat. Where was the fruit, the vegetables, the high-quality proteins, and fats?

I wish I could say that my own daughter's lunch was a paragon of dietary virtue, but I remembered arguing with her that very morning about what she should pack. I watched as she slid her almost-healthy lunch under the table and stealthily traded it for some honest-to-goodness junk food.

Speaking with mothers all over the country, I hear the frustration in their voices as they talk about how difficult it is to get kids to eat healthy foods. From every corner of their world, kids are bombarded with messages about the wrong foods. From sugary breakfast cereals to soft drinks to fat-laden snack packs to canned entrées (is SpaghettiOs an entrée?) to cookies and candy, the marketing assault goes on and on.

It is difficult enough for a mother to stand up and fight the culture, day after day, year after year. It is impossible for a child to fight it—especially when the messages they receive come from their favorite TV character or from their school lunchroom.

Kids eat poorly before they go to school, but after they get into school, eating habits decline still further. The average child eats just one serving of fruit (one-half in the form of fruit juice) and only one-half serving of vegetables each day. According to one study, no children eat the recommended five servings of vegetables per day. These averages range across all economic ranges, but when poorer children are evaluated, their eating habits are much, much worse. In families so poor there is often not enough money to buy food, children "drank substantially more juice, drinks, soda pop, and Kool-Aid." On the average, chronically hungry children drink nearly two-and-a-half times more Kool-Aid than children who are not chronically hungry.[14]

It might be argued that Kool-Aid is cheap; it fills growling tummies inexpensively. Of course, water is cheaper than Kool-Aid and is far more "nutritious" than antinutrition Kool-Aid, which robs the body of nutrients by using its precious resources to metabolize the huge amounts of sugar in it. How much cheaper it would be if low-income moms and dads gave their kids water to drink and spent their limited food dollars on raw carrots, real potatoes, chicken, and fish. It certainly would provide the brains of their children with more to munch on.

In New York City, the ultimate urban landscape, many families on food stamps do this at the dozen-plus "greenmarkets" made up of hundreds of farmers, bakers, and fishermen from the outlying metropolitan area who have grown, raised, caught, and made their goods.

Thirty children from my daughter's middle-class school, ranging in age from eight to eleven, completed a one-day food diary for me, and what they entered on these journals clearly reflects the trends we see in supermarket sales. When I made my request for the food diaries with the teacher, her face reflected disgust. "Carol, you'll be shocked at what you see. I talk to these kids constantly about what they bring for lunch, but it makes no difference. Maybe you can make a difference."

STUDENT #1:
Breakfast: Waffles
Lunch: Goldfish crackers, sandwich, chips, and more goldfish crackers
Dinner: Meatloaf

STUDENT #2:
Breakfast: Cereal and milk
Lunch: Pretzel, milk, and dessert
Dinner: Fish and salad
Beverages: Pop

STUDENT #3:

Breakfast: Cocoa Krispies, peanut butter, Cap'n Crunch
Lunch: Soft pretzel, juice, applesauce, goldfish crackers
Dinner: Meatballs, bread, water, corn

STUDENT #4:

Breakfast: Cereal with milk and juice
Lunch: Apple, cake, sandwich, chips
Dinner: Potato
Snack: Cookies and 1 apple

STUDENT #5:

Breakfast: Granola Chewy Bar
Lunch: Cookies, peanuts, hamburger, fries
Dinner: Ribblets
Beverages: V8 Splash (Strawberry Kiwi), root beer

What shocked me almost as much as the food was their spelling and handwriting. At breakfast most kids ate sugary cereals (S'Mores, Honey Nut Cheerios, and Lucky Charms were the favorites listed). Several kids ate waffles with syrup, one kid ate yogurt, one ate a banana, and several enjoyed a piece of toast with butter and jam.

One little boy knew exactly how much he ate: "Count to 3 sekonts [*sic*] and that is how much I ate." One boy swore he ate a half-pound of oatmeal, but he probably had the healthiest breakfast of all. Except for my daughter. I'm proud to say that morning she enjoyed a bowl of oatmeal, a half bagel, a quarter glass of pineapple juice, and a quarter of an orange. Not the best—but definitely not the worst.

When children fast all night, then miss a good-quality breakfast, their thought processes are slower. They make more mistakes, and have more difficulty remembering details. Part of the problem comes from lower blood-sugar levels; part may also come from inadequate supplies of micronutrients that produce brain energy.[15]

Fewer children than ever are eating breakfast,[16] and the quality of their breakfast is declining. One benefit of eating breakfast at school is that it seems to improve school attendance and reduce tardiness,[17] but that says something about us as parents, doesn't it?

For lunch, the scenario deteriorates dramatically. The kids who ate the school lunch actually ate better than the kids who brought their lunch from home. Just some of the foods these kids packed for lunch included pretzels, cheese sticks, pizza, peanut-butter-and-jelly sandwiches, potato chips, fish crackers, Go-Gurt, muffins, and other goodies (some indecipherable words). One child brought carrot sticks (that and a potato were the only vegetables consumed among all twenty-seven kids) and the school lunch provided five children with applesauce. Three kids brought an apple from home; my daughter brought a few pieces of an orange. Out of an entire class of twenty-eight children, these were the only fruits eaten for the day.

Do things get better at home? Do they eat a well-balanced dinner? Not really. Only six children ate what looked like a home-cooked meal (meatloaf, fish and salad, teriyaki chicken with stuffed peaches(?), stew). The other children either couldn't remember what they ate the night before or ate prepared foods like pizza, cereal, burritos, and macaroni and cheese. They washed dinner down with soft drinks and topped it off with sugary desserts. Only four kids could remember eating vegetables.

Clinical nutritionists know that the accuracy of food diaries is questionable, especially when they are done by third-graders who barely remember what they ate ten minutes ago, let alone the night before. These diaries do reflect shopping trends, however. They mirror just what the statistics tell us, that on any given day, most children eat no vegetables at all.

As children get older, do their eating habits improve? Unfortunately not. A sixth-grade teacher asked her children to complete a three-day food diary for me. The eating habits of the younger children are reflected in their older siblings. The only difference between the older and younger children is that the older kids ate larger portions of the same junk food.

Summarized, here is what these eleven- and twelve-year-olds ate, on two consecutive days: for breakfast, they ate Instant Breakfast (chocolate), Sugar Smacks, pancakes and syrup, Cap'n Crunch, Cocoa Roos mixed with Cheerios and "flooded with 2% milk," cinnamon bread, French toast with syrup, and so on. Only two kids took vitamins. (One child apparently wanted to make a point with her diary: "Organic Fruity Crunch with pills and vitamins, with organic milk with organic pills with organic vitamins . . .") Most ate high-sugar cereal. Four children ate fruit or drank fruit juice, and one child ate eggs; some kids ate nothing.

If the children chose the school lunch program, like their younger siblings, they ate better than if they brought lunch from home—sometimes. On the day the school served pretzels, nut mix, and fruit for lunch, the kids fared no better at school. They ate lots of chips, cookies, pop, Go-Gurt, and other assorted stuff. Among the twenty-two children who completed the diaries over two days, thirty fruits were eaten (most of the fruit was eaten by just a few kids who had several servings) and nineteen vegetables were eaten (including the lettuce on their greasy hamburgers). Most kids drank several servings of sweetened beverages, including soft drinks, chocolate milk, fruit juice, and artificial fruit beverages. A couple kids drank water. Nearly every kid ate several servings of candy, cookies, and ice cream.

None of the kids included any sources of essential fatty acids at all, and only a few children enjoyed protein other than the cheeseburgers they ate with the school lunch. Only seven children ate a home-cooked meal for dinner. Part of the results are skewed, because some of the sixth-grade girls play basketball and on one of the nights they traveled out of town for a game and stopped at McDonald's on the way home for their evening meal.

Perhaps they would have eaten better if they had gone home to eat—but possibly not. Their classmates who went home to dinner were likely to eat a meal prepared outside the home or made from packaged foods.

These kids eat a lot, but what they eat cannot support a healthy body, let alone a healthy brain. The research shows that this classroom is a

---

"Nutrition experts" often boast of the quality of breakfast cereals, saying that they are of higher quality now than they were several years ago when fat content was much higher. What is not taken into account, however, is that when food processors remove fat from a food, they put sugar in its place—and market it as "Low Fat!" thus promoting the idea that low fat equates to healthy. It never does.

Kellogg's should feel proud of its health food origins. Will Keith and John Harvey Kellogg realized that the diet of fellow Americans was contributing to degenerative diseases, and at the turn of the century, they started experimenting with the processing of grain. They started with whole wheat, boiling it and running it through metal rollers to create a "doughy substance." One evening they cooked a batch of the wheat, then forgot about it for two days. When they ran this dough through the rollers, small, thin flakes came out the other end, and the idea for wheat flakes was born.

At first, William Kellogg signed his name to each box of his cereal to assure customers they were getting a quality product.

The Kellogg Corporation tries to assure us that "the unique brand of enthusiasm and devotion to creating breakfast products that are both tasty and nutritious still prevails at the Kellogg Company today."[18] But today many cereals such as Froot Loops, Cocoa Puffs, and Honeycomb contain more sugar, ounce for ounce, than soft drinks.

microcosm of the eating habits of American children. Children eat only about one-quarter of the vegetables recommended to them, and one quarter of those vegetables is french fries.[19] Only a few children actually meet the dietary goals set by the government, and many of us in the nutrition profession feel that government standards are inadequate to promote vibrant health, especially brain health.

Interestingly, my daughter helped me decipher the food diaries and she expressed surprise at what she saw. But her last comment before she raced outdoors to play was a real eye-opener. "Mom," she said. "No wonder these kids always go a little crazy after lunch . . . Miss Redman gets really upset because she can't quiet them down."

The High-Sugar, Low-Nutrient Diet

Cereal manufacturers would like you to believe that they are interested in promoting your kids' health. Kellogg's assures browsers on their Web site that they are so interested in nutrition that they've established the "Nutrition University," where you can learn how healthy their products are. They boast that Kellogg's Froot Loops has twenty-five percent of the daily requirement of iron, Kellogg's Cocoa Krispies has ten percent of the daily requirement for calcium, and Kellogg's Apple Jacks has twenty-five percent of the daily requirement for zinc.

Actually, if a cereal is the major portion of the breakfast meal, which it usually is, it should contain at the very minimum one-third of the daily requirement of all the nutrients. In fact, it might be better, if comparing sugar content, to give your kid a soft drink for breakfast than a bowl of breakfast cereal. Ounce per ounce, most breakfast cereals contain more sugar than soft drinks.

How healthy is your child's breakfast? Does it meet the minimum need for at least one-third the daily allowance of essential nutrients? How much simple sugar does he consume each morning? The following table lists some nutrients for two popular breakfast cereals, and the Homemade Granola with Fruit recipe in Chapter 8.[20] Compare this table with the RDA table on page 92.

Nutrient	Nature Valley Granola	Kellogg's Frosted Flakes	Homemade Granola with Fruit and Nuts (see Chapter 8)
Calories	503 kc	138 kc	563.4 kc
Saturated fat	13 gr	00 gr	5.202 gr
Sugar	30.9 gr	16 gr	17.23 gr
Protein	11.5 gr	1.33 gr	17.52 gr
Thiamin	.39 mg	.499 mg	.967 mg
Riboflavin	.19 mg	.565 mg	0.258 mg
Niacin	.83 mg	6.65 mg	2.777 mg
Vitamin A	7.91 IU	200 IU	95.3 IU
Vitamin D	00 IU	1.33 IU	00 IU
Vitamin E	3.39 mg	.399 mg	16.63 mg
Vitamin K	00 IU	00 IU	4.663 IU
Vitamin C	00 mg	19.9 mg	2.43 mg
Folate	85 mcg	133 mcg	84.31 mcg
Vitamin B_{12}	00 mcg	.08 mcg	00 mcg
Calcium	71 mg	13.3 mg	186.8 mg
Magnesium	116 mg	5.32 mg	208 mg
Iron	3.78 mg	2.39 mg	6.019 mg
Zinc	2.19 mg	.20 mg	4.037 mg

While the sugar content of the Homemade Granola with Fruit and Nuts looks high, the only refined sugar in the recipe is a little honey. The other sugars come from unsweetened dried fruits that are also rich in minerals and vitamins. The sugars in the processed cereals are from sucrose or table sugar and various other forms of simple sugar. Kellogg's Frosted Flakes has no fiber, while the Homemade Granola contains a healthy 7.058 grams of fiber per serving. The Nature Valley Granola contains slightly more than 4 grams of fiber per serving.

The influence of the high-sugar diet on brain chemistry is enormous, ranging from hyperactivity, depression, fatigue, inability to focus and concentrate, and on and on. However, just reading the studies about sugar can make you crazy, because they are contradictory. A review article about the connection between sugar and behavior states that "little evidence supports the claim that refined sugar intake significantly influences behavior or cognitive performance in children . . ."[21]

Conversely, an article published in the *South African Medical Journal* stated: "Sugar can lead to hyperactivity, irritability, tiredness, lack of energy and depression."[22] Whom are we to believe?

Following sugar as it wends its way through a young child's body, we can begin to understand where some of the confusion (and the truth) in the research lies. It is not as complicated as the experts would lead us to believe. The amount of sugar that our young children consume on a daily basis does indeed play a huge role in cognition and mood.

FOLLOWING SUGAR THROUGH THE BODY

When a child wakes up in the morning after sleeping for ten or more hours, his blood sugar is naturally low. Even if he had a protein-rich snack before he went to bed the night before, digestion has long since delivered it to the bloodstream and into the cells, and now his blood sugar has dropped down to the bottom range of normal.

Teddy bear in hand, the boy toddles into the kitchen where Mom is setting out his favorite breakfast of cereal, toast, and orange juice. Though it boasts of fortification with vitamins and minerals, his cereal contains over fifteen grams (about five teaspoons) of sugar per serving. His toast is covered with strawberry jam, which contains more sugar and other sweeteners than actual fruit. Another five teaspoons of sugar. Even if his orange juice does not contain added sugars, it is still pure carbohydrate, which rapidly digests down into simple sugar. Within minutes, his entire "power breakfast" surges into the bloodstream in the form of glucose, unimpeded by slower-digesting protein or fat.

Such a load of blood sugar is dangerous for the brain. Although the brain is fueled by sugar, it can't handle excessive sugars, so the pancreas leaps to the rescue, dumping insulin into the bloodstream to remove excess sugars before they can "burn" the brain. At each meal, the pancreas senses how much insulin is needed, even before digestion and absorption are complete, so an insulin reaction can happen very quickly. Large amounts of insulin are released—then, just as rapidly, sugar is pulled out of the bloodstream and deposited in his liver. When his liver is full, the excess sugar is stored as fat, contributing to the rising epidemic of obesity in this country.

Suddenly, as though someone pulled an electrical cord out of a socket, he runs out of steam. Due to the high sugar content of the breakfast, the insulin response was exaggerated, so his blood sugar plummets. His sugar is too low and the brain starts to panic. He gets cranky, headachy, irritable. He can't concentrate. Sometimes he falls into a chair and stares listlessly at the TV; at other times his adrenal gland spits cortisol into the bloodstream in a desperate attempt to raise blood sugar. The extra cortisol makes him hyperactive and damages the hippocampus, his memory center. His energy is "false," but his mom sees hyperactivity, obstinacy, and defiance.

If he has access to the refrigerator or pantry, he may pull out all the sugary foods he can get his hands on and stuff them into his mouth, just to get his sugar up. It will work briefly, but insulin again kicks in and drops his sugar. The cycle continues, all day long.

Look back at the food diaries of the third-grade children. Their Cocoa Puffs or Cap'n Crunch breakfasts (or their skipped breakfast) have sent their blood sugar roaring into high gear, and by the time lunch rolls around and the next load of sugar hits the bloodstream, it is impossible for them to work productively in the classroom. No wonder Miss Redman is frantic come midafternoon, after the kids purchased snacks from the school vending machine.

The B complex vitamins are required to metabolize these sugars; unfortunately, the brain enzymes are also dependent upon the B-complex vitamins. Unless these essential nutrients are abundantly provided in the diet, there simply aren't enough to go around. If the B-complex vitamins and minerals are busy handling the onslaught of sugar, they aren't available to the brain for its functions, leading to a functional deficiency that can show up as learning and behavior disorders.

Does sugar affect the brain? Definitely. Just ask Miss Redman or any schoolteacher. Ask Mom.

MINERALS AND BRAIN HEALTH

One of the hottest trends in the supermarket industry includes packaged entrées such as Oscar Mayer Lunchables, Kraft Handi-Snacks, and Top Ramen soup mixes. Maruchan markets a series of dried soups, as does Nissen and other companies. Many supermarket chains have their own private-label products that mirror the design of the well-known brands.

Put aside the incredible array of synthetic flavoring and coloring agents and preservatives for the moment and ignore the fact that these meals are so deficient in basic nutrition that companies like Oscar Mayer should be embarrassed to put its corporate name on the package. The nutritional content of these entrées is sure to send the delicate mineral balances of our kids' immature bodies into chaos. These meals are high in sodium, low in potassium, low in magnesium, low in zinc, low in B complex, and low in virtually every nutrient except sodium.

From to the Center for Science in the Public Interest (CSPI), here is a list of ten foods you should NEVER eat:

1. Quaker 100% Natural Oats & Honey Granola (one-half cup is coated with three teaspoons of sugar and more fat than a McDonald's hamburger)
2. Gwaltney Great Dogs Chicken Franks (loaded with fat)
3. Entenmann's Rich Frosted Donut (as much fat as nine strips of bacon)
4. Nissen Cup Noodles with Shrimp (over 1,070 milligrams of sodium, plus loaded with more fat than a one-ounce bag of potato chips)
5. Frito-Lay Wow! Potato Chips (fried in Olean, the artificial fat that has sent people to the emergency room with severe cramps or diarrhea)
6. Oscar Mayer Lunchables ("It would be hard to invent a worse food than these combos. . . .")
7. Häagen-Dazs Ice Cream (more than twice the fat of most regular ice cream—forty-six grams of fat in one cup of Butter Pecan)
8. Campbell's red-and-white-label soups ("brimming with salt")
9. Rice-A-Roni Chicken & Vegetables (one cup has 1,470 milligrams of sodium; Vegetables? We found nine peas in a two-cup box!)
10. Contadina Alfredo Sauce (one-third stick of butter on each cup of pasta . . .)

An overview of the various roles these nutrients play in brain health will help us understand the problem with Lunchables and other packaged kids' entrées.

Vitamins and minerals play an important role in the function of the brain. The real work of the brain is done by enzymes that speed the activ-

CSPI also lists ten super foods that you should DEFINITELY eat:
1. Sweet potatoes (loaded with carotenoids, vitamins, potassium, and fiber)
2. Whole-grain bread (higher in fiber and nutrients than white or "wheat" bread)
3. Broccoli (lots of vitamin C, carotenoids, and folic acid)
4. Watermelon (good source of vitamin C and carotenoids)
5. Beans (inexpensive, low in fat, and rich in nutrients; lots of fiber, too)
6. Cantaloupe (lots of vitamins A and C)
7. Spinach and kale (lots of vitamins, minerals, and fiber)
8. Oranges (lots of vitamins and fiber)
9. Oatmeal (inexpensive, lots of fiber, rich in B complex for the brain)
10. Fat-free (skim) or one-percent-fat milk (I may disagree here)

ity of the brain cells. Chemical reactions that could take hours or days without enzymes are performed several million times faster in the presence of these worker chemicals that are constantly recycled and reused. Enzymatic reactions are driven by vitamins (particularly vitamin C and the B complex) and minerals (magnesium, calcium, potassium, zinc, and others).

The body spends a great deal of its metabolic energy preserving the delicate balance of minerals in the blood, often at the expense of the bones when dietary mineral levels drop so low that the balance is tipped the wrong way. This is why assessing mineral levels using blood tests is worthless. Minerals are not stored in the blood; they are stored in the bones and soft tissue, and when the blood supply drops low and more minerals are required to replenish it, they are pulled out of storage to restore mineral levels in the blood.

First, we will look at some minerals to see how they are used in brain function and throughout the body, and then we will take another look at Lunchables and other kids' entrées to see how they measure up against the body's needs.

Magnesium

Magnesium is used in over three hundred enzymes, many of which are brain enzymes. It is also used to produce cellular energy. Magnesium and calcium work together in the muscles; magnesium causes muscles to relax, while calcium causes the muscles to contract. Magnesium is essential in DNA and RNA synthesis and transcription, part of our internal genetic code. Magnesium works in opposition with calcium in nerve excitability.

Low levels of magnesium are linked to overexcitability, aggressive behavior, alcoholism, anxiety, attention deficit, autism, dementia, depression, fatigue, insomnia, learning disabilities, organic mental disorders, PMS, and schizophrenia.[23] One author wrote that "magnesium is an important therapeutic agent for psychiatric disorders. Magnesium is valuable in hypnosis, sleep disturbance, excitability, panic attacks, hyperkinetic children, anxiety states, psychogenic asthma, heart syndromes, and anxiety. It is an effective muscle relaxant and has influence on nerve excitability."[24]

Magnesium deficiency is not uncommon,[25] since it is found mainly in raw nuts and seeds, legumes, whole grains, and dark-green leafy vegetables, foods that most young American children avoid. Excessive amounts of calcium (from excessive milk drinking, for example) reduce the amount of magnesium available in the cell, so even if magnesium intake is adequate, oversupplying the body with calcium can produce the same effects as those from low magnesium.

The following chart lists three popular entrée and snack items (Handi-Snacks Cheez N Crackers with Bacon, Campbell's Chicken Noodle Soup, and Oscar Mayer Ham with Fruit Punch Lunchable) with their nutritional profile, as provided by the manufacturers:

Nutrients	HS Cheez N Crackers	C's Chicken Noodle Soup	OM Lunchable
Calories	130 kc	14.97 kc	360 kc
Protein	4 gr	.749 gr	17 gr
Saturated fat	4 gr	.077 gr	4.5 gr
Sugar	0 gr	0 gr	40 gr
Vitamin A	60 IU	14.97 IU	60 IU
Thiamin	.03 mg	.023 mg	0 mg
Riboflavin	0.68 mg	.017 mg	0 mg
Niacin	.4 mg	.299 mg	0 mg
Folate	0 mg	.256 mcg	0 mg
Vitamin B$_{12}$	0 mg	.017 mcg	0 mg
Vitamin C	0 mg	0 mg	0 mg
Vitamin D	0 IU	0 IU	0 IU
Vitamin E	0 IU	0 IU	0 IU
Vitamin K	0 IU	0 IU	0 IU
Sodium	410 mg	224.6 mg	1150 mg
Potassium	40 mg	6.519 mg	0 mg
Calcium	100 mg	0 mg	350 mg
Magnesium	0 mg	.567 mg	0 mg
Iron	0.36 mg	.09 mg	0 mg
Zinc	0 mg	.047 mg	0 mg

Iron

Iron is used as an oxygen shuttle, carrying oxygen from the lungs to every cell in the body, piggyback fashion. It is common for children to be iron-deficient, especially when their eating patterns do not include red meat.

Deficiencies in iron are often associated with poor cognition and behavior, as cited in many studies. Nonheme iron (iron derived from vegetable sources) is not easily absorbed; nor is heme iron easily absorbed in the absence of adequate amounts of vitamin C. Children can therefore "inherit" iron deficiency from their days as a formula-fed infant unless the diet has been made very adequate in iron, vitamin C (which aids in iron absorption), and several of the B-complex vitamins.

A study conducted in the New York City area showed that about one-third of children may be deficient in iron, associated with mental and psychomotor impairment during the first two years of life.[26] One possible cause? Cow's milk. Studies have shown that intestinal blood loss is increased by thirty percent in infants fed whole cow's milk. The study went on to say that "iron deficiency early in childhood may lead to long term changes in behavior that may not be reversed with iron supplementation, even though the anemia is corrected. A number of dopamine D-2 receptors in the rat brain are reduced when the experimental animals undergo a transient period of iron deficiency during infancy, and are not subsequently restored with iron supplementation."[27]

Older children seem to be no better off when it comes to receiving adequate amounts of iron in the diet. While we often think of "iron-poor blood" as a geriatric problem, in children iron-poor blood leads to impaired physical development, "failure to respond to test stimuli, short attention span, unhappiness, increased fearfulness, withdrawal from the examiner, and increased body tension."[28]

Sodium

Because of "bad press" over the past few decades linking sodium with heart disease, we don't often think favorably of sodium. However, sodium is an essential nutrient and is carefully balanced in nature with magnesium and potassium to efficiently produce cellular energy. For the purposes of our discussion, sodium plays two important roles in the body: maintaining normal muscle irritability and operating the sodium potassium pump that pulls nutrients into the cells and pulls waste materials out of the cells.

The dietary sodium-to-potassium ratio should be about 1:2.5; in other words, if we consume one thousand milligrams of sodium, we should balance the sodium with twenty-five hundred milligrams of potassium. If the sodium-to-potassium ratio is thrown off by too much sodium in relation to potassium, the entire energy production system of the body is disrupted, producing fatigue, overproduction of adrenal hormones, and mental symptoms like alcoholism, depression, and organic mental disorders.[29]

Excessive levels of sodium throw off the water balance, resulting in bloating from edema or water retention, but the emotional characteristics can range from tiredness, loss of stamina, weakness, and lassitude, to anger.

Zinc

Zinc is one of the unsung heroes of the brain and is commonly undersupplied in the American kid's diet, simply because most of it has been removed in the processing of foods, and the only other abundant dietary source is red meat or oysters. The USRDA for zinc is fifteen milligrams per day, eight milligrams for children under the age of four. The average child, however, receives less than he needs.[30] Many nutritionists believe that we need far more zinc than the RDA.

Zinc is used in hundreds of enzyme reactions throughout the body, but it is particularly important that the brain receive adequate supplies because many brain enzymes are zinc dependent. Zinc is used to metabolize carbohydrates, helps balance blood-sugar levels, and lessens the requirement for insulin. It is essential for the proper functioning of RNA and DNA, our essential genetic material. Without adequate amounts of zinc, cell division and replication cannot take place. Zinc is a structural part of hormones and helps stabilize membrane and structures in the cytoplasm of the cell.

Zinc breaks down and metabolizes protein in the digestive system but helps put proteins together inside the cell. It is essential in the formation of bone and skin and supports the immune system. Providing optimal levels of zinc in the diet speeds the metabolic rate of the body by promoting thyroid activity. Without adequate supplies of zinc, the ability to taste and smell is impaired, leading to lowered appetite. Zinc opposes toxic metals like mercury, pushing them out of the body before they can cause damage to the brain and nervous system.[31]

What happens, then, when we are in constant short supply? The body uses its nutrient resources much the same way we use our financial resources: When we have enough money in our bank account, everyone gets paid. When we are short, we pay the most urgent bills first, then cross our fingers, hoping more money will appear so bill collectors don't call. When adolescent monkeys are deprived of zinc, they become lethargic, especially around the time of growth spurts. They have more difficulty paying attention.[32]

Zinc deprivation leads to eating disorders like anorexia nervosa and bulimia, two serious problems that become more common as children become teenagers.[33] Clinicians have linked low levels of zinc with frequent frontal headaches, with depression severe enough to stimulate thoughts of suicide, and with aggressive, angry, hostile behaviors that often result in physical violence.

"Oscar Mayer shares your concern about nutrition," they write in their promotional pamphlet Lunchables Nutrition Facts.

Lunchables contain thirteen teaspoons of sugar (fifty-two grams of carbohydrates altogether), enough to send your child's blood sugar soaring. This marketing nightmare contains seven forms of sugar, seven forms of sodium, nineteen different chemical additives, and hydrogenated fats to clog up his or her arteries.

You're not doing any better if you buy your child Campbell's soups for lunch. Designed for a meal on the run, just one can contains over 1,000 milligrams of sodium, two teaspoons of sugar, and MSG. Nearly all the natural nutrition found in vegetables has long since been cooked out, leaving very little to nourish your child's brain. Campbell's Vegetable Soup hardly qualifies as a serving of vegetables.

When zinc levels are low, overall nutrition begins a downward spiral as zinc-deficient children begin to crave sugary foods and shun protein-containing foods. The reason they avoid protein foods is that zinc helps balance blood sugar; when zinc is in short supply, blood-sugar levels wobble out of control, making the child feel that he must eat sugary foods to elevate it. Zinc activates enzymes that are critically important for the digestion of protein. If the body cannot digest protein, it will reject it until zinc levels have restored enzyme function to normal. These kids may say they "hate meat" or "hate beans," and binge on foods made from grains, or other foods high in carbohydrates (not usually vegetables).

Food Additives

Since so little natural goodness is left in these highly processed junk foods, these brand-name companies add chemicals to make your child think he is getting good food.

FDA regulations say that "food additives are substances which may by their intended uses become components of food, either directly or indirectly, or which may otherwise affect the characteristics of the food. The term specifically includes any substance intended for use in producing, manufacturing, packing, processing, preparing, treating, packaging, transporting, or holding the food, and any source of radiation intended for any such use."[34]

But the following are excluded from the definition of an additive:

1. substances generally recognized as safe (GRAS) by qualified experts

2. substances used in accordance with a previous approval (prior sanction) under either the Federal Food, Drug, and Cosmetic Act; the Poultry Products Inspection Act; or the Federal Meat Inspection Act

3. pesticide chemicals in or on raw agricultural products

4. color additives

5. new animal drugs

Pesticide chemicals, color additives, and new animal drugs are subjected to similar safety requirements of other sections of the law.

Here is a partial list of the artificial ingredients added for coloring, flavoring, or preservatives:

sodium lactate (associated
  with panic attacks)
sodium phosphate
sodium erythorbate
sodium nitrite
sorbic acid
Oleoresin paprika
artificial flavors (unnamed)
partially hydrogenated soybean oil
sodium bicarbonate
sodium acid pyrophosphate
monocalcium phosphate
calcium propionate
artificial color (unnamed)
xanthan gum

apocarotenal
vanillin
sodium stearoyl lactylate
sodium alginate
annatto
sodium aluminum sulfate
fumaric acid
potassium sorbate
sodium propionate
calcium sulfate
Yellow dye #5
TBHQ
Red dye #40
sodium benzoate

Unless you have a degree in chemistry, the secrets of the food additives will not be revealed easily. The Center for Science in the Public Interest provides a great deal of information (www.cspinet.org). They can't monitor the three thousand chemicals that are purposely added to food products, but they do hit the high points, and the high point is whether or not additives cause cancer. Seldom is anything said about whether or not these substances produce endocrinological or neurological problems.

However, if you're patient and creative, you can find information about the more common additives (start with the FDA Web site at www.fda.gov). Their resources and search engine will help lead you in the right direction. On a Web site I found devoted to sodium benzoate, a manufacturer wrote that "this product is hazardous under the criteria of the federal OSHA Hazard Communication Standard 29CFR 1910.1200." It does not, according to the California Proposition 65, cause "cancer, birth defects or other reproductive effects." According to the FDA, it has GRAS (Generally Regarded as Safe) status and is used as a preservative in a variety of food products. It is added to margarine to retard flavor reversion.[35]

Sodium lactate, a substance added to many meat products, precipitates panic attacks in susceptible individuals.[36] When sodium lactate is given intravenously, adrenal hormone levels are increased.[37] Whether or not these high cortisone levels induce the panic attacks is unknown.

In a study patients who were diagnosed with multiple chemical sensitivity syndrome (symptoms typical of panic disorders, chest tightness, shortness of breath, palpitations, paresthesias [abnormal touch sensation in the absence of touch, such as tingling or burning], light-headedness, and mental confusion) were given either a normal saline solution placebo or an infusion of sodium lactate, which is known to produce symptoms of panic disorders. Every patient who received the sodium lactate infusion experienced a panic attack.[38]

Only the chemists at Oscar Mayer know how much sodium lactate is in a box of Lunchables or other processed foods. Amounts of additives are not listed on the label, so it is difficult to determine if the children or adults experiencing recurring panic attacks are actually responding to levels of sodium lactate in the food.

Another common food additive is annatto, extracted from the seeds of the tree *Bixa orellana,* and commonly added to cheeses, snack foods, beverages, and cereals to produce a yellow color. Numerous studies have shown that annatto often produces allergic symptoms like skin rashes and large wheals on the skin. In one patient written up in the *Annals of Allergy,* his morning breakfast of Fiber One cereal with milk produced these symptoms, plus severe low blood pressure. Annatto is also known to cause blood-sugar levels to rise precipitously, producing damage to the energy-production sites in the liver and pancreas.[39]

Tartrazine is another food additive known to cause behavioral disturbances in children,[40] and this is only the tip of the iceberg, so to speak.[41]

We do not have the space to cover all the potential problems caused by the additives in children's foods, and more research is needed to determine their safety, especially in terms of brain health. One thing is known, however. Even if these chemicals really are benign, even if they inflict no temporary or permanent damage on your child's brain, even if they simply pass through the liver and are excreted out of the body, they do your child no good.

Nutrition is a precious gift. Our kids don't need chemicals. They don't need artificial stimulants to increase energy. They don't need Lunchables . . . or Campbell's soups . . . or Cup O'Noodles, or any other artificial lunch. They need food to nourish their brain, to build health and vitality.

ALLERGENS IN THE DIET

There is a huge debate going on right now in the nutrition profession about allergies and how common they are, particularly when it comes to the consumption of our favorite foods. Our most common foods are wheat and dairy products. We eat them nearly every day in the form of milk, cheese, bread, pasta, cereals, cakes, and cookies. Apart from eating a huge amount of nonfoods and sugars, the second problem we see is the overconsumption of what some nutritionists consider to be the most allergenic foods in the Western diet: wheat, corn, and dairy.

The controversy is over whether or not food allergies are as common as is believed, and the answer is yes or no, considering how the word *allergy* is defined and your point of view. Defined in the strict sense of the word, an allergy relates to a specific immunological reaction, that is, exposure to the antigen (the allergen), which causes the body to produce specific antibodies like IgE, IgA, IgG, and so on. An allergy is an immune-system response.

Defined in a broader sense, the idea of intolerance is added. The reaction may not involve the immune system, per se, but may cause the body to respond negatively with a variety of symptoms. If an individual lacks an enzyme needed to digest a particular food or substance in the food, he may experience diarrhea or constipation as a consequence. For example, many people are intolerant of dairy products because their bodies do not produce lactase, the enzyme that digests lactose, or milk sugar.

Using the broader definition, allergies or food intolerances are extremely common, ranging from two percent to over twenty percent of the population. An article in *The Lancet* magazine stated, ". . . doctors who regularly use elimination diets know recognized food intolerance is just 'the tip of an iceberg' because the remainder may be causing chronic symptoms unrelated to food until 'unmasked' by a break in exposure . . . [T]he authors believe the estimate of the prevalence of food intolerance . . . is a serious understatement."[42]

The most common offenders are wheat, corn, and dairy, then chocolate, peanuts, soy, shellfish, and the list goes on from there.[43] This is bad news for the typical American mom, who feeds her child the same type of breakfast that little Junior enjoyed. Every morning, Junior is loading up on foods that send his brain into a frenzy of activity or otherwise create mental havoc.

Diagnosing allergies and food intolerance can be dauntingly difficult. Reactions may occur immediately or may occur up to seventy-two hours later, depending on which immune body stimulates the reaction or what generates the intolerance. An IG reaction, for example, is called "delayed onset reactivity" and might occur hours or days after the child or parent has forgotten what he ate. The intolerance is particularly difficult to diagnose correctly if the food is eaten every day or, in some cases, every meal. In defense, the body often sets up a craving for the allergenic food and symptoms of the allergy are temporarily relieved by eating the food. A vicious cycle is created, broken only by suffering through withdrawal symptoms.

Several years ago I worked closely with a group of individuals who wanted to clean up their diets and lose weight. In our first support-group meeting, I handed them a two-week menu that included no wheat, corn, dairy, sugar, carbonated beverages, or processed foods, and asked them to follow it religiously for two weeks. Two weeks later when we returned, I asked them how they were feeling. "Fine," they said. They all felt wonderful and loved the program.

When we started talking I learned that the first three days were extremely unpleasant as they went through reactions similar to withdrawal from a drug. They described symptoms like extreme fatigue, headaches, nervousness, trembling, apathy, and anger. No one would have guessed that they were withdrawing from wheat, dairy, and sugar foods.

We normally think of allergies as hives, diarrhea, stuffy nose, sinus infections, or repetitive sneezing, but an allergen can attack any part of the body with any type of symptom. An allergy that attacks the brain is called a cerebral allergy. I saw firsthand the results of cerebral allergy in my own daughter as I took her to a clinician for allergy testing. We were home-schooling her at the same time. She was in the third grade, and her favorite class was spelling, a subject at which she excelled. Because the testing would take several hours, I brought work for us both.

The technician placed a few drops of an antigen under her tongue and left the room. My daughter took out her notebook. I began to dictate spelling words, just as we had done in the past. At first, she sat quietly and wrote the words in careful, neat handwriting, but within a few minutes, she began to giggle. I told her to settle down and get back to work, which only increased the giggling. I tried to be patient, but she grew more and more disruptive. Now she was hiding her pad so I couldn't see her work.

I scolded her sternly. "Caryl Anne, sit down and do your work." With that, she threw her pad directly at me and collapsed onto the floor, giggling uncontrollably. I stared in disbelief as my well-behaved child was out of control. Then the technician walked in. "I can't believe her. Look at her. She never acts like this!" The technician smiled and said, "I think she is very allergic to glycerin. She's having a reaction." She placed a desensitizing drop under the tongue, and within moments, Caryl Anne sat down quietly and resumed her work.

The technician gave me a drop of a substance under my tongue and again left the room. My work involved simple arithmetic, and I started to calculate. I did a multiplication problem, checked my work—it was wrong. I repeated it, rechecked—and it was wrong again. After failing a fourth time, I put my head down on the desk and burst into tears. Cerebral allergy reaction to car exhaust. When I was desensitized, I was able to complete the calculation without difficulty. In our case, the problem was toxins in the environment, but with many people, the problem is the foods they frequently enjoy.

William Philpott, M.D., the author of *Brain Allergies,* writes:

"The emotional symptoms evoked on exposure to foods and commonly met chemicals range from mild central-nervous-system symptoms such as weakness, dizziness, blurred vision, anxiety and depression, to gross psychotic symptoms such as catatonia, dissociation, paranoid delusions and visual and auditory hallucination . . . inability to read or write . . . hyperactivity, weakness, sleepiness, insomnia . . . and many other such reactions were observed."[44]

The problem of food allergies gets more complex with each passing year, possibly due to the increase of genetically altered foods and the addition of other toxins.

If we were pouring large glasses of ice-cold raw, organic milk into our children's glasses, we might not see as many problems. Pasteurized, homogenized, bovine-growth hormone, and antibiotic-laced milk is not the equivalent of fresh, organic, raw milk, rich in essential fatty acids, protein, and enzymes that deliver the nutrients to the bloodstream in a form the body recognizes. When we discuss wheat or corn or soybeans, we're not discussing the foods that our ancestors ate. Wheat today isn't what it was two hundred years ago.

When I started researching this section of the book, I was unable to find any primary research done on the consequences of feeding children genetically altered foods and what possible allergic or other reactions they may experience. Research simply isn't being done to see if changing the protein structure of a plant influences brain chemistry—least of all by the biotech companies, like Monsanto and Nestlé, that are buying up seed crops around the world.

Several years ago, a young client of mine was presented with an "adverse personality." This nine-year-old boy was constantly in trouble, in school, at home, in church. He was loved and disciplined by his parents, but they saw trouble ahead. His father joked that "he'll probably end up in jail," but his eyes revealed deep concern for his boy.

Upon testing, we found that he was intensely allergic to wheat. Within days of removing every grain except rice from his diet, this normally disruptive child settled down, brought his grades up, said good-bye to the principal's office, made friends around the neighborhood, and, in general, became a pleasant, friendly child.

One day a few months later, he came home from school in a familiar rage. He'd been sent back to the principal's office for fighting. After considerable probing by his baffled mother, he confessed to eating one Wheat Thin for lunch—and that set him off like a firecracker.

It gives me a certain amount of angst to say bad things about milk for growing children. I had my own cow named Betsy, a gentle, brown-eyed creature who provided me and my family with gallons of fresh, raw milk that we drank for breakfast, poured on our bowls of oatmeal, and gulped with dinner. We skimmed the rich layer of cream off the top and churned it into butter. Occasionally, we made homemade ice cream. Why my parents started selling Betsy's milk to the creamery and replaced it with pasteurized milk is a mystery. The first few times I purchased a carton of milk at school for the afternoon milk break, it made me sick to my stomach. It wasn't anything like what I enjoyed at home.

The advertisements, especially the ones with our favorite TV and movie stars sporting the familiar white mustache, say, "Yes, milk does a body good." My response is, "If you are a calf, yes. If you're a person, no." Especially if the milk is pasteurized and homogenized.

There is considerable evidence that over eighty percent of the world's population is intolerant to dairy products.[45] In the 1930s, Francis M. Pottenger, Jr., M.D., did a series of experiments on cats. After studying nine hundred cats over a ten-year period, he found that the only diet that supported the health of his cats was raw milk and raw meat.

He found that by substituting heat-processed milk for raw milk, even when it was the milk from their mothers, physical and mental degeneration occurred, increasing with each subsequent generation. Kittens of the third generation of pasteurized milk failed to survive six months, and after four generations, cats were unable to reproduce at all.

Parasites and vermin abounded in the processed milk–fed cats. They developed skin diseases and allergies, from five percent in cats fed the raw milk diet to over ninety percent in the third generation of artificially fed cats. Their bones became soft and pliable.

Pottenger also noticed startling changes in the personalities of the cats. He noted that they suffered from "adverse personality changes . . . Females became more aggressive while males became docile." The type of physical and mental deterioration that Pottenger observed in cats on deficient diets paralleled the human degeneration that Dr. Price found in tribes and villages that had abandoned traditional foods.

He found that it took four generations on raw milk and raw meat to bring the cats back to normal—but only if he used cats from the first and second generation. After the third generation, the cats were infertile or unable to give birth to living offspring.[46]

The physical degeneration he discusses is beyond the scope of this book, but notice the ominous words: "The cats suffered from adverse personality changes. Females became more aggressive while males became docile." We are not cats, obviously. I'm not advocating putting our children on a totally raw diet. Even if I did, it wouldn't happen. However, there are a few things that we need to seriously consider:

1. The milk supply is becoming increasingly contaminated with hormones that wield a powerful influence on our own levels of hormones. Little to no research has been done on how these hormones affect the endocrine system in young, growing bodies. Genetic testing is now underway to boost the estrogen content in milk even higher.[47]

2. If pasteurized, homogenized milk produces such devastating effects on young cats, is it possible that the same effects may be happening in our children?

3. If the protein/fatty acid blend of cow's milk is not appropriate for infants, is it any more beneficial for older children? If unpasteurized, unhomogenized milk were only a small part of the diet, the risk may be lower in older children than it is for infants for whom milk is the sole source of nutrition.

4. Testing the neurotoxic effects of these highly processed dairy foods has not been done. This area of research desperately needs to be done. If we are going to continue feeding our kids processed dairy products, we need to learn just what these products do to our bodies and brains. Only then can we really decide if "milk does a body good."

What Else Is There?

We've gotten so used to behaviors that were once unknown or disapproved of that we don't think twice when our young children lie limply in a semivegetative state for hours, staring with glazed eyes at a flickering screen. They don't have either the energy or the imagination to go outside and play. Our classrooms pulsate with hyperenergetic kids who can't sit still longer than a few minutes. Teachers have to "perform" to keep students' attention, and schools purchase TVs and videos and movies and computer games to occupy minds that can't focus on Shakespeare or write a coherent sentence.

"Our society is changing," we explain to ourselves. It's a changing world, all right. But many of us certainly aren't getting smarter. We have enough evidence. More science would be nice, but it isn't necessary. The evidence that what we eat affects how we think and how we feel is already here. It shows that whether or not we eat breakfast makes a big difference in whether or not we can spell or perform double-digit multiplication calculations.

It shows that if we don't make changes we're going to spend more money on teachers for remedial reading or remedial math. We're going to hire more security guards to keep trouble under control. We're going to have to continue installing metal detectors in the high schools. We're going to hire more and more counselors to try to help our kids cope with life—largely because we aren't spending our money on food that nourishes their brains, food that gives their brains something to think with.

We're either going to spend money on better-quality food or we'll spend it on higher school taxes to pay for the extra services to cope with kids whose brains are deteriorating faster than we can fix them.

Many mothers can tell you when their kids are "sugared out." What moms have trouble with is defining "sugared out." To say that the typical American child drinks over one liter of soft drinks per day often causes no more than a shrug because, well, "What else is there to drink?"

Countless times I've been asked that question after teaching a seminar on healthy eating. After I've shared the dangers of a high-sugar, high-soft-drink, highly processed diet, my audience asks, "If my kids can't drink milk or pop, what else is there?" When I respond, "Water," they look even more confused. That's it?

NUTRITION PRIMER FOR YOUNG CHILDREN

As a mother of four children, I learned firsthand how early children express food preferences. When my first child was born, I was certain that as I prepared delicious, homemade meals for her, she would appreciate my efforts and eat them happily. She would be thrilled to know that her mother provided the very best foods for her.

When it came time to introduce her to solid foods, I carefully blended chunks of chicken breast, fresh vegetables, brown rice, and herbs into a savory stew, then whizzed it up in the blender. I poured meal-sized portions into freezer cups and froze them for later use.

At first, she ate it willingly. But one afternoon when I reheated it for lunch, I inadvertently got it a little too warm. It wasn't hot enough to burn her, but she was scared. Eventually, she refused to eat anything but ice cubes, chicken nuggets from Kentucky Fried Chicken, Cheerios, hard-boiled or scrambled eggs, and mashed bananas. I was certain she would be permanently injured. To this day, she is my pickiest child, but I never stopped keeping after her and reminding her I was the mother.

Now, after raising four children who have provided a variety of mothering experiences, I encourage young mothers and fathers to take responsibility for what their children eat. You must take your rightful authority in the kitchen. The influences on children's eating behaviors are diverse and pervasive.

In school, children are exposed to peer pressure. They see what classmates pack into their lunch bags and don't want to take a leadership position in the lunchroom. They naturally try to copy what they see on TV. They will usually, at every opportunity, try to get Mom to compromise her position and pack as much junk into their lunches as possible. If that doesn't work, they'll barter their healthy lunches for the junk.

I wish I could offer five simple guidelines on how to get your kids to eat healthfully, but that simply can't be done. Kids are too complicated. It takes persistence, a living example, your own knowledge of your child's personality, and a constant reminder that what you are doing is going to help them in the years to come.

There are, however, general rules that will reduce the junk foods and increase the brain-healthy foods that your children eat. (Also see Chapter 8 for healthy meals and snacks.)

General Shopping Guidelines:

- Buy organic. Reduce the exposure to harmful chemicals as much as possible.

- Do not purchase soft drinks of any kind, except for rare occasions. If the children want something carbonated occasionally, purchase sparkling mineral water and add unsweetened fruit juices for flavoring.

- Do not purchase candy. They will get far too much candy at school, birthday parties, and other occasions.

- Do not purchase cookies or cakes except for special occasions like birthday parties. If you feel you must allow them an occasional store-bought cookie, designate one night as "Treat Night" and allow them a small cookie or other treat of their choice. For school lunches and snacks, make your own cookies, reducing the sugars in the recipe.

- Encourage your children to snack on fresh fruit, raw nuts and seeds, carrot sticks, homemade popcorn, etc.

- Do not buy any prepared lunch or dinner entrées that contain artificial ingredients. You can purchase lunch boxes that are divided into sections into which you can place your own nutritious lunch items, but don't fall into the trap of purchasing the harmful prepared meals that other children are buying.

- There are a number of companies that are developing healthy kid lunches. See Appendix I in the back of this book for more information.

- Plan to serve at least one family meal each day. Sometimes you may enjoy making a festive breakfast with the kids. At other times, you will want to sit down to dinner together. It is often difficult to assemble the entire family because of work schedules and after-school sports activities, but kids need the togetherness of the family over a wonderful meal.

Some of my fondest family memories are our times in the kitchen. Several months ago, one of my daughters asked if she could help prepare Sunday dinner. We selected a fairly exotic menu: ossobuco, mozzarella and tomato salad, roasted red peppers with anchovies, risotto, and cream puffs.

Another daughter set the dining room table with a tablecloth, our company dishes, and a vase of fresh flowers. Then we all sat down to enjoy the meal and the family. As they learn to cook, we spend precious time together.

My daughters know how to make pancakes, waffles, crepes, and oatmeal. Sometimes they have the option of preparing the entire meal themselves (they are paid $2.00). The preparation and enjoyment of good food have become part of our family traditions.

One of the most valuable tips in preparing healthy meals for the family is planning the menu in advance. Each weekend I go over our family's schedule for the week, then plan the meals around the schedule. Grocery shopping is done from the list. If some of the menus can be prepared in advance, I schedule time in the kitchen to do this. Many meals can be prepared in large quantity, frozen, then reheated on a night when time is short or when I am tired. The advantage of preparing several meals at once is obvious: I only dirty the kitchen once.

We allow our children to help us select restaurants, but we set the guidelines: no fast-food chains and no greasy spoons. They now help us select restaurants that serve fresh vegetables with each meal along with a healthy protein. They are encouraged to order salads and fresh fruit. They select water or herbal teas for their beverage.

Nutritional Guidelines for Young Children

During this critical period of life, your child's brain is continuing to gain weight through dendrite and axon growth. The myelin sheath is being laid into place around the dendrites, forming a fatty-acid conduit for the transmission of nerve signals. Neurotransmitters and neurohormones are being formed to transmit messages. Children's brains are extremely active because they are constantly learning. The materials for each of these brain constituents come from the diet. Optimum brain development can only take place when all essential nutrients are in generous supply, so care must be given when planning meals.

You'll want to use the the recipes in this book as a starting place, but you'll soon want to plan your own meals. It is not difficult to feed brain-healthy meals to your child, once you understand the Nutrition Rules.

I use these Nutrition Rules with my young clients:

1. When your child heads out the door each morning on his way to school, it is important that his brain be fueled for a day of logic, of memory, and of concentration. He can't think clearly if his brain is muddled by a load of simple sugars or by skipping the breakfast meal. He needs protein

to think. He needs minerals and vitamins to think. He needs essential fatty acids to think. He needs enough blood sugar to fuel his brain, but not so much that insulin surges create blood-sugar swings throughout the day.

Children are often not hungry in the morning, but don't let them skip meals. Offer fresh fruit or homemade applesauce, along with their vitamin and mineral supplement. My children are occasionally allowed to eat breakfast cereals that contain no more than three grams of sugar per serving.

If they are a little hungrier (and you've gotten up on time), prepare fresh oatmeal with fresh or home-frozen fruit. You may also enjoy making crepes and stuffing them with fresh fruit or unsweetened frozen fruit. Whole-wheat crepes are also delicious with fruit-only jam. Other breakfast suggestions may include breakfast burritos, scrambled eggs, or a protein shake made from soy or rice protein. "Spike" their protein drink with flax-seed oil to provide some of those essential oils that are so good for their brains.

Vitamin and mineral supplements should be taken with breakfast, because supplements are energizing. If your children do not eat several tea-spoons of unprocessed oils each day, you may wish to slip a fish oil or flaxseed oil capsule in with their supplements.

Other healthy breakfast ideas include breakfast parfait (with organic, low-sugar yogurt and homemade granola), fried egg sandwich on whole-

---

Even if your child is consuming a great diet, I believe it is critical to augment his diet with a carefully selected vitamin and mineral supplement. Check your local health food store for the best quality. Choose a product that provides at least 100 percent of the RDA for the vitamins and minerals (the label lists this information), and a substantial base amount of the other essential nutrients for which an RDA has not yet been assigned.

If your child is struggling with behavior or mood disorders, you may wish to consult a nutritionally oriented physician or a clinical nutritionist about a vitamin B complex, magnesium, zinc, antioxidant nutrients, iron, and essential fatty acids (fish oil, flaxseed oil, or a combination of EPA/DHA).

wheat toast, salmon hash, or brown rice pudding. (Recipes for many of these breakfast treats can be found in Chapter 8.)

2. Lunches can be dicier with kids. Children tire of sandwiches each day, so when the school lunch menu looks reasonably healthy, you may allow them to purchase hot lunch at school. They will enjoy that occasional treat.

My daughters enjoy taking salads to school for lunch. We purchase salad "kits" that include a grilled chicken breast, fresh greens, and dressing. Other times they prepare a salad at home, and add grilled salmon or smoked salmon as their protein and fat source. We purchase the peeled, baby carrots to add a little crunch to the lunch. Sometimes my girls bake homemade cookies for dessert.

Remember the information about cerebral allergies and how your child's favorite foods are often the foods to which he is allergic? Ask your doctor for an IgG or IgE blood test to determine his possible food allergies.

Many practitioners prefer to use the pulse test to check for potential food intolerances. The pulse test can be done in your own home, following these instructions: Before your child gets out of bed in the morning, take his resting pulse for fifteen seconds, then multiply it by four to get his sixty-second pulse rate.

While he is still lying in bed, let him eat a little of the food you are testing (I recommend you start with wheat, dairy, and corn, one food per day). Ten minutes later (still resting), take his pulse again. If it is elevated or suppressed by more than just a few beats per minute, it is likely that his body is responding negatively to that food.

Eliminate it for one month and evaluate his mood or behavior through the month. If he seems to be doing better, reintroduce a tiny portion of the food and note any behavioral or mood changes. *Warning: If your child is severely allergic, he may experience an exaggerated response after having not been exposed to the allergen for a period of time.* Please consult your medical doctor before reintroducing the food back into your child's diet.

Determining your child's allergies or intolerances can be difficult, especially if he is reactive to several foods or environmental substances simultaneously. It is important to consult with a nutritionally oriented physician or nutritionist for help in determining your child's allergies or food intolerance.

They are not allowed to drink sweetened beverages for lunch. Sugared beverages create thirst and make concentration more difficult. We encourage them to fill athletic bottles with ice water for their beverage.

3. My husband and I enjoy working out at the gym each afternoon, and the girls love to join us. Sometimes I have dinner ready for the family after school before we head for the gym. When I am working, however, and cannot get dinner ready this early, I often prepare a meal ahead of time that can be reheated. Sometimes I pay one of the girls to prepare a simple meal (we pay $2.00 for a full meal preparation). Sometimes we take the family out to dinner. We've learned to be flexible.

As with most families, time is short. We don't always plan our days carefully. Dinner isn't always perfect. Home-prepared meals are important, though, and we schedule them in wherever possible, usually several times per week. And when we eat our meals out, we opt for nutrition, not price or convenience. We choose the healthy restaurants that cater to our needs over the junk-food restaurants.

Conclusion

We've looked at dietary trends in young children and in the back of our minds probably knew that they aren't eating well, but until we saw it on paper, we didn't realize how bad it was. And we didn't realize that companies were producing food products that are actually dangerous to our bodies and brains.

We can change it. We can provide our children with the nutrition they need to run and play, to sit still and concentrate in class, to interact socially with other children, to develop a healthy sense of spirituality. We still carry the purchasing power of the family, after all. We buy the groceries. We prepare the meals. We can do better, and we WILL do better. Start today and teach your children how to eat to nourish their brains.

What about our teenagers, though? They are struggling as they have never struggled before. Is their angst a product of skewed hormones and a dysfunctional culture, or have their brains been harmed, too?

5

Feeding the Adolescent Brain

Our children are showing signs of what researcher Weston Price, D.D.S., foresaw as a trend in the degeneration of the human species—from the radically depleted and processed diet consumed in the past 80 or so years . . . His research . . . proved that a devitalized diet . . . [erodes] moral and sexual behaviors . . . what an intolerable burden we have placed on our children. Does anyone care?

—IRENE ALLEGER[1]

There was no hint of trouble until Cassie entered the sixth grade. Until that time, she had been home-schooled, and her parents were delighted with their companionable daughter. Her three younger sisters looked up to her, both physically and socially. As the oldest, she was the acknowledged leader of the pack, and they often slept in her room.

As Cassie entered the sixth grade, her personality began to suffer. She became morose and moody. She stopped playing with her sisters. She snapped at them, calling them ugly names. She kicked them or pushed them down when she was angry, which was nearly all the time.

Her parents set reasonable limits: "You may not talk ugly to your sisters. Go to your room until you can control yourself." She would stomp off to her room and slam the door, reappearing hours later with the same hateful glare. Her mother joked grimly that a "black cloud hovers over your head."

One night, the entire family went out to dinner. It was an evening in early spring. The younger sisters jostled noisily for the best seat at the table. Cassie quietly took a seat, head down, looking furtively around at the neighboring tables.

Finally, she leaned over to her mom and whispered, "Mom, why are they all looking at me?" Her mother glanced around. Other families' conversations filled the room.

"No one is looking at you," she whispered back. "They're all enjoying time with their families."

She looked around again. "They're all looking at me."

That mother's heart sank with dread. She thought of all those other mental symptoms: the anger, depression, violent behaviors. The bright conversation of the other girls swirled around her, but she couldn't hear it.

During the drive home after dinner, her daughter started talking about a famous rock star who had committed suicide. Her husband let her talk about it for a few minutes, then asked, "Cassie, what do you think about what he did?"

For a moment she was quiet, then she started sobbing. "Daddy, if I could do what he did, I would. I don't want to live anymore. I wish I could die!"

When they got home, Cassie's father ushered the other girls into the house and his wife took Cassie out into the backyard to talk.

Cassie stood with her head downcast, her hands in her pockets, her face miserable. "Sweetheart, what has happened? Has someone hurt you? Has someone touched you?"

She looked at her mother impatiently. "No, Mom. Of course not. No one has hurt me."

"What, then?"

"I don't know, Mom. I just don't want to live. I want to die."

Her mother finally said, "I'll find help for you. No matter what it takes, we'll solve this problem. Daddy and I will fix it."

When she walked back into the house to talk to her husband, he was busy. He had a gun collection that he had enjoyed for years. Every once in a while, he'd go down to the range and shoot at some targets. Only once, in their thirteen years of marriage, had he actually gone hunting. That was the extent of his hobby.

Tonight, he was going through the house, making sure that every weapon was secure and that the house was safe for his daughter. But how could he remove all the danger? There were butcher knives and matches. What could he do with those?

Cassie's mom put a plan together. Tomorrow, she'd make an appointment with her pediatrician and find the problem. Surely other kids had gone through this. Maybe this is a normal rite of passage. Maybe all preadolescent girls go through this type of depression. It must be her female hormones kicking up a fuss.

The next morning, she made an emergency appointment and pulled Cassie out of school to get her in. The doctor gave a perfunctory examination, then spoke with the mother. "Nothing wrong. She's a healthy girl."

It was when I started working with Cassie, who was only ten and in the spring of her life, that I began to understand the real problem of mental illness. When we see families struggling with preadolescents and adolescents who are out of control, self-medicating with drugs, threatening suicide, displaying the obstinate, defiant types of behavior, consumed with eating disorders, burning and cutting themselves, refusing to groom themselves, acting out in hundreds of bizarre, antisocial ways, we rush to judgment. It is the fault of the parents, society, the schools.

It all makes sense. There is, though, the question that no one seems to be considering and that is even more fundamental than questions about the culture. "What about our food?"

I have long studied the nutritional needs of the body and considered how our American food culture is depriving our children of the nutrients they need to build strong, healthy bodies. I had never, however, delved into nutrition for the mind until I worked with Cassie. I had never seriously considered the question, either. It was easier to blame Mom and Dad or the ever-culpable culture.

WHAT DOES THE TEENAGED BRAIN REQUIRE?

During adolescence, a child's body metamorphoses into that of an adult. The child grows from eighty to one hundred pounds up to two hundred pounds in just a few short years. At the same time, the endocrine system is revving up, transforming a nonsexual or a presexual person into a sexual person through hormones that influence the reproductive organs. These hormones also shape the landscape of their emotional lives. The social and family milieu is thrown into disarray as the child squirms for more and more independence.

Meeting the nutritional challenges of the teenaged body can be tough—especially when you, as a nutritionally aware parent, are swimming against the current and are trying to get decent food into your child's mouth. To complete this transformation successfully, teenagers have to go beyond minimum government standards and eat a very high-quality diet.

We've seen in previous chapters the importance of essential fatty acids for brain development. The brain of the adolescent is still laying down myelin tissue, so requirements for Omega-3 and Omega-6 fatty acids remain high. They need saturated fat, so the cell membrane of the neuron remains strong. Roughly eighty percent of the dry weight of myelin is fat or lipids. The fatty acid blend is complex. Different types of fats bond with proteins to form specific molecules, each of which is unique and essential. Some of the complexes comprising the myelin are cholesterol, cerebrosides, sulfatides, ethanolamine phosphatides, lecithin, sphingomyelin, phosphatidylserine, phosphatidylinositol, and plamalogens.[2] Providing an abundant supply of fatty acids and amino acids is of critical importance to adolescent brain health, as it is with younger children.

Your child's brain has been growing and developing, fed by the foods he has enjoyed through his infancy and childhood. If his diet hasn't been the best, it isn't time to give up. During these next few years, his brain will continue to lay down new tissue, form new networks of axons and dendrites, built by the foods he will eat during his teenage years. He will have to get those good fats up into the brain where they can settle into myelin and support brain function for the rest of his life. This period of life is of critical importance, nutritionally speaking.

He's got to have dietary fats to produce steroid hormones like testosterone, estrogen, and progesterone that are flooding the body. Hormones practically drive the teenage psyche; fats are used to build those hormones.

He needs protein, too. Fifteen to thirty percent of his brain, brain compounds, and nervous system are composed of proteins (themselves constructed from essential amino acids); about thirty percent of the teenage diet should be good-quality protein. Every day, all ten essential amino acids (arginine, histadine, leucine, isoleucine, lysine, methionine, phenylalanine, threonine, tryptophan, and valine) are carried through the blood-brain barrier to be laid down into the nerve tissue. Some of those proteins will become part of the structure of hormones or neurotransmitters, delivering messages throughout the body and the brain.

The calming neurotransmitter, serotonin, for example, is derived from tryptophan. Dopamine, the neurotransmitter that gives sensations of pleasure, is derived from phenylalanine. Thyroid hormone is synthesized from tyrosine, a nonessential but vitally important amino acid that also helps produce dopamine, the neurotransmitter that receives signals of pleasure.

Minerals and vitamins activate the enzymes that perform much of the work of the brain, making it run faster and more efficiently. The metabolic conversion that transforms tryptophan into serotonin or tyrosine into thyroid hormone requires minerals and vitamins as cofactors. While some of the minerals like iron, iodine, magnesium, and zinc, or vitamins like the B complex or vitamin C, are high-profile in terms of research, there are scores of individual nutrients, each one fulfilling a unique and critical role in the functioning of this complex organ. When even one is missing some function goes undone, some structure remains unbuilt, and while the effect may not be noticed immediately, over time the implications of nutrient deficiencies are serious.

The Recommended Dietary Allowance (see the table on page 142) for adolescent boys and girls is incomplete. RDAs have been established for only a few nutrients. It simply outlines what level of nutrition is needed to prevent overt deficiency diseases like rickets or beriberi.

Every building, though, needs a floor. Think of the RDA as a floor of nutrition. It is where everything must start; below RDA level is gross deficiency.

WHAT DO TEENAGERS EAT?

Children's eating habits are terrible, but as they grow, they become even worse.[3] Like their younger siblings, teens really don't eat fruits or green vegetables at all, except perhaps the iceberg lettuce sandwiched between the slice of tomato and the pickle decorating the hamburger they purchase at the local fast-food restaurant.[4] About one-half of all meals are consumed away from home, primarily in a fast-food restaurant.

Over two hundred middle and high school students, from different schools, completed food diaries for me. These diaries provide a great deal of real-life information. Read through some of these food diaries to see if you think the nutritional needs of teenagers are being met:

Recommended Dietary Allowances (RDAs) for Adolescent Boys and Girls[5]

Protein

	Age (Yrs)	Weight (kg)	(lb)	Height (cm)	(in)	Protein (g)
Males	11–14	45	99	157	62	45
	15–18	66	145	176	69	59
Females	11–14	46	101	157	62	46
	15–18	55	120	163	64	44

Fat-Soluble Vitamins

		Vitamin A (IU)	Vitamin D (IU)	Vitamin E (IU)	Vitamin K (IU)
Males	11–14	1,000	10	10	45
	15–18	1,000	10	10	65
Females	11–14	800	10	8	45
	15–18	800	10	8	60

Water-Soluble Vitamins

		Vitamin C (mg)	Thiamin (mg)	Riboflavin (mg)	Niacin (mg)	Vitamin B_6 (mg)	Folate (mg)	Vitamin B_{12} (mg)
Males	11–14	50	1.3	1.5	17	1.7	150	2.0
	15–18	60	1.5	1.8	20	2.0	200	2.0
Females	11–14	50	1.1	1.3	15	1.4	150	2.0
	15–18	60	1.1	1.3	15	1.4	200	2.0

Minerals

		Calcium (mg)	Phosphorus (mg)	Magnesium (mg)	Iron (mg)	Zinc (mg)	Iodine (mg)	Selenium (mg)
Males	11–14	1,200	1,200	270	12	15	150	40
	15–18	1,200	1,200	400	12	15	150	50
Females	11–14	1,200	1,200	280	15	12	150	45
	15–18	1,200	1,200	300	15	12	150	50

SARAH

	Day 1	Day 2
Breakfast	1 cup General Mills Trix cereal ½ cup 2% milk	1 cup General Mills Trix cereal ½ cup My*T*Fine 2% milk
Lunch	2 slices Fred Meyer bread with 4 tablespoons Jif Creamy Peanut Butter 3 tablespoons Smuckers Red Raspberry Jelly 1 cup 2% milk	1 BK Broiler from Burger King (one 3 oz. chicken breast) 1 piece lettuce 2 tomato slices on a bun
Dinner	2 slices Fred Meyer bread 3 oz. Fred Meyer brand tuna 2 tablespoons Kraft Miracle Whip 1 cup Snapple lemon iced tea	2 slices Fred Meyer bread 2 oz. Bumblebee tuna 2 tablespoons Kraft Miracle Whip ¾ cup Campbell's Beef with Vegetables Chunky Soup
Beverages		1 cup Minute Maid Fruit Punch 12 oz. Dr Pepper

JOHN

	Day 1	Day 2
Breakfast	2 scrambled eggs 1 sausage (pork) 1 hash brown potatoes	1 bowl Honey Nut Cheerios with milk
Lunch	Nothing	Cinnamon roll
Dinner	Taco Bell (2 burritos, 1 soft taco) 1 large Mountain Dew	1 peanut-butter-and-jelly sandwich 1 hard-boiled egg water
Snack		Chips Crackers

I selected two days of diaries and analyzed them for nutrient content. Compare this analysis with the RDA on page 142 and you'll begin to understand why teens have such a hard time *thinking* and *feeling* appropriately. Keep in mind, this chart was analyzed using information from the manufacturer regarding the nutritional content of the meals. This information has not been verified by an independent laboratory.

JOHN		SARAH	
Nutrient	*Amount*	*Nutrient*	*Amount*
Calories	1649	Calories	1087
Protein	109.2 gm	Protein	52.26 gm
Carbos	86.84 gm	Carbos	135.6 gm
Fat	94.55 gm	Fat	38.60 gm
Vitamin B$_1$	1.195 mg	Vitamin B$_1$	1.040 mg
Vitamin B$_2$	4.607 mg	Vitamin B$_2$	1.155 mg
Vitamin B$_3$	24.16 mg	Vitamin B$_3$	20.48 mg
Sodium	2906 mg	Sodium	2307 mg
Potassium	1606 mg	Potassium	899.2 mg
Iron	16.14 mg	Iron	11.06 mg
Calcium	348.5 mg	Calcium	304.1 mg
Magnesium	132.5 mg	Magnesium	82.53 mg
Zinc	12.04 mg	Zinc	5.590 mg

I selected these diaries at random. Some are worse and some are a little better. None is good. A number of observations need to be made regarding the diaries:

1. Very few of the kids were served a home-cooked meal at any time during the day. Twenty to twenty-five percent had a prepared meal in the evening, but even this is deceptive because many of the meals were composed of Hamburger Helper, canned vegetables, and the like.

2. While breakfast is usually eaten, it is nearly always a bowl of sugared cereal (see previous chapter for a profile on commercial cereals) or an entrée from a fast-food chain. Virtually no one eats a prepared breakfast.

3. In the meals in the above diaries, only a few vegetables were served, even counting the wilted lettuce and tomato on the hamburger, the veggie burger, the canned vegetable soup, and the canned corn. Only one salad

appeared anywhere. A couple glasses of juice are sprinkled throughout (juice is not the nutritional equivalent of fresh fruit).

4. Where is the water? Maybe the kids forgot to include the water they sipped through the day, but I doubt it. I've met few kids who drink water; they think it either tastes bad or it's too boring.

5. Where are the essential fatty acids? There aren't any. Ditto high-quality protein; it is missing, too.

6. How can we expect these kids to enjoy vibrant mental health when they aren't even beginning to meet minimum nutritional requirements?

We've always thought that, at this age, the influence of friends is much greater than the influence of parents, but according to current information, parents actually have more control than friends over what their teenagers eat. One study noted that "we found clear resemblance in habitual fat and food intake between parents and their adolescent children and between spouses. Friends do not seem to have a lot of influence . . ."[6] In this case, the good news is also the bad news. According to the research, as terrible as teens' eating habits are, they very much resemble our own.

The School of Public Health at the University of Minnesota completed an ambitious study of more than thirty thousand adolescents, assessing health status, health behaviors, and psychosocial factors. Although the study didn't delve into many nutritional issues, the following trends appeared:

"Major concerns identified included high prevalence rates of inadequate intake of fruits, vegetables, and dairy products; unhealthful weight-control practices; and overweight status. For example, inadequate fruit intake was reported by 28% of the adolescents and inadequate vegetable intake was reported by 36%. Among female adolescents, 12% reported chronic dieting, 30% reported binge eating, 12% reported self-induced vomiting, and 2% reported using diuretics or laxatives."[7]

After asking her class to complete a twenty-four-hour food diary and looking over the results, one teacher moaned in despair. "There goes one whole semester of nutrition education down the drain." She looked depressed. And why not? Her degree is in home economics; she understands fundamental nutrition and knows how to teach it. But the kids just aren't getting it.

I tried to comfort her: "You're trying to fight the American food culture. That isn't easily done."

What Are Our Schools Teaching Our Kids?

It's too easy to point our fingers at Mom and Dad and say, "Mom, it's your fault your kid misbehaves in school. Dad, you're to blame that your son is behaving outrageously, or is suffering from some sort of mental illness." We parents do need to take the responsibility to feed our children nutritious food (and eat nutritious food ourselves as role models) and start putting good meals on the table, three times a day. We have become so distracted by crushing responsibilities and time pressures that we place good nutrition at the bottom of our "To-Do List."

We're also tired of fighting the food battles day after day. We're tired of saying "no" in the supermarket, over and over again. We're tired of explaining that, yes, their favorite sports heroes unashamedly promote the latest junk food to hit the market but no, we're not going to buy it. We're tired of the whole thing.

It would be helpful if the schools came beside us and taught the same message about good nutrition that we're trying to teach. But your school district is just as culpable as the rest of the culture. The local institutions that pride themselves on teaching skills and behaviors that will serve our children as they leave the sacred halls of academia and enter the "real world" are teaching your children a lot more than scholastics.

There is big money to be made in the school food service department, particularly in vending machines and the selling of branded merchandise, or in fast-food franchises set up in the place of the school kitchen. Nearly

$6 billion is spent by elementary and high schools in the United States on foods served at school. Over $750 million annually is spent on vending machine sales alone, bringing huge dollars into the school coffers. What is sold in the vending machines? If you think the schools stock healthy snacks in the machines, you live in a dreamworld. Top sellers are soft drinks, coffee, juice and pseudo-juice drinks, candy, chips, pretzels, cookies, and even french fries. Nonsparkling water accounts for a small fraction of soft drink sales.[8]

While some school districts make a perfunctory attempt to limit the amount of junk the kids consume, let's face it: Motives are driven by profit, even when administrators know that the consequences of offering low-nutrition snacks can be severe. Sadly, when decisions about whether or not to bring in the vending machines must be made, registered dietitians often help make the decision. Dietitians should be leading the charge against junk food, but it seems their eyes cloud over when presented with more dollars to plug into their programs.

One food service director bragged, "We profited $50,000 net the first year, and it's more than double that today."[9]

The American School Food Service Association is the national trade association that serves food service departments in school districts. Its goals are lofty, or so states their pamphlet titled *The Little Big Fact Book:*

> For more than 50 years, school food service and nutrition professionals have fostered the educational, physical and social well-being of our nation's school children. Every school meal served is more than an isolated investment in a child; it is an investment in America itself.
>
> Improper nutrition is not simply an issue of socioeconomic status; hunger does not discriminate. Any student who skips a meal, who has no access to breakfast or lunch or who fails to make healthful food choices risks incurring serious learning and health deficits. School nutrition programs help to ensure the maximum return on the billions of dollars spent for public education, which will enhance America's future productivity.

Why, then, are the top advertisers in the food service magazines the junkiest foods on the market? In the trade magazine *School Foodservice & Nutrition,* top advertisers are General Mills, Chef Boyardee, Red Baron Pizza, Lipton's Cup-A-Soup, Gehl's Nachos, Nabisco cookies and crackers, Tyson Fried Chicken, Pizza Hut, and Otis Spunkmeyer chocolate chip cookies.

School food service is a huge industry, serving over 94,000 public and private schools with a "captive audience" of 51 million children and young adults.[10] Administrators feel they are competing with the fast-food chains and wonder how they can pull those dollars into their programs instead of seeing it spent in the restaurants. They even bemoan the dollars lost to kids who attempt to bring a healthy lunch from home. An article in *School Foodservice & Nutrition* pleads, "Would you like to coax a few more Burger King devotees, or are you looking longingly at the lost-revenue parade of brown-baggers as they pass your lunch line each day?"[11]

I'm sure many food service workers would like to improve the nutritional content of the foods they put on students' trays. No one likes to think they are harming their young charges, after all. But when it all comes down to the final decision, the dollars decide the school lunch program and what goes into the vending machines. The health of your child's brain has nothing to do with it.

The school food service program, including vending, used to be the responsibility of the principal, but this task was taken over by the professionals. "Where once vending was managed by principals seeking supplemental income, now amid the vending machine clatter, you can hear the sound of coins jangling right down to the bottom line of school food service department budgets."[12] One reason food service personnel wrested control of the vending machines was ostensibly to improve nutrition; they apparently believed that their school principals weren't stocking enough healthy foods in the machines and wanted to do better, so to speak.

Maybe that is the motivation of some, but according to the industry, money still talks; nutrition walks. They know the students want to drink soft drinks. They would, if given the choice, eat fast foods rather than healthy foods, and why not let the schools benefit from the dollars to be gleaned from rich manufacturing companies?

One food service director found himself in a difficult position: His school board was demanding more return for the food service operations. They were looking at red ink lining the bottom of the financial sheet. When the soft drink detail men showed up at his office door, he listened.

When they offered a $200,000 signing bonus and a lucrative stipend of $100,000 per year for ten years, plus a generous commission rate from the sale of drinks, he took it. The program became so profitable for the school district that he subsequently brought in vending machines for snacks and cold-food items. He already has picked out a machine that makes hot french fries in forty-five seconds for $1, and has his eye on a hot-air popcorn machine. He's looking to vend fresh fruit and ice cream.[13] What a deal.

In case food service directors lack imagination for how to get their kids to buy more junk food, food manufacturers offer their own fresh ideas. General Mills offers to let you "earn cash for your school" just by purchasing a whole list of junk cereals and other pseudofood products: Bowlpak Cereals, Yoplait Original and Yoplait Trix Yogurt, Betty Crocker Fruit Roll-ups, Betty Crocker Fruit by the Foot, Betty Crocker Fruit String Thing, Nature Valley Granola Bars, Golden Graham Treats, and Gushers. They aren't real generous, however. Just ten cents earned for every case of food service box-top logos.

The USDA requires a serving of grains with kids' meals, and Darlington Farms offers a way to get kids to eat grain: Give them cookies. According to their advertisement in a recent publication, "We've finally found a way to get kids to eat bread. Darlington Farms cookies are a great way to give students (and the USDA) the grain requirements they need.

Our cookies are home-style baked to be soft and chewy and well, they're a little more exciting than a slice of bread . . . And as far as brussels sprout brownies and turnip turnovers, well, we'll have to get back to you on that one."

Whom are they kidding? Since when did a cookie become the nutritional equivalent of whole-grain bread?[14]

When your kids leave the school building each day and walk home, they are bombarded with another segment of the food culture that contributes to their deteriorating mood and cognition—fast-food chains.

Our teens are eating the worst possible foods, starting with breakfast and continuing on throughout the day. While some studies seem to indicate that breakfast contributes a significant share of nutrition, other studies disagree. According to a study published in the *American Journal of Clinical Nutrition,* breakfast consumption is declining, particularly in older adolescents age fifteen to eighteen.[15] What concerns me as much, however, is that when kids do eat breakfast, it is primarily empty calories.

American teenagers are poorly nourished in most minerals, primarily calcium, iron, zinc, copper, and magnesium, and many vitamins, including B_{12}, vitamin D, folic acid, and others—all of which play a critical role in brain health.[16]

While other studies show that supplies of sodium, potassium, phosphorus, and others are adequate,[17] I'm baffled. From where are they possibly getting the potassium? Potassium is found primarily in vegetables and fruits—they don't eat vegetables and fruit. I'm sure they get enough sodium—too much sodium. Sodium is liberally added to highly processed foods, of which they get too much.

HOW DO DEFICIENCIES AFFECT THE TEENAGE BRAIN?

Theories about adolescent nutrient deficiencies don't mean very much until we see how the deficiencies translate into poor school performance and ugly behavior. Poor nutrition isn't just theory; it really does take its toll on the mental health of your child in a very tangible way. While we can't discuss every nutrient in the context of brain health, we can touch on a few of the better-researched nutrients and learn what their deficiencies mean to our teenagers.

Iron Deficiency and Teens

American girls (and boys) are at risk for iron deficiency because they do not routinely enjoy iron-rich foods except hamburgers. Menstrual cycles pull several milligrams out of the blood supply each month, depleting iron stores even further.

How does iron affect cognition and mood? Iron circulates through the blood as a type of ferry service, carrying life-giving oxygen to every cell in the body. The body doesn't need very much; the average adult male has about 49 mg/kg of body weight (or about 3.5 grams), and the average adult female has about 38 mg/kg of body weight (or about 2.5 grams).

When iron stores are depleted, anemia results, with symptoms of fatigue and apathy. Studies around the world show that iron-deficient kids have difficulty paying attention, are uncoordinated, and don't develop at the same rate as iron-adequate kids.[18]

Iron doesn't act alone. Low-iron status can aggravate the signs of fatty acid deficiency, decreasing the total weight of the brain. Low iron reduces the rate at which prostaglandins are developed[19] and lowers the production of key energy enzymes and neurotransmitters that send messages between nerve cells. Some of the neurotransmitters affected by low-iron status include noradrenaline, serotonin, and dopamine; a deficiency in any or all of these neurotransmitters could cause depression or other mood disorders.[20]

Magnesium Deficiency

In the last chapter, we saw the various roles that magnesium plays in the body. Magnesium is a fascinating mineral. It is used to regulate receptor sites for neurotransmitters, and is active in the hippocampus, the emotional center of the body.[21] It is used in the production of ATP, or cellular energy; it activates scores of enzymes, and so on.

Magnesium influences on behavior can be very visible. People with low stores of magnesium are often sensitive people, easily thrown into emotional states like anger, depression, frustration, agitation, or fears. They tend to be frightened of people or situations that do not affect most people.

Magnesium-deficient people crave chocolate but can crave other sweets as well. Sometimes the eyelids will twitch periodically, or young girls will experience severe muscle cramping during their menstrual cycle. Many symptoms of PMS may actually be magnesium-deficiency symptoms, since the body burns more magnesium during the week preceding menses.

Low magnesium can cause hyperactivity, because in the presence of calcium and inadequate amounts of magnesium to counterbalance the stimulating effects of calcium, the nervous system is in a state of constant excitation. These hyperactive people can't calm down because their nerves are agitated; there is not enough magnesium to quiet the nerve signal. Their minds race, their bodies can't stop moving, they pace the floor, they interrupt constantly, their minds are never at peace.

Magnesium-deficient people are constantly tired, because the diminished production of ATP cannot meet the energy demands of the body. They often experience jumpiness in the muscles before going to sleep, where their whole body convulses as it begins to relax into the sheets. And yet, as tired as they are, they awaken in the middle of the night. Their minds are unable to shut back down and rest, their muscles are tight, and they lie awake until dawn. Sometimes they drift back off to sleep before they must get up, but when the alarm goes off, they are exhausted. They feel as if they didn't sleep a wink all night. Their bowel movements are infrequent and hard like pebbles.

Do any of these symptoms sound like your teenager? Magnesium deficiency is very common in adolescents and children, because the best food sources of magnesium are dark-green leafy vegetables, tofu, wheat germ, and cashews, foods that teenagers abhor. Ironically, chocolate is a fairly good source of magnesium, although it would make more sense to crave tofu, since tofu contains over twice the amount of magnesium found in cocoa powder!

Teenagers seldom eat the foods that supply the richest amount of this mind-calming mineral, but what compounds the problem is when too much calcium is consumed in relation to magnesium. When adolescents drink substantial quantities of milk and leave the broccoli or kale sitting coldly on their plates, calcium levels are elevated and magnesium levels are depressed, causing even more of an imbalance. Magnesium-deficiency symptoms become even more pronounced.

Zinc Deficiency

Another nutrient that seems to be lacking in the juvenile brain is zinc, a trace mineral that boasts of a powerful influence on many systems in the body, including the digestive, immune, and neurological systems. We saw in Chapter 4 that zinc is a very versatile mineral, supporting nearly every organ and system in the body.

Zinc shines in the nervous system, where it activates over two hundred enzymes that drive the work of the brain, particularly the hippocampus, the part of the brain that performs memory tasks.[22] Zinc is also a structural part of the brain, helping lay the fatty acids down properly into cell membranes. Zinc, along with calcium, is needed for neurotransmitter release; large amounts of zinc are located inside the synaptic vesicles and released when the nerve cell fires.[23]

As one study put it, zinc-deficient people can't think. "Evidence from both animal and human studies suggests that zinc deficiency may lead to delays in cognitive development . . . zinc deficiency may lead to deficits in children's neuropsychologic functioning, activity, or motor development, and thus interfere with cognitive performance."[24]

Unfortunately, most Americans, including children and adolescents, are deficient in zinc because it has been stripped out of the grains used to make breads and cereals, and the other primary sources of zinc, oysters and red meat, are not eaten frequently enough to ensure even meeting the RDA. The RDA for zinc ranges from ten milligrams per day for children to fifteen milligrams per day for adolescents. Many nutritionists believe the RDA is far too conservative in its estimates of zinc needed and that upward of thirty milligrams may be needed to promote health. But just as magnesium should be opposed, or counterbalanced, by calcium, copper opposes zinc, and we get far too much copper in the diet, exaggerating the possible consequences of zinc deficiency.

The diet of the typical adolescent doesn't even reach the recommended daily allowance for zinc; the average teenager gets from five to ten milligrams of zinc in the diet, and only about twenty percent of dietary zinc is actually absorbed.[25] While the RDA is about fifteen milligrams per day, many clinicians believe that, given the enormous variety of tasks that zinc must perform, upward of thirty milligrams may be necessary to prevent the zinc-deficiency symptoms listed below.

When I first went into clinical practice, I saw numerous clients whose hair showed excessive levels of copper and extremely low levels of zinc. The symptoms they primarily complained about were crushing depression, frequent headaches, confusion, poor memory, and cravings for bread. But most notable was the depression, accompanied by extreme confusion and the feeling that "life is just too difficult to live." They felt that the slightest challenge posed an impossible hurdle to cross. It was difficult for them to make and stick with decisions. Part of the indecision could have come from severe depression; depression can make the brain feel sluggish or apathetic because mental energy is in short supply.

The fuzziness of thinking in my copper-toxic/zinc-deficient clients was deeper than simple depression. It rendered them nearly unable to function at all. They were angry, vengeful people. They held their hostility in front of them like a shield, protecting them from close relationships with other people. Where magnesium-deficient people may be weepy, clingy, or hiding in seclusion, the zinc-deficient, copper-toxic person can be verbally abusive.

Zinc-deficient people don't smell or taste food very well, so they lose their appetite. They develop eating disorders of all types, sometimes refusing to eat anything at all for long periods of time or choosing only the junkiest of the junk foods.

According to some researchers, zinc deficiency may frequently accompany periods where hormone levels are transitional, as in prepuberty or

> Michael Schmidt, author of *Smart Fats: How Dietary Fats and Oils Affect Mental, Physical and Emotional Intelligence*, says it is particularly important to give adequate amounts of zinc during the first three months of prenatal life because that is a period of rapid growth of brain tissue, and zinc works with fatty acids to properly myelinate the dendrites and axons of the nerve cells. If that tissue is not properly deposited, functionality of the nerve cell is hindered.

adolescence, or later in adult life after giving birth, going on birth control pills, approaching menopause, or beginning hormone replacement therapy. Excessive amounts of estrogen in the absence of adequate amounts of progesterone can tip the zinc:copper ratios toward excessive copper, and it is this imbalance that can help cause the extreme mood disruptions in the teenager.[26]

Deficiencies in the B Complex

The teenaged diet is grossly inadequate in most vitamins, but because of teens' excessive consumption of sugar, they are particularly undersupplied in the B complex vitamins that must metabolize the sugars. A list of the typical B complex–deficiency symptoms sounds like most teenagers today:

- Fatigue
- Indigestion
- Malaise
- Skin eruptions
- Muscular weakness
- Disorientation
- Confusion
- Anorexia
- Memory loss
- Anemia
- Depression

Following is a chart showing the nutrient content of a sample teenage girl's and boy's diaries:

GIRL'S CHART		BOY'S CHART	
Nutrient	*Amount*	*Nutrient*	*Amount*
Calories	1452 kc	Kilocalories	1379 kc
Protein	59.82 gr	Protein	46.03 gr
Fat	57.72 gr	Fat	29.92 gr
Sugar	72.80 gr	Sugar	76.60 gr
Vitamin A	630.4 IU	Vitamin A	297.7 IU
Vitamin E	4.821 mg	Vitamin E	.718 mg
Thiamin	1.011 mg	Thiamin	.911 mg
Riboflavin	1.532 mg	Riboflavin	1.033 mg
Niacin	28.59 mg	Niacin	20.49 mg
Folate	60.76 mcg	Folate	154.7 mcg
Vit B$_{12}$	5.383 mcg	Vitamin B$_{12}$	.89 mcg
Vitamin C	19.78 mg	Vitamin C	205.2 mg
Vitamin D	3.825 mcg	Vitamin D	2.55 mcg
Vitamin K	14.64 mcg	Vitamin K	9.885 mcg
Sodium	1677 mg	Sodium	2407 mg
Potassium	1379 mg	Potassium	3758 mg
Iron	11.08 mg	Iron	33.62 mg
Calcium	600.5 mg	Calcium	1640 mg
Magnesium	105.7 mg	Magnesium	293.4 mg
Phosphorus	604.1 mg	Phosphorus	405.6 mg
Zinc	2.862 mg	Zinc	2.603 mg

You can compare these two charts against the RDA chart on page 142.

Sodium, Potassium, and Other Nutrients

In the previous chapter we discussed the impact of the high-sodium diet on the younger child. Sodium becomes an even bigger problem in the teenage brain when emotions are running wild as part of their hormonal life. We cannot, however, isolate one or another mineral or vitamin and believe that represents the entire story. Nutrient deficiencies never occur in singles. Nutrients are bound together in nature, working in synergy and balance. Stimulating nutrients like calcium and sodium are blended with calming nutrients like magnesium and potassium to give the body and brain a sort of peaceful energy, purposeful vigor, and calm attentiveness.

In natural food, potassium is typically about 2.5 times higher than sodium or more, emphasizing its importance in the body. Magnesium is just slightly lower than calcium. Most natural foods or natural diets contain about eight times more zinc than copper. Vitamins accompany the minerals in the natural diet because vitamins work hand in hand with minerals; neither vitamins nor minerals work in solitude. And they all blend with proteins, carbohydrates, and fats, because in synergy and balance, the body is well nourished.

When the nutrients are pulled out of their natural balance and deprived of their fellow workers, when stimulating minerals like sodium, calcium, and copper are elevated and the body is deprived of the calming minerals like potassium, magnesium, and zinc, the brain cannot work. It simply cannot, any more than we could work if half of our tools were missing. It is easy to see, from the diaries and nutrient tables of typical teenagers, that a substantial portion of their "brain tools" is missing.

WHY DO TEENAGERS OFTEN SELF-DESTRUCT?

It is not difficult to imagine that deficiencies could cause subtle changes in cognition or behavior. Making simple improvements to the diet could easily improve grades and make our teenagers feel a little happier about life. What we have discussed so far in this chapter are the little things: slightly lower grades, little outbursts of defiance, a tendency toward pessimism, PMS.

We also have to consider the larger issues. What about behaviors and learning disorders that are so serious that they endanger the child's life or send him to jail? What about serious mental disorders like anorexia nervosa, bulimia, suicide ideation, obsessive-compulsive behaviors, mental retardation, and the like? What about extreme anger, self-mutilation, drug use and abuse, and alcoholism? What about sexual promiscuity?

Twenty-five percent of all teenagers will engage in activities so severe that if they even survive adolescence, some form of permanent damage will haunt them the rest of their lives.[27] When these conducts begin to emerge in a teenager, parents are thrown into the most frightening time of their lives. They replay every event in their family's life that they can remember.

"What did we do to cause this type of behavior in our child? Where did we go wrong?"

Dr. James Dobson, Ph.D., and founder of Focus on the Family, comforts parents of troubled teenagers by saying, "It's time we admitted that the children of some very loving, caring parents can go wrong, too.

"In years past, if a kid went bad, he was a bad kid. Now society claims it is parents who must have bungled his childhood in some way. Well, maybe, and maybe not. Adolescents are old enough to make irresponsible choices of their own, and some do stupid things despite the love and care they receive at home.

"I do not seek to exonerate parents who have short-changed their kids and treated them badly. But someone should speak on behalf of those good-as-gold moms and dads who have done the best they can for their rebellious children. They deserve a pat on the back, not a slap in the face."[28]

Have we seriously considered that our food culture is harming our kids? Take a child and deprive his brain of adequate nutrition through his entire life, dump him into a hostile, unstable social scene, and pull away the pillars of his support network (his family—he pulls away from them).

Then load up his breakfast cereal with stimulants, feed him more stimulants at lunch, snack, and dinner, and at the same time, rob him of the very nutrients he needs to process the stimulants. Toxic chemicals from his food target his endocrine system and prevent his natural hormones from locking into place. Inject other toxic chemicals from his food into his nervous system that prevent neurotransmitters from relaying messages back and forth. This is a recipe guaranteed to make him or her crazy.

When these kids try to destroy themselves and the others around them, they are continuing down the path they started down when they were born, continuing the self-destruction of their own brain cells. Because we can't physically examine brains until autopsy, it is difficult to pinpoint exactly when and how the damage occurs, but from outcome studies that compare the test scores of teenagers who eat well and teenagers who eat the typical American diet[29] we can assume that some physical damage has been done or that something is not functioning correctly in the brain.

What we are likely seeing is a composite effect, coming from an onslaught of dietary events that started even before they were born and didn't stop as they passed through childhood and adolescence. With the exception of less than ten percent of children who were breast-fed by well-nourished mothers for twelve months or longer, every other child exits infancy with less-than-optimal brain development. These kids will never live up to their genetic potential. We won't even know what their potential was.

What does a nutrient chart look like when a teenager eats a "healthy" diet?

Breakfast	Midmorning snack	Lunch	Midafternoon snack	Dinner
1 cup Homemade Granola with Fruit (See Chapter 8)	2 raw apples	Chicken salad (grilled chicken on green salad, with olive oil and vinegar dressing)	2 homemade bean and cheese burritos (See Chapter 8)	Broiled halibut (5 ounces)
				Steamed broccoli
½ cup 2% milk				Coleslaw
1 banana				1 orange

Nutrient	Amount
Kilocalories	1872
Protein	104 gr
Fat	65.03 gr
Carbohydrates	235.3 gr
Vitamin A	1123 IU
Vitamin E	28.98 mg
Thiamin	1.782 mg
Riboflavin	1.532 mg
Niacin	26.06 mg
Folate	465.9 mcg
Vit B_{12}	2.411 mcg
Vitamin C	247.7 mg
Vitamin D	1.313 mcg
Vitamin K	229.5 mcg
Sodium	1426 mg
Potassium	3978 mg
Iron	17.10 mg
Calcium	842.8 mg
Magnesium	547.4 mg
Phosphorus	1641 mg
Zinc	8.925 mg

SERIOUS PROBLEMS

Jake presented problems right from the very beginning. The first three years of his life were chaotic. His birth mother, hooked on narcotics, didn't care for her son. His birth father was equally unreliable, and when Jake was just a couple of years old, he went into foster care and was adopted a year later.

His adoptive parents had no idea what they were getting into, but within a few months they realized their son had serious problems. He seemed angry all the time, lashing out at people for little provocations. When he went to kindergarten and then into elementary school, the behavioral problems escalated, but now they were accompanied by a complete disinterest in schoolwork.

They attributed his problems to the instability of his infant and toddler days, but they also pulled huge amounts of guilt onto themselves. Friends and neighbors added to their guilt with little comments: "Well, if it were my child . . ." When the inevitable telephone calls from the principal came, week after week, year after year, they tried everything they knew to turn him around—discipline, loving guidance, church attendance. But Jake fell deeper and deeper into antisocial, destructive behaviors that escalated even higher when he entered junior high and high school.

Most parents blame themselves until they meet other frightened, frantic parents whose lives have been torn apart by a child. They compare their parenting skills against the techniques used by parents of successful kids and find little difference.

I recently interviewed Jake and asked him to recall his earliest memories. He said, "I have always been angry. My earliest memories are of feeling angry, for no reason, at everyone . . . I have always been tense, on the edge. My mind never stops, never shuts off, even when I lie down to sleep at night. It torments me. I do drugs to try to shut my mind off, to help me relax, to give me some temporary peace . . ." In some respects, the junk food becomes a type of self-medication against the inner pain. Sugar and salt can sometimes temporarily relieve the tension, but when used long-term, hasten the downward spiral of the symptoms.

Research is mounting that nutrition and violent behaviors are inextricably linked. One study found that twenty subjects with marginal deficiencies of thiamin were impulsive, highly irritable, aggressive, and sensitive to criticism. After their diets were supplemented with thiamine, the subjects' behavior improved significantly.

Research shows that iron deficiency is directly associated with aggressive behavior in young men and that iron deficiency is nearly twice as prevalent in incarcerated adolescents as in their nonincarcerated peers. Iron deficiency may cause behavioral impairment by diminishing dopamine transmission and is linked to behavioral disorders,[30] and while iron deficiency is more common in young adolescent girls than boys, boys, too, can suffer from iron deficiency that leaves them vulnerable to mental and social disorders.

Low levels of certain amino acids are also connected to bad behavior. Serotonin, synthesized in the body from tryptophan, is a calming transmitter. Studies show that rats fed diets depleted in the amino acid tryptophan become more aggressive toward mice. In addition, research on vervet monkeys found that tryptophan-free diets increased aggression in males, while high-tryptophan food reduced aggression in both males and females. High-sugar diets that are also low in high-quality protein can lead to deficiencies in this essential amino acid and others.[31]

Other studies show that deficiencies in essential fatty acids cause violent behaviors by changing the concentration of EFAs in neurotransmitters. Deficiencies in the essential fatty acid docosohexaenoic acid (DHA) is strongly correlated with violent behaviors; subjects with low levels of DHA tended more toward violence and alcohol dependence.

One study noted that "violent subjects had significantly higher lifetime violence and hostility ratings . . . than nonviolent subjects."[32] Remember that the dietary source of DHA is fish; most adolescents simply don't eat fish.

Dr. Stephen Schoenthaler of the California State University, who has written a number of research papers on nutrition-related violence, strongly believes that antisocial behaviors can be greatly reduced, both in a prison population and in the population at large, just by making changes in the diet.

"We have demonstrated that vitamin-mineral supplementation raises low blood vitamin concentrations," Schoenthaler says, "corrects abnormal brain function owing to low blood vitamin status, and ultimately produces better behavior and less violence among juvenile delinquents." He goes on to say that supplementation may not even be necessary if juveniles are counseled to take responsibility for selecting a good diet, and that "the literature suggests that about a 45% reduction in violence is possible by diet change alone."[33]

The implications of this information are frightening and hopeful. What would happen if we turned our backs on the American food culture and *fed our children wholesome foods that feed their brains?*

A study in Great Britain found that of nine children with persistent antisocial, disruptive, and/or criminal behaviors, all tested positive for food intolerance and allergy, and when the allergens were removed, their antisocial behavior ceased.[34] They settled down to become "normal kids." Two of the kids who subsequently discontinued the program and began eating their allergenic foods again reoffended and were institutionalized.

Depression As a Causal Factor

Adults have enough life experience to know that bad times come and go, like the good. Our daily routines of life provide comforting structures that shore us up during the worst of seasons. Work and children may be the best therapies of all.

Adult responsibilities provide an anchor as we go through turbulent times. Adolescents, on the other hand, have no such anchor, no such life experience. When they sink into depression, they don't know that these feelings may be a temporary phase of life, or that they'll feel better after the hormone storm has subsided, or when they wake up in the morning.

When their diets have deprived their brains of the molecules needed to make calming, soothing neurotransmitters and they feel overwhelmed with negative feelings, they don't hide in bed. They lash out in anger. They drink more soft drinks and eat more junk food that temporarily makes them feel better but escalate the bad mood. Negative emotions cloud im-mature thinking. Pepsi and Twinkies and McDonald's hamburgers may be a form of self-medication against a pain they can't manage.

While depressed adults may withdraw from the world, teenagers fling their moods at the world. Research shows that adolescent depression spawns a whirlwind of destructive behaviors, including alcohol and drug use, sexual promiscuity, self-mutilation, and violence. Coping skills are limited. Doing "something bad" temporarily relieves the psychic pressure that has built up, and for a little while, they feel better.

The speed at which this descent takes place can be frightening to a parent who is watching from the outskirts of his child's life. Just a few short weeks or days ago, everything seemed to be going well.

Violent, self-destructive behaviors in adolescents are often the result of depression for which they have no resources to resolve.[35] Researchers have been working to make stronger links between nutrition and behavior, no easy task. There is a growing mound of research showing that nutrition does indeed influence brain chemistry, and thus influences cognition and behavior. Proving it with the type of scientific certainty that scientists like to see, however, is not easy. Our very personal biochemistry is altered day in and day out by our environment and our food. Nutritional require-ments shift from day to day, based on the changing needs of the body.

When researchers find that, out of one hundred or so children, fifteen make significant intellectual and emotional gains when supplementing the diet or changing eating habits, twenty-five make modest improvements, and the rest remain unchanged, they may have discovered that the first group was incredibly malnourished and responded positively to good nutrition. The first group responded to the supplemental nutrition in a statistically significant way. The second group also showed some improve-ment, and the third group didn't alter the statistical record.

A report in *The Lancet* may have hit upon this very thing. When Cal-ifornia schoolchildren were given either a placebo or a multivitamin and mineral supplement, there was no difference in test scores in the placebo group. In the supplemented group, there was a 3.7 point increase in non-verbal intelligence, but even more interesting, forty-five percent of the subjects gained an astonishing fifteen or more points in nonverbal intelligence. Forty-five percent of those students really needed the extra nutrition.[36]

That seems to be how the numbers work out across the board. In the kids who eat better, just adding a multivitamin or mineral doesn't make a statistical difference. But in the kids who eat poorly, that little bit of added nutrition makes an astonishing difference.

According to Dr. William Walsh, Ph.D., of the Pfeiffer Treatment Center and Health Research Institute in Illinois, the critical issues in behavioral and mental disorders lie in the biochemistry of the brain, and violent behaviors can be triggered by bad nutrition. He relates that when he began to study prisoners incarcerated for violent offenses over twenty years ago, he believed their problems were caused by social events, primarily in the family. But as he met the parents of his patients and found them to be sensitive, intelligent, caring people whose hearts were broken by the misbehavior of their children, he wondered if other factors were at work in these individuals, especially when he met the siblings of these violent people and found them to be hardworking, stable, well-adjusted people.

Dr. Walsh believes that poor nutritional habits don't start the underlying biochemical mischief but trigger it in susceptible people who, for genetic reasons, start out at a biochemical or nutritional deficit. If some children are born with a genetic tendency toward mental or behavioral illness, those illnesses might never be expressed or expressed only mildly if the nutrition is optimum.[37]

When teenagers indulge their junk food tastes, the problem is not confined to the damage caused by what they are eating. It is compounded by the good foods they don't eat when they're eating the bad food—the bad supplants the good. Researcher and naturopathic physician Dr. Ian Bier, who has worked on numerous projects studying the association between nutrition and brain chemistry, believes that this two-pronged approach is what causes so much damage.[38]

When teenagers aren't eating fresh, organic vegetables, their mineral intake is inadequate. The body's ability to digest protein is reduced because minerals fuel the enzymes that digest protein. Undigested protein ferments in the intestinal tract and inhibits the absorption of other nutrients and sends toxic materials into the system. The liver has to deal with those toxic materials. If mineral levels are inadequate to supply the brain enzymes, brain activity is reduced.

If fresh, organic fruits and vegetables are not eaten, vitamin intake is low, which reduces the enzyme activity in the brain. Neurotransmitters are synthesized from and fueled by vitamins. Deficiency in vitamin B_3 (niacin) causes serotonin to be undersupplied. And on and on. It's a domino effect that continues to tumble wildly when children choose junk food instead of nutritious food.

It is difficult, however, to point to a specific cause and say "this food" causes "that mental problem." Statisticians can often find correlations but not causes. They can't positively say that Pepsi causes hyperactivity or that high-sodium potato chips and french fries cause angry, hostile behavior. Unfortunately, researchers don't study potato chips and anger, because food-processing companies don't fund that type of research.

Until that is done, we have to rely on our knowledge of the body and our knowledge of food trends and try to fit those pieces together. We have to use existing studies and ask ourselves some hard and obvious questions. If hostile, antisocial behaviors can be reduced by forty-five percent in a prison or school population just by changing the diet, is it possible that dietary changes could reduce some of the hostile, antisocial behaviors of your child?

Remember the results on mood disorders that were achieved in our high school breakfast drink study? If just drinking a nutrient-dense breakfast drink can improve overall mood in schoolchildren, what would happen if you took away your kid's high-sugar, low-nutrient breakfast cereal and gave his brain something good to feed on before he trudged off to school? While we can't say with the preciseness that statisticians like to achieve that your kid's diet is to blame when he acts out in school or the home, we have what is considered fairly good evidence that nutrient-deficient diets are strongly correlated to antisocial behavior and decreased intelligence.

SOLUTIONS: THE ADOLESCENT NUTRITION PRIMER

Once your son or daughter enters the world of junior high or high school, he or she encounters new forms of peer pressure. Your daughter's hormones are fluctuating wildly from one day, one week to the next, and with it, uncontrollable cravings for sugars and chocolate. Your daughter wants to be fashionable, beautiful, popular, athletic, smart, funny, and social. She also has to be thick-skinned to avoid the barbs of the hundreds of PMS-ing girls around her.

Your son's hormones are racing out of control, too, and he has no idea how to deal with the new pressures he is feeling. In grade school, he only had to deal with getting reasonably good grades and playing low-key sports with his friends. Now he has to get good grades to get into a good college or to stay on the varsity team. If he plays sports, he has to be good or be cut.

Trying to talk to teenagers about nutrition is nearly a wasted effort. With all the other noises clamoring for attention, they can't hear another voice, asking them to avoid the vending machines, asking them to eat salad instead of a McDonald's hamburger, asking them to drink water instead of Pepsi. Since their eating habits are often driven by the culture, it will take time to introduce new foods into their routine and to remove offending foods.

Go at it slowly and discuss your plan with your teenager to enlist as much cooperation as possible. Use the following step-by-step guide to establishing good eating habits in your teenager. Each step in the sequence should be done for about two weeks before going to the next step:

STEP ONE: As a clinical nutritionist, I have found that making changes to the eating habits can be accomplished more easily if the body's nutritional needs are first met with supplements. We have to make up for past deficiencies. Minerals reduce the craving for sugars, for example. Good-quality oils reduce the cravings for fatty foods. I usually start my clients on supplements before asking them to change the diet. Philosophically, it probably isn't the best thing, but it simply works better!

Start your child on a good supplement program, using vitamin and mineral supplements that provide a "healthy" amount of all the B complex, the rest of the vitamins, and high doses of minerals. Make sure they supply at least 250 milligrams of magnesium, 250 milligrams of calcium, 25–35 milligrams of zinc, 5–8 milligrams of iron (especially if your child is a girl), and 200 micrograms of chromium. A good supplement will reduce many of the cravings for inappropriate foods and help balance blood sugar.

Purchase a separate essential fatty acid supplement (fish oil or flaxseed oil), and include one to two grams of the oil per day with his other supplements. It is unlikely that you will find this combination in a single bottle of the typical daily supplement.

He will be taking several capsules per day. Give them to him with breakfast and dinner.

STEP TWO: Ask your teenager to drink a protein breakfast drink each morning before going to school. Make sure the protein drink you choose does not contain aspartame (which we discuss in the next chapter), sucrose, or other poor sources of sugar. It should contain between fifteen and twenty grams of protein per serving. Add one to two tablespoons of flaxseed oil or olive oil before whizzing it up in the blender.

If your child enjoys physical activities, you can gain compliance more easily by purchasing a "sports drink" from your local health food store or sports store. Many of these are quite good. Check with your local nutritionist or a nutritionally trained physician for their recommendations on the type of drink to use.

STEP THREE: Purchase an athletic water bottle for your teenager and ask her to drink at least two of those containers of water each day, throughout the day. If she prefers more flavoring in the beverage, squeeze a fresh lemon or lime into the water.

STEP FOUR: Prepare a salad for your child for at least one meal each day. If she prefers to eat her salad at school for lunch, terrific! Add some tuna fish, sliced chicken or turkey breast, or some other form of protein to complete the meal. Ask her to use an olive oil–based dressing on the salad for added beneficial oils. The salad should contain several types of raw vegetables, preferably brightly colored vegetables.

If your child will not take the salad to school, make sure she gets the salad for dinner or as an after-school snack.

STEP FIVE: Ask your child to reduce the amount of soft drinks she is drinking each day by one-half. If she is drinking two cans of Pepsi each day, ask her to reduce it to one can per day, for example. She may substitute sparkling mineral water if she chooses. After the soft drinks have been reduced, ask her to eliminate them completely, or drink one soft drink per week.

STEP SIX: Stop buying all junk snacks. No more store-purchased cookies, ice cream, candy, soft drinks, or packaged foods. Purchase fresh fruit and carrot sticks for snacks, or purchase snack items from the health food section of your local grocery store or natural food store. Ask your son or daughter to make homemade treats each week, and reduce the amount of sugar in the recipe by one-half (they usually can't taste the difference). You may also wish to use sugar substitutes like date sugar or fruit-only jam as a sweetener.

Eliminate all products containing aspartame, MSG, or other artificial ingredients. If you feel this is too harsh, designate one day of the week as "treat day" and allow a little junk food on just that one day.

You can assume that your son or daughter will still find sources of junk food, but at least you'll be comforted that the amount of junk they are eating will be substantially reduced. Just make sure you provide plenty of fun, delicious alternatives and make them easily accessible.

STEP SEVEN: Plan your family meals carefully to include as many Mom-, Dad-, or kid-prepared meals as possible. Do some cooking on the weekend for the following week. Restructure as much of your life as possible to enjoy time in the kitchen with your child.

Following these steps, you'll slowly introduce new foods into your child's diet. One mom recently shared how choices are presented to girls in different age brackets by Girl Scout leaders. When a leader offers a snack to a young child (ages six to eight), they are given two choices: "Would you like popcorn or would you like a cookie?" When it comes time to offer a snack to an older child (ages nine to twelve), their range of options may be expanded: "What would you like for a snack today?"

When offering a snack to a teenager, it once again becomes "Would you like popcorn or a cookie?" Teen counselors say this is the best way to discuss options with a teenager. Their minds are so full of their changing world that they simply cannot focus on another thing. They cannot handle wide-open choices. Life needs to be made simpler for them until they have passed through much of the turbulence they are experiencing and can focus on expanded goals.

Their brains must be provided with the same balance of nutrients as their younger siblings get, but in greater amounts. It is important that you provide them with both healthy meals and healthy snacks, since many of their calories will come from snacks. Most teenagers have a considerable amount of money to spend, and they will spend it on junk food wherever it is available. They do not need to have you buy it. We make it a policy to never keep soft drinks, cookies, candy, cakes, or convenience snacks around the house.

The healthy snacks that are kept around our house include baby carrots, nut mixes from the health food section of the grocery store, dried fruits, fresh fruit, and occasionally, tortilla chips. We purchase baked potato chips. We also enjoy bean dips or vegetable dips with the chips. Once each week we allow the children to indulge in homemade pie or cookies, or pie and ice cream at Grandpa's house. Sometimes we split dessert at a restaurant, as long as good nutritional habits are being developed consistently, at home, in school, and hopefully, with friends.

When taken with a good-quality vitamin and mineral supplement, (see Appendix I), your child's brain will be well nourished, even in minerals that activate the enzymes and vitamins that function as cofactors with the enzymes.

Choose the drink based on both taste and quality, making sure that the drink provides at least fifteen grams of protein and a fairly low amount

I strongly recommend that your teenager drink a high-quality protein drink each morning for breakfast or after school as a snack. (Check with your nutritionist for recommendations.) Using the protein drink provides several benefits:

1. It is quick and simple to prepare.
2. It provides a balance of protein, carbohydrates, and fats. His blood sugar will remain stable so he will be better able to concentrate on his work through the morning.
3. The balance of nutrients also reduces the need to snack on sugary foods to keep blood sugar up.
4. The balance of nutrition will make it easier for your son or daughter to control his or her weight, making it less likely he or she will slip into anorexia, bulimia, repetitive dieting, or other eating disorders.

of refined carbohydrates like sugar, and does not contain aspartame. It should also contain at least one-third the daily requirements of vitamins and minerals. Another bonus to the drink would be other nutritional foods that have been added, such as spirulina, green foods, and fiber.

Because oil is a fragile food and cannot be added when the drink is manufactured, it must be added just before you blend it. I use flaxseed oil to provide both Omega-3 and Omega-6 fatty acids, adding about one to two tablespoons per serving. When the drink is mixed in a blender, the oil emulsifies and is not detected by taste or mouth feel.

If your child prefers to eat "real food" for breakfast, choose foods that provide a blend of protein, carbohydrates, and fats, not just simple sugars as in most breakfast cereals. Chapter 8 has several kid-tested recipes that can be enjoyed for breakfast.

The question is often asked: If we eat a good diet, do we need to take supplements? The truth is that very few of us eat a "good" diet, even if we agreed what that means. We are all exposed to levels of stress and pollution for which we are ill-prepared. When we are faced with greater-than-usual stressors, our bodies require greater-than-usual nutrition. Stress takes a nutritional toll on teenagers, as it does on adults.

It is an unusual teenager who will eat a consistently excellent diet or who will take nutritional supplements without being reminded daily. My children are no exception. I've given them nutritional supplements from the day they could swallow them. I've tried relinquishing to them the responsibility for taking them, but so far I still have to lay them out each morning. My younger children usually take them if they are simply laid out in a conspicuous place. My older children often have to be "hand-fed," i.e., I have to place the vitamins in one hand, and a glass of water in the other hand, and watch until they take them. Whatever works, do it. Your child's mental health will flourish when his brain is fed.

Expect to see changes in your child's demeanor or ability to focus and concentrate in school. Don't be discouraged if your plan doesn't go smoothly. Keep working at it, and within a few months you will have taught your child a great deal about how to care for himself for the rest of his life.

Conclusion

After we have passed through our teenage years, life settles down a little. Will our brains recover from the previous two decades of bad nutrition? If we have escaped the clutches of the Gerber baby, Tony the Tiger, and Ronald McDonald, maybe we can breathe a little easier. We're adults now. What are the mental challenges of adulthood? Perhaps the first challenge is that we need to save our brains from approaching senility.

6

Feeding the Adult Brain

*Why do you spend money for what is not bread,
and your wages for what does not satisfy? Listen
carefully to me and eat what is good, and delight
yourself in abundance.*

—ISAIAH 55:2

After we pass through the turbulent teenage years and enter our twenties, life takes on a new dimension. Adolescence is the period of time when we establish independence. Then, suddenly, we're on our own, off to college or to business. We find our way in the world. We study a profession or learn a trade. We establish a family and settle into it. We come "into our own," as the saying goes.

With adulthood come responsibilities, duties, and possibilities that must be successfully completed if we want to lead a successful life. Among that list is giving birth to the next generation. Reproduction is a significant part of a woman's life and energy. If a mother chooses to breast-feed for a year or more, childbirth is a two-year stint. During those two years, she has to meet high demands for calories and nutrients to maintain her own health, and at the same time, provide for a child who is growing at an exponential rate.

Childbirth isn't the only task of adulthood. The next fifty years will be spent in industry and hard work. Strength and vitality have to be maintained through periods of enormous stress and frustration. Parents juggle the pressures of making a living for a growing family, taking care of responsibilities around the house, and being a good father and mother. Many parents work a second job just to keep food on the table. Trying to keep up with these expectations is exhausting.

Although physical growth is complete, the body does not lie dormant. The body is a dynamic organism, constantly changing, constantly repairing. Everything looks the same, with gradual signs of aging appearing as decade after decade passes. But every second in life, cells are being born, are dying, and are being reborn. New tissue is being laid, old tissue is carried out.

Billions of new red blood cells are manufactured in the core of bone tissue every day. Every two to three days, each cell lining the digestive tract dies and is reborn with new materials brought in from the outside. Minerals are carried out of the bone matrix and deposited into the bloodstream, then drawn from the bloodstream and laid down into the bone matrix again. It is, in the words of Deepak Chopra, as though you were living in a house in which bricks were constantly being removed and replaced. In time, a new house will have been constructed, a house that looks and "feels" the same but is completely different.

In his book *Quantum Healing,* Chopra wrote:

> The Greek philosopher Heraclitus made the famous remark, "You cannot step into the same river twice, because the river is constantly being changed by new water rushing in." The same holds true for the body. All of us are much more like a river than anything frozen in time and space.
>
> If you could see your body as it really is, you would never see it the same way twice. Ninety-eight percent of the atoms in your body were not there a year ago. The skeleton that seems so solid was not there three months ago. The configuration of the bone cells remains somewhat constant, but atoms of all kinds pass freely back and forth through the cell walls, and by that means you acquire a new skeleton every three months.
>
> The skin is new every month. You have a new stomach lining every four days, with the actual surface cells that contact food being renewed every five minutes. The cells in the liver turn over very slowly, but new atoms still flow through them, like water in a river course, making a new liver every six weeks. Even within the brain, whose cells are not replaced once they die, the content of carbon, nitrogen, oxygen and so on is totally different today from a year ago.[1]

Scientists believe that nerve cells don't undergo the type of renewal experienced by other cells, that once the neuronal tissue is laid into place, it is there for life. The brain's capacity for regeneration is limited.[2] Once neuronal damage has taken place, little recovery should be expected, even if that damage is brought on by the simple pressures (and pleasures) of life. Because we cannot expect active regeneration to take place, it becomes even more important, therefore, to minimize the damage.

Are we doing all we can to slide into our senior years with as many brain cells intact as possible?

Not even close. We engage in "antinutrition." Instead of minimizing the damage to our nervous system, we are accelerating the damage by the very foods (or nonfoods) that we are stuffing into our mouths. We are, in the words of an unknown sage, digging our graves with our forks. The lifestyles that we have chosen have made good nutrition even more difficult. At a time of life when good nutrition is imperative, we're so busy shifting our focus elsewhere that we don't have time to eat properly.

THE STARBUCKS GENERATION

Millions of American men and women live exhausting, stress-filled lives. The toll that stress exacts on the physical body is extreme; the toll it exacts on the mind is just as extreme. The adrenal gland is our "stress" gland, responding to stressors in our environment and body by flooding the bloodstream with supraphysiological doses of adrenal hormones like cortisol that affect virtually every part of the body, including the brain. When we are confronted with acute, severe stressors, cortisol secretion is an appropriate response and could save our lives by increasing blood pressure, increasing blood flow to the extremities, hyperactivating our brains, and so on. Cortisol is an important hormone to our survival under these conditions and is secreted and withdrawn within short periods of time.

After the stress condition has been resolved, cortisol drops, blood pressure drops, blood flow normalizes, and the body returns to normal. But one author wrote: "It is an ideal system for allowing an organism to deal with short-term physical stress, and that is exactly the sort of stressors that organisms face most of the time. Stress-related disease appears most likely to emerge when the stress-response is activated for too long . . . and when it is activated for no physiological reason in the first place (i.e., psychological/social stressors)."[3]

The types of stress with which we are confronted are not short-term. They are not typically physical. They are psychological and social. They go on, day after day, year after year. The body responds to these inappropriate stressors with lower levels of cortisol that have similar effects, i.e., higher blood pressure, increased blood flow, etc., but more important to this discussion, chronically elevated cortisol has marked effects on the brain. Cortisol influences learning and memory, makes us more vulnerable to depression, causes us to eat inappropriately, and increases our aggression. Current stress levels wear down cognition and mood.

Extended doses of cortisol destroy the brain by damaging the hippocampus, the area that lays down both short- and long-term memory. Under the influence of high levels of cortisol, neurons in the hippocampus die rapidly. Ironically, part of the function of the hippocampus is to shut off adrenal hormone production, but when stress is increased, this braking mechanism often fails, flooding the body with more and more adrenal hormones, and producing more and more damage to the hippocampus.[4]

When stress continues day after day, the body responds to the ongoing stress deep within the body, compromising such brain functions as memory. But the adrenal gland cannot keep up the pace forever. Eventually, it simply wears out. Where the adrenal gland has been hyperactive, now it becomes hypoactive. When the adrenal gland loses its capacity to respond to stress, we spiral downward, sucked into a whirlpool of exhaustion. We feel chronically exhausted. We gain weight. We feel like our lives are falling apart, that we can't cope.

What do we do? Do we cut back on our stress? Do we take care of our adrenal glands by eating better food? No. We drown our anxieties in more work, eating, buying more toys, drinking alcohol, taking drugs—anything other than slowing the pace. The cost would not be nearly as severe if our diets were designed to compensate for the added stress, but our diets are themselves victims of the high-paced society that we live in.

Meal planning and preparation becomes just another stressor. Instead of planning our foods carefully and enjoying the process of meal preparation, instead of savoring a meal with people we love as we would a glass of wine, we see good nutrition as yet another impossible task to squeeze into an overcrowded schedule. Talk about good nutrition to a busy mom and you see another wave of guilt sweep over her face. "Please, don't I have enough to do?"

How do we respond to the stress? We drink coffee.

Think of the mule master who is confronted with a heavy workload and a stubborn mule. The master must get his work done, but his mule lies on the ground, looking up with peaceful but determined eyes. He won't budge. The master speaks kindly and nudges him with his foot. The mule sinks farther into the grass and stretches his legs. The master gets a little impatient, speaks sharply now, and the nudge becomes a gentle kick. The mule grunts and lays his chin on the ground.

In desperation, the master gets a whip and flogs the mule. Not brutally, but it stings the mule's backside. He slowly rises to his feet, gives a relenting sigh, and shuffles off to do his master's bidding. He isn't happy. But he's moving.

The master is your body. The mule is your adrenal gland. You overworked your "mule" for the past twenty years and it can't move. Your coffee cup is the whip. Can't get up in the morning? Whip your body into action with a cup of coffee. Never mind that the stress is gnawing away at your brain, that cortisol continues to pump through your veins, destroying your hippocampus, and ignore the fact that if you don't take care of it, you'll have no memory left when you reach your "golden years."

The Starbucks Revolution

The original Starbucks store was a tiny little coffee shop located in a trendy area of downtown Seattle, called Pike Place Market. The company putzed along for over ten years in one tiny location that offered a fresh cup of coffee to tourists and Seattle-ites enjoying the open-air atmosphere in the market, along with fish shops, gift shops, restaurants, and bake shops. In 1982, Howard Shultz joined the company as director of retail sales and marketing, and started providing Starbucks beans to local restaurants and hotels.

In 1983, Shultz took a trip to Milan, Italy, where his entrepreneurial eyes saw fifteen hundred espresso bars flourishing and he decided his Seattle customers would enjoy this part of Italian culture. When he returned to the States, he presented a business plan to the partners at Starbucks. They formed a new corporation, and the rest is history. From one location in 1983, Starbucks grew rapidly, first in Seattle; Chicago; Vancouver, B.C.; then Portland, Oregon; Los Angeles; and across the United States like a firestorm. Currently, there are over two thousand locations and more are springing up, but in the meantime, other companies have seen the Starbucks success and have opened similar operations.

Just how widespread is coffee drinking? The average American drinks over twenty-six gallons of coffee per year, but perhaps more germane to the discussion is caffeine itself. Coffee has over three hundred chemicals; caffeine is only one of them. There are about seventy-five milligrams of caffeine in the average cup of coffee, but in espresso, the caffeine content jumps upward to over one hundred milligrams.

On any typical day, nearly fifty percent of the American population drinks coffee, averaging over three cups of the black stuff per day. Tea also contains caffeine. Although tea leaves actually contain more caffeine than coffee beans, a cup of tea usually contains less caffeine because it is not prepared as strongly. Cola drinks also contain caffeine. There are about thirty-five milligrams of caffeine in the standard 280-milliliter serving. About sixty-five percent of all soft drinks sold contain caffeine, and the average American drinks over 576 twelve-ounce cans of soft drinks per year.[5]

Apart from the fact that coffee pulls minerals out of storage in bone tissue and hastens its excretion from the body (increasing the potential for osteoporosis, PMS, menopause symptoms, gastrointestinal disturbances, and increased blood pressure), coffee is not kind to the brain, either. Coffee is an addictive drug, in the same category as cocaine and amphetamines, affecting the same parts of the brain as cocaine, although different and weaker.[6]

Consider these caffeine facts:

- Caffeine is the most widely used psychoactive drug in the world today.

- At least eighty percent of the world's adult population uses enough caffeine-laced beverages and foods to affect the brain.[7]

- Caffeine enhances the effects of dopamine (i.e., enhances sexual arousal and performance,[8] increases hypersensitivity, hyper-responsivity,[9] large-muscle activity, and so on).

- Caffeine increases the energy metabolism throughout the brain but simultaneously reduces the amount of blood flowing to the brain, so while the brain's energy requirements are higher, there is less energy pumped in to meet the demand.

- Caffeine increases the stimulating neurohormone, noradrenaline, and reduces the calming neurotransmitter, serotonin.[10]

- Coffee increases the excretion of calcium from our bones, hastening the onset of osteoporosis.

- Coffee increases the risk of birth defects.[11]

- Coffee increases blood pressure, increasing the risk of heart disease.[12]

Several years ago I interviewed a naturopathic doctor about fatigue. I asked for his recommendations, expecting him to discuss such issues as eating better-quality food, drinking more water, taking dietary supplements, and possibly using herbs. Instead he said very quietly, "We are tired because we demand too much of our bodies. Fatigue is a sign that we need to slow down. Our lifestyles are far in excess of our body's ability to handle. If we are tired, we need to rest, not take something to mask the fatigue."

At the time, I was working ten to twelve hours per day, then going home to my husband and four children. I tried to meet their needs, but my needs were overwhelming. I was exhausted. Instead of using stimulants, I needed to rest.

- Coffee is implicated in seizure disorders.[13]

- Coffee contributes to insomnia, depression, and anxiety disorders.[14]

- Caffeine is addictive.

Just how addictive is caffeine? In a study published in *JAMA*, researchers evaluated ninety-nine subjects; sixteen had been diagnosed as "caffeine dependent." The daily average caffeine intake was three hundred fifty-seven milligrams, but nearly twenty percent consumed less than the national average (two hundred ten milligrams). Ninety-four percent had withdrawal symptoms and ninety-four percent continued to use caffeine, despite knowing that physical or psychological problems were related to caffeine.

Over eighty percent had been unsuccessful in controlling or cutting back on coffee consumption, or had a persistent desire to reduce their intake. Seventy-five percent had developed a tolerance for caffeine. A significant number in the study suffered "functional impairment" when reducing their intake.[15]

Drinking coffee and tea and soft drinks laced with caffeine, indulging in large amounts of chocolate, taking prescription medications that contain caffeine—it all adds up. Most of us are consuming well over two hundred milligrams of caffeine per day. In fact, the daily per capita con-

The following items are the top products sold in the supermarket, by dollar value in billions. Figures are 1996 figures:	Frozen dinners/entrées 4.4
	Ice cream 3.7
	Cookies 3.4
	Soup 3.3
Carbonated beverages $11.1	Candy/mints 3.0
Milk 9.2	
Cold cereal 7.4	Vegetables are twenty-third in the list,
Bread 6.6	after luncheon meats, dog food, and toi-
Cheese 6.2	let tissue. Fresh fruit and seafoods don't
Chips and snacks 5.7	even make the list in the top fifty sellers
Cigarettes 5.4	in this country.[16]
Beer and ale 5.2	

sumption of caffeine is about two hundred ten milligrams, with about sixty percent from coffee; tea and soft drinks each account for about sixteen percent. The world's annual consumption of caffeine is about 120,000 tons. About twenty percent of adults in the United States and Canada consume more than three hundred fifty milligrams per day and are considered "addicted."[17]

But this may be one case in which we are being helped in our addiction by a powerful industry: the coffee industry. Coffee is one of the top monied industries in the world. Retail sales for the specialty coffee industry have grown from just $44 million in 1969 to over $3 billion in 1999. Total coffee sales are expected to reach over $5 billion by the turn of the century.

In 1969 there were just fifty specialty coffee stores in the United States; in 1999, there were over twenty-five hundred stores, along with over five thousand specialty food stores, over five thousand gift shops, over nine thousand other stores that sell coffee, and over ten thousand coffee cafes. These numbers do not include espresso carts, food service locations in hospitals, businesses, schools, and mail-order facilities.[18] And it doesn't include the pots of coffee we brew in our own machines.

What fuels this explosive growth? Our own diminishing energy levels and the marketing hype of sophisticated companies that convinces us that self-medicating with an addictive substance is the answer to our energy crisis.

THE SWEET BRAIN POISON: ASPARTAME

Possibly nothing of a nutritional nature is quite as controversial or confusing as the question of aspartame, sold under the brand name of NutraSweet and Equal as a noncaloric sweetener. Where is aspartame found? In instant breakfasts, breath mints, cereals, sugar-free chewing gum, cocoa mixes, coffee beverages, frozen desserts, gelatin desserts, juice beverages, laxatives, multivitamins, milk drinks, pharmaceuticals and supplements, shake mixes, soft drinks, tabletop sweeteners, tea beverages, instant teas and coffees, topping mixes, wine coolers, and yogurt.

- Is aspartame safe?
- Does aspartame assist in weight loss?
- Does aspartame cause cancer?
- Does aspartame impair brain function?

These questions have been bandied back and forth for decades, and meanwhile, this billion-dollar product remains on the market as one of our most popular food additives.

Aspartame was discovered in 1965 by a chemist from the G. D. Searle company, which is now a subsidiary of Monsanto, the largest biotechnology company in the world. It was thought that the perfect sweetener had been found. Although two hundred times sweeter than sugar, it nonetheless had no calories, and because it was composed of two amino acids, it was thought to be perfectly harmless. Searle immediately submitted aspartame to the FDA for approval, and in 1974, was granted approval for limited use based on initial tests.

Monsanto paints aspartame in glowing terms, stating that "NutraSweet has become one of the most highly valued and widely used sweeteners in the world, known for it's [sic] clean taste and amazing sweetness (180–200 times sweeter than sucrose). NutraSweet also quickly became a highly valued ingredient among people with diabetes because it literally changed their lives, allowing them to enjoy foods that are sweet and tasteful without ingesting sugar. Now that time has proved the value of this product, we are happy to continue to present the sweetener of the millennium from the company who [sic] invented it."[19]

The FDA declares that aspartame is safe for use in foods. It has not found any consistent pattern of symptoms that can attributed to the use of aspartame. The FDA acknowledges that aspartame can be problematic for people who are allergic to the substance or who were born with the genetic disease phenylketonuria (PKU), for those with advanced liver disease, and for pregnant women with high levels of phenylalanine in the blood. Other than those conditions, FDA has given aspartame its blessings.

But if you carefully read the FDA's disclaimer, the term "consistent pattern" means that symptoms are so diverse that a pattern cannot be established, not that there is no basis for the complaints. Note the words, "clearly show safety problems." Legal nuances are used to confuse the reader, not to clarify the issues. The FDA's definition of "clearly" may differ remarkably from yours. What is aspartame? Aspartame is a combination of two amino acids: aspartic acid and phenylalanine. If these amino acids are essential for human health, aspartame should be as natural as an ear of corn or a salmon fillet, shouldn't it? That is what marketers want you to believe.

As we read in the chapter on infant formulas, unbalancing the body's delicate balance of amino acids can impose serious consequences on the brain, even in adults. Both deficiencies and excesses have negative influences on brain chemistry. Phenylalanine (PHE), a powerful amino acid with extensive usage in the brain, produces a number of neurotransmitters and is, of course, present in food. For example, cheese, tuna fish, soybeans, red meat, dairy products, and poultry supply hundreds of milligrams of PHE per serving.

Defenders of aspartame claim that the amount of the amino acid in it is so small that one would have to drink enormous amounts of aspartame-containing beverages or devour wagonloads of other products to produce any type of negative brain experience. To produce the mental retardation of the genetic metabolic disorder called phenylketonuria (PKU), for example, blood levels of phenylalanine have to reach levels substantially above what one could possibly achieve even by drinking large amounts of soft drinks.

High levels of phenylalanine may not be necessary to produce brain dysfunction, however. According to some researchers, "Phenylalanine may have neurologic effects at a blood and brain concentration well below the neurotoxic levels associated with PKU. The basis for this premise is that elevated phenylalanine concentrations may reduce normal neurotransmitter (serotonin) levels and consequently affect behavior and mood and even induce seizures."[20]

The seizures and other mental symptoms commonly associated with aspartame consumption may be related not to high phenylalanine levels but to low serotonin levels resulting from high PHE consumption, and certain individuals may be more susceptible to these subtle changes in brain nutrition than others.

In fact, of the thousands of adverse reactions reported to the FDA, most concerned abnormal brain function, i.e., depression, fatigue, irritability, insomnia, vision problems, hearing loss, anxiety attacks, slurred speech, loss of the sense of taste, tinnitus, vertigo, and memory loss. Also included were a number of chronic illnesses, including brain tumors, multiple sclerosis, epilepsy, chronic fatigue syndrome, Parkinson's disease, Alzheimer's, mental retardation, lymphoma, birth defects, fibromyalgia, and diabetes.[21]

Phenylalanine is not the only problem with aspartame. The other amino acid in aspartame is aspartic acid, a nonessential amino acid synthesized from glutamate that acts as a major excitatory transmitter in the human brain.[22] Note that PHE reduces serotonin levels in the brain (serotonin is a calming neurotransmitter); aspartic acid further stimulates the brain. It is likely the combination of the two amino acids causes seizures and other "excitatory reactions" in the brain, not one or the other.

Large quantities of aspartic acid in the brain produce brain lesions in experimental animals,[23] and while it is rapidly washed out of the plasma, continual doses (drinking aspartame every day, for example) may produce cellular damage. Studies attempting to assess the safety of aspartame have not been done on the long-term, high-dosage intake of artificially sweetened foods, and no studies could be found to determine which individuals may be more susceptible to aspartame-induced brain damage.

The story continues to unfold as aspartame passes through the digestive tract and is digested into methanol or wood alcohol, which happens most readily when aspartame is heated (as when it is part of a "food product" like Jell-O, for example, or is improperly stored at high temperatures, as often happens in warehouses in hot climates). When heated above eighty-six degrees, free methanol is produced and is rapidly absorbed into the bloodstream. One liter of an aspartame-sweetened beverage can produce about fifty-six milligrams of methanol. When several of these beverages are consumed in a short period of time (one day, perhaps), as much as two hundred fifty milligrams of methanol are dumped into the bloodstream, or thirty-two times the EPA limit.[24]

Symptoms of methanol poisoning include headaches, ear buzzing, dizziness, nausea, gastrointestinal disturbances, weakness, vertigo, chills, memory lapses, numbness and shooting pains in the extremities, behavioral disturbances, and neuritis (inflammation of the nerves). According to the Aspartame Consumer Safety Network information, "The most well known problems from methanol poisoning are vision problems including misty vision, progressive contraction of visual fields, blurring of vision, obscuration of vision, retinal damage, and blindness."

During the 1991 Gulf War, in a marketing campaign disguised as a spirit of patriotism, all military personnel were provided free supplies of aspartame-laced soft drinks (along with experimental vaccines, nerve gas antidotes, and personal insecticides). Keeping in mind that aspartame degrades into methanol in temperatures exceeding eighty-six degrees and temperatures in the Gulf region were far higher, soldiers were potentially exposed to criminally high levels of methanol. Is methanol poisoning from aspartame the possible cause of the "Gulf War Syndrome," which has affected more than 50,000 military personnel? This is a question that needs to be answered, not only for the unfortunate victims of this syndrome but also for those of us who have struggled with symptoms for which we find no causes, related possibly to the artificial sweeteners in our favorite foods.

One group of professionals most concerned about aspartame usage is airline pilots. In 1988, the Aspartame Consumer Safety Network installed a private hot line to receive inquiries from pilots who are in jeopardy of losing their flying licenses because of seizure episodes from the use of aspartame. Since 1988, more than six hundred calls have been made to the confidential hot line. One caller noted that "after just two cups of NutraSweetened hot chocolate, a pilot experienced blurred vision so severe he was unable to read instruments on his panel and very narrowly avoided a tragic landing. Safely on the ground, he related his story to the coworkers in his office. Two of them recounted similar symptoms experienced after brief exposure to aspartame."[25]

Monsanto passed my request for comments on aspartame to their subsidiary, NutraSweet. To date they have not responded to my inquiry.

Monsanto, of course, remains unconcerned about this information. They even recommend that you give NutraSweet to your children. On their Web site, they write, "You can be extremely confident when your child consumes NutraSweet brand sweetener because NutraSweet is made of the same components found in the foods we eat everyday [sic] such as meat, milk, fruits, and vegetables.

"The American Medical Association has agreed with the FDA and many other regulatory agencies around the world that NutraSweet is safe for consumption by people of all ages, including children and pregnant women."

This last statement is interesting, considering that the FDA Web site recommends that pregnant women with high levels of phenylalanine stay away from aspartame. No mention of this possible problem is made.

They say that "it is not possible to consume too much NutraSweet brand sweetener. To your body, what's in NutraSweet is the same as what's in peaches, milk and most other foods you eat everyday [sic]. No limit is needed . . . It is calculated that a 132 lb. adult could consumer [sic] 3,000 mg. of aspartame (i.e., 85 packets of Equal or 18 cans of diet soda) every day of her life and it wouldn't make a bit of difference."[26]

The Center for Science in the Public Interest (CSPI) urges caution when considering using aspartame-laced products, writing "Aspartame (Equal, NutraSweet), made up primarily of two amino acids, was thought to be the perfect artificial sweetener, but questions have arisen about the quality of the cancer tests, which should be repeated. Some persons have reported adverse behavioral effects (dizziness, hallucinations, headache) after drinking diet soda, but such reports have not been confirmed in controlled studies. If you think you've experienced adverse effects due to aspartame, avoid it. Also, people with the rare disease PKU (phenylketonuria) need to avoid it. . . ."

Monsanto elicited the support of the Massachusetts Institute of Technology (MIT) to confirm that "despite the high consumption of aspartame, the forty-eight normal subjects showed no changes in mood, memory, behavior, electroencephalograms (which record the electrical signals of the brain) of physiology that could be tied to aspartame . . . although some subjects reported headaches, fatigue, nausea and acne, the same number of incidences were reported by subjects taking placebo and sugar as those taking aspartame . . . Dr. Spiers noted that these findings corroborate the results of another recent study with preschool and elementary school children that discovered no effect on their moods, activity levels, behavior or thinking after they consumed high doses of aspartame."[27]

The research project was paid for by a grant from the NutraSweet Company, paid to the Center for Brain Sciences and Metabolism Charitable Trust. While research projects sponsored by manufacturers are not inherently unethical and researchers are not necessarily biased in favor of their benefactors, there is a growing mound of evidence showing that, of the hundreds of studies done on aspartame, tampering with the results eliminated the negative data. Tampering with data is not unknown in the scientific community. For example, the Center for Science in the Public Interest charged in 1998 that studies showing the safety of saccharin were untrustworthy because the review committee was dominated by industry employees and consultants.[28]

Many of the studies on aspartame were laden with design flaws.[29]

LOW BLOOD SUGAR AND ASPARTAME/ SUGAR COMBINATION

Aspartame was brought to market to lower America's consumption of sugar and reduce calories, but neither goal has been achieved. Sugar usage skyrockets, with the average American consuming over two hundred pounds of both sugar and artificial sweeteners per year. This hand-in-hand consumption of two sweet substances may pose still another risk to the health of the brain that is not often discussed: low blood sugar.

When large amounts of sugar flood the bloodstream, the body reacts by releasing insulin from the pancreas to keep blood sugar levels within a narrow range. Both excessive and low amounts of blood sugar damage the brain. When huge amounts of sugar are consumed over the course of a lifetime, the pancreas loses its ability to regulate blood sugar levels precisely, often overreacting to the presence of sugar.

Nutritionists call this condition "carbohydrate sensitivity." Growing evidence suggests that carbohydrate sensitivity is a common problem leading to a number of health disorders, including diabetes and heart disease. Because too much insulin is dumped into the bloodstream, blood sugar levels plummet, plunging the individual into hypoglycemia. In an attempt to drive blood sugar levels back up, more sugar is eaten, causing blood sugars to soar, again stimulating the pancreas to send more insulin and remove more sugars. A vicious cycle sets in that leaves the hapless person vacillating wildly between high sugars and low sugars.

When sugars drop too low, the adrenal gland sends cortisol into the bloodstream to signal the liver to pull stored sugars out of the liver and deposit them into the bloodstream. Excess cortisol causes symptoms of headache, panic attacks, irritability, anxiety, depression, poor concentration, and poor memory.[30] Hypoglycemia is a common cause of learning

---

Is It All in Their 7,000 Heads?

Over the past fifteen years, more than seven thousand complaints of adverse reactions to aspartame have been filed with the FDA, including reactions like headaches, dizziness, and mood changes. Aspartame complaints account for about seventy-five percent of all reported adverse reactions to substances in food received by the FDA since 1981.

Americans consumed about 3.5 pounds of aspartame per person in 1983, and in 1991, consumption rose to seventeen pounds per person. According to a study reported in *Nutrition Week*, "Critics state that high concentrations of phenylalanine in the body can cause severe mental retardation in children, and aspartic acid, in high doses, can act as a neurotoxin and promote hormonal disorders."[31]

For a free copy of the FDA report, "Summary of Adverse Reactions Attributed to Aspartame," send a self-addressed, stamped envelope to Center for Nutrition Information, 910 17th St., NW, Suite 413, Washington, D.C. 20006.

disorders and depression.[32] People who tend toward hypoglycemia learn how to avoid the situation by eating more frequent meals and so on.

When aspartame is thrown into the picture, a slightly different permutation of the hypoglycemic reaction is created. Remember that low blood sugar is caused by an insulin response to elevated blood sugars—eating too much sugar. What happens when aspartame-laced soft drinks (nonsugary treats) are consumed in the place of real sugar? Aspartame is two hundred times sweeter than sugar, so tiny amounts produce a similar sweet sensation in the mouth. The body may not know the difference between sugar and aspartame, and respond to the sweet taste with its usual insulin response, pulling already low or normal blood sugar levels down precipitously. The association between aspartame consumption and hypoglycemia in susceptible individuals has not been studied adequately, and more research is needed.

> CRAZY MAKER
> ★
> **AWARD**
>
> ADULT DIVISION/
> THIRD PLACE:
> The Low-Fat/Diet Industry, for promoting the low-fat cooking style, and producing food products that are so deficient in essential fatty acids that the physical structure of the brain is in jeopardy.

THE LOW-FAT-DIET FRAUD

Possibly no one is more complicit in provoking brain damage than the low-fat-diet/health industry. At the turn of the century, heart disease was so rare that many physicians had never treated a heart patient, but with the growth of the sugar and processed-fat industries, heart disease flourished as big medical business, and money poured into research facilities trying to "find a cure." Even with top-dollar attention, heart disease is still one of the top three killers in the Western world.

One of the first symptoms of heart disease can be sudden death, and because drugs and surgery were enjoying little success in pulling down fatality rates, medical professionals started looking at diet for a preventive and a cure. In autopsies, they saw cholesterol caking the inside of the arteries. Doctors who scheduled a blood draw on a patient who had just indulged in a McDonald's hamburger could watch the grease float to the top of the vial. They concluded that if cholesterol were removed from the diet, it would remove itself from the bloodstream. Heart disease is beyond the scope of this book, and we will leave the discussion of the correlation between low-fat diets and heart disease in the hands of others. However, several individuals rose to the challenge of finding ways to bring down the heart disease death rate by manipulating the diet. One of the first and most prominent of these individuals was Nathan Pritikin.

Ann Louise Gittleman, author of a number of books on health and nutrition, worked at the Pritikin Center as a nutritionist for several years and came to respect Pritikin's passion for health. Pritikin himself suffered from heart disease, and when he "cured" his heart problem by using a low-fat diet, he immediately set to work convincing the American public that their love affair with fat was killing them. Pritikin was the first major voice of the low-fat healthy philosophy.

Pritikin's influence spread rapidly throughout the medical community. Soon he was joined by scores of clinics, doctors, books and magazine articles, and, of course, food technologists in promoting this diet paradigm. The low-fat diet became medical dogma and was embraced with religious fervor. Research projects sprouted in universities all over the world. Vegetarianism fell into lockstep with the low-fat gurus, making it nearly a sin to eat steak or roast a salmon fillet on the backyard grill.

Fat became the enemy. "We need fats in only very small amounts," Pritikin stated,[33] and he put his clients on a diet that contained only ten percent calories from fat. Gittleman believes that because Pritikin was an open-minded student of nutrition, he would have learned of the beneficial oils and become more balanced in his fat recommendations had he lived longer. Unfortunately, he died several years before the pendulum swung back toward a more balanced approach to protein/carbohydrate/fat ratios.

Dr. John McDougall, M.D., wrote, "Essential fats are made only by plants . . . as long as the need for an essential fat is met by eating plant foods, the likelihood of having too little fat in the diet is never a problem . . . All fats—saturated and unsaturated—are involved in the growth of certain kinds of cancer cells."[34] In another best-selling book, McDougall wrote, "After we eat a meal high in any type of fat, our blood cells can actually stick together in clumps that plug the blood vessels . . . All fats, including cold-pressed vegetable oils, promote the growth of cancers in animals . . ."[35] McDougall recommends a diet that contains less than five percent of total calories from fat.[36]

Nathan Pritikin had no formal background in nutritional biochemistry; McDougall is a medical doctor, and we can assume he took at least one course in biochemistry in medical school. Were they right? Is the low-fat diet the answer to all our health ills?

The low-fat diet did clean out the arteries, reducing the incidence and severity of heart disease. It did enhance energy, clear the skin, and boost the immune system. In addition to improving the odds of heart disease, it appeared to reduce the risks of certain types of cancer like breast cancer and colon cancer. Researchers found that diabetes could be improved on the low-fat protocol. It was hoped they had found the way to defeat the top three killers in the Western world—heart disease, cancer, and diabetes.

Food processors and marketers saw a huge opportunity. The low-fat industry sprang into action, bringing to market such culinary treats as potato chips, cottage cheese, yogurt, candy, breakfast cereals, pastries, frankfurters, packaged entrées—all newly low fat.

We forgot that fat is an essential part of the diet and that if dietary fats are restricted, other nutrients are poorly absorbed because fat escorts nutrients across the intestinal mucosal border. Dietary fat often accompanies protein, and in the quest to eliminate fat, we restricted protein as well.

It would be one thing if this nutritional revolution took place in the middle of a well-nourished culture. Yet it took place in the center of a culture already obsessed with sugary, refined food stripped naked of its natural, nutritional value. Instead of improving the nutriture of the Western culture, low-fat food faddists removed a pillar of good health.

Pritikin, McDougall, and other low-fat prophets of the low-fat message fail to distinguish between the good and the bad fats. Medical doctor or not, McDougall's information about fat is simply wrong. All fats do not promote cancer, all fats other than plant-based fats are not harmful, and to bring the dietary fat content down to less than five percent is not only virtually impossible, but ludicrous to any serious student of nutrition.

HOW THE LOW-FAT DIET AFFECTS COGNITION

As we read earlier, virtually all of the development of the brain occurs before the age of twenty. All of the neurons have been formed; the axons and dendrites have sprouted in the areas of the brain most stimulated by the environment. The nervous system throughout the body is in place, and thankfully, cells of the nervous system do not die and regenerate like cells in others parts of the body. The brain is protected from toxins that harm the rest of the body by the blood-brain barrier, which blocks most foreign substances from entering this sensitive region. Hopefully, that part of body construction was successfully accomplished, that the brain has been adequately nourished up to this point.

However, just as we know that formation of the brain is essentially complete after the age of eighteen, we also know that the environment of the brain is a dynamic environment. The brain's demands for nutrition are insatiable. The demand will continue, unabated, throughout life.

The brain uses over twenty percent of the total body's oxygen supply, for example. Oxygen is pumped into the brain region in the blood, piggybacked onto iron-bearing molecules. Millions of enzymes are formed and used every day to carry on the work of the brain. Enzymes are protein complexes that are activated by minerals and vitamins that must be in constant supply in the bloodstream. Neurotransmitters and hormones are synthesized from fatty acids, proteins, carbohydrates, vitamins, and minerals. Neurotransmitters transmit information signals across the synaptic gap at speeds that are accelerated by fatty acids. Hormones send chemical messenger signals around the body to individual cells. The hormones are fatty acid–based and lock onto receptor sites that are composed of proteins and fatty acids.

In other words, while the structure of the brain is essentially complete, carbon, oxygen, and hydrogen molecules are being replaced by incoming materials, but even more, its work is ongoing, performed by molecules that are constantly being degraded and resynthesized. Think of your brain as a factory. The brain tissue itself (the nerve tissue) is the building: the walls, the plumbing fixtures, the electrical wiring, the windows, the doors. The work of the factory is done by millions of workers. Workers quit, they are fired, they get sick, they die. Turnover is expected and common. New workers are constantly being hired and trained to replace the workers who left.

The workers use tools to produce materials made from raw materials brought into the factory. In this case, the raw materials are stimuli received by the sensory organs (eyes, ears, taste buds, skin, and nose); the finished products are thoughts and feelings. The tools are scores of nutrients and the workers are enzymes. Even though the factory building will remain for several decades, repairs are often needed. Bricks fall out; insulation wears out, wiring breaks. Repairs are done by the workers. The activity never ceases; the demands never end.

If materials are in short supply, the body must decide how to use its limited resources. If fatty acids are not being supplied, the body must choose between using the available fats for hormones, for neurotransmitters, for repairs, for skin integrity, or hundreds of other uses. If the diet doesn't provide enough magnesium, the body must choose between maintaining heart function, transmission of nerve signals, maintaining bone density, or producing cellular energy. If adequate amounts of protein have not been consumed, hundreds of potential structures or functions may go unbuilt or undone. Fatty acid deficiencies can have serious, long-term effects on the brain, and severe mental disorders can result from consuming a low-fat diet. For example, as Omega-3 fatty acid levels fall, rates of depression increase. In countries where fish is consumed frequently, Omega-3 fatty acid levels are high and rates of depression are low, even in areas of the world that don't get much sunlight. Note these "fat facts" as they relate to the brain:

• Depression has been linked to low levels of a fatty acid called phosphatidylserine.[37]

- A number of studies have made the correlation between depression and low levels of cholesterol. For example, an interesting study published in the British medical journal *The Lancet* reported that more than one thousand males between the ages of fifty and eighty-nine took tests to determine their levels of depression and simultaneously had their cholesterol levels checked. Depression was three times more common in the group with low plasma cholesterol than in those with the higher concentrations.[38]

- The same low-cholesterol effect has been noted in younger women who were otherwise healthy.[39]

- Low cholesterol has also been associated with panic disorders accompanied by depression.[40]

- Deficiencies in other fatty acids have been implicated in depression and other mental defects.[41]

This information about fats and the mind is particularly distressing because the low-fat-diet paradigm came from the people we trust the most: the medical profession.

THE NEW INDUSTRY: HOME REPLACEMENT MEALS

Food manufacturers stay on top of cultural trends and produce products that fill a real or perceived need in the marketplace. No one knows better than advertising executives that mothers and fathers are stressed, short on time, and desperate to make life a little easier. It is likely that some of these very advertising executives are mothers and fathers themselves. They certainly don't have time to prepare a leisurely meal in the kitchen at the end of a twelve-hour day.

Because of this perceived need, a few creative people scattered throughout a few advertising offices created a national market for packaged foods, called home meal replacements, or HMRs.

Over the past few years, we have watched the amount of expensive supermarket freezer space expand to accommodate increasing numbers of packaged frozen entrées, and they now occupy a huge amount of space in your local supermarket. Some of the most aggressive companies include Swanson's, Stouffer's, Marie Callender's, Healthy Choice, Taco Bell, Red Baron Pizza, and the like. These entrées are designed for the adult market. Then there are the Kid Cuisine frozen entrées, packaged and marketed to introduce kids to packaged foods early in life.

The problem with these packaged foods goes beyond the idea that meal preparation is an important social event in the family and that we need to go back to our roots. It goes to the heart of our discussion of nutrition and the brain. These convenient foods are not benign. They are incredibly damaging to our brain chemistry.

The first nutritional problem is that they are deficient in essential fats, fats that feed the brain. In fact, in the "healthier" entrées, fats have been purposely and artificially removed or reduced to give the illusion that the meals are good for you. To make up the missing taste from the fat, sugars were added. Many of the entrées contain a quarter cup of sugar per serving or more.

The second nutritional problem is that there really is so little nutrition. Only a fraction of some essential nutrients are present at all. For example, only a few have more than a few milligrams of a couple of the B complex, virtually no vitamin C, and only a smattering of the essential minerals.

What is astonishing about these entrées is the amount of sodium they contain, the third major problem. The sodium (salt) content ranges from a few hundred milligrams to nearly two thousand milligrams in a single meal, far in excess of what the body needs or can use. Over the past few decades we have learned something of the importance of maintaining proper sodium in the blood because some individuals with high blood pressure are susceptible to excessive sodium.

In natural food, sodium is balanced against potassium, or more accurately, most foods provide about three to seven times more potassium than sodium. Potassium is used in the production of cellular energy, is used as a cofactor in many enzymes, helps regulate nerve transmission and muscle contraction, and so on. Potassium is incredibly important for heart function because of its ability, with magnesium, to regulate the rhythm of the heartbeat.

Sodium and potassium drive the cellular sodium-potassium pump that pulls nutrients into the cells using an electrical current created by the electrically charged ion potassium inside the cell. The electrically charged sodium ion is outside the cell, in the blood. The pump also drives waste materials out of the cell into the bloodstream for elimination.

The sodium-potassium pump is an incredibly fascinating part of cell biology, and wields an enormous power over the production of cellular (and subsequently whole-body) energy. Sodium is concentrated on the outside of the cell and potassium is concentrated on the inside of the cell. Both minerals leak through the pores in the cell membrane so the pump operates continuously to exchange sodium ions, which have entered the cell, for potassium ions outside the cell. The pump, a protein embedded within the walls of the membrane, is operated by cellular energy (ATP).

The pump measures about six by eight nanometers, or slightly more than the thickness of the cell membrane. Each pump can exchange three sodium ions on the inside of the cell for two potassium ions on the outside, at a rate of about two hundred sodium ions and about one hundred thirty potassium ions per second. Most neurons have between one hundred and two hundred pumps per square micrometer of membrane surface, but there can be up to one thousand or more pumps in some parts of the cell wall.[42]

A typical nerve cell has about one million sodium pumps with a capacity to move about two hundred million sodium ions per second. This activity produces the electricity that runs the body, and it is by this pump that nerve activity is driven. The electrical voltage passes along the axon until it reaches the end, much as a flame travels along the fuse of a firecracker. The voltage pulls the nerve signal along the axon to release the neurotransmitters at the synaptic gaps. It is easy to see why the balance between sodium-and-potassium must be maintained and why it is important that the mineral balance not tip in the direction of sodium.

When sodium and potassium levels are reversed, the kidneys have to work overtime to try to dump the excessive sodium and restore the mineral ratios. The adrenal hormone aldosterone is used to help balance intra-cellular sodium-to-potassium ratios so that energy production is not slowed.

Scientists recommend that about 3,500 milligrams of potassium and about 500 milligrams of sodium be supplied in the diet daily. If we ate what nature provided, this potassium-to-sodium ratio would be easily ac-complished. Most natural foods contain far more potassium than sodium. For example, one stalk of celery contains about 1,500 milligrams of potas-sium and about 34.8 milligrams of sodium. One cup of shredded Romaine lettuce provides about 162 milligrams of potassium and about 4.48 mil-ligrams of sodium, and one large carrot provides about 684 milligrams of potassium and about 74 milligrams of sodium. The numbers are heavily weighted toward potassium. These ratios are drastically reversed in the frozen entrées. We see that the difference in mineral ratios in these processed foods is not insignificant; there is a huge difference.

Could you eat one-half of a Celeste frozen pepperoni pizza? That por-tion size contains nearly 2,000 milligrams of sodium and about 600 mil-ligrams of potassium. (Magnesium, zinc, copper, manganese, etc., are virtually nonexistent, as is vitamin C and the B complex.) In one serving of Stouffer's Chicken Divan entrée, the sodium-to-potassium ratios are similarly reversed, with over 800 milligrams of sodium and 400 milligrams of potassium.

Sodium loading begins in early childhood with the Oscar Mayer Lunchables and the Campbell's soup preparations designed for young children, continues through the teenage years with french fries, McDon-ald's and Burger King hamburgers, and potato chips. Foods designed for children and teenagers are loaded with sodium. When we grab the most at-tractive package in the frozen entrée section of the supermarket and pre-pare it for dinner, the sodium loading continues.

What influence does this mineral imbalance have on the brain? In rats, we understand high levels of serum sodium (called hypernatremia) lead to brain lesions, defects in the myelin sheath, neuron cell death, and dehy-dration of the brain tissue.[43]

We know that high levels of sodium in the form of sodium lactate are instrumental in triggering panic disorders in susceptible people, and it is probably the load of sodium in the sodium lactate molecule that triggers the panic attacks.[44]

What may happen, in the face of day-to-day, continuously high levels of sodium in the diet and the bloodstream, is that we experience a type of acute hypernatremia—not enough to kill us or cause the myelin sheath to lose its integrity, but enough to keep our sodium potassium pump slightly dysregulated and throw off the electrical system of the brain.

The first signs of excessive sodium are restlessness, lethargy, and irritability. Water is pulled from the brain cells, shrinking the cells. Remember that enzymes function only in the presence of water, so enzyme function can be impaired. As water is pulled out of the tissues, thirst is created, which corrects the hypernatremia theoretically. If water were consumed in response to the thirst, it is possible that the sodium damage would not occur or, at the very least, would be minimized.[45]

Americans don't drink very much water. We drink coffee, a beverage that pulls even more minerals out of the tissues and excretes them in the urine. Americans drink soft drinks that are often loaded with more sodium and which further unbalance the mineral stores. We drink V8, loaded with sodium. We drink everything but water, which would pull the excess sodium out of the blood and out of the brain. We defeat the body's own mechanism of balancing the critical sodium-to-potassium ratios by overindulging in these entrées and beverages that contain so much sodium, and then by not drinking water to flush it out of the system.

If excessive levels of sodium lead to brain lesions and the destruction of the myelin sheath in rats, it also may lead to brain lesions and destruction of the myelin sheath in humans. While research needs to focus on this concern, we know from existing research that extreme hypernatremia in infants leads to seizures, extreme neurologic damage, and ultimately death.[46] It is likely that lower but continuous levels of high sodium have an effect on the adult brain as well.

SOLUTIONS: THE ADULT NUTRITION PRIMER

For those of you who are struggling with depression, memory loss, difficulty in performing cognitive tasks, or other mental disorders, I offer a word of hope. There is no question that we are frightened when we feel we are losing brain function. Now that we understand how intimately brain chemistry and nutrition are associated, we can feel a certain power over our brain health. We can alter our diets and make a huge difference in the way we feel and think.

Can we design a nutrition program to feed our brains? Yes, we can, but only by turning our backs on the American food culture. Use the menus and recipes in Chapter 8 to start your day-by-day nutrition plan. Think of this section as a nutrition primer. Follow the menus and recipes in this book carefully for several weeks. Purchase cookbooks that feature natural, organic foods and stretch your culinary imagination. Many resources are available to help you transition your kitchen into a brain-healthy kitchen.

It goes without saying that if you are serious about feeling better mentally, you will need to stop indulging in your favorite junk foods that poison the brain. Diet sodas will have to be eliminated (drink water instead). Say good-bye to the Campbell's Soup elfin (make your own soup). The average American may eat 23.3 gallons of ice cream per year; you won't (you'll enjoy a fresh fruit tray or fresh fruit sorbet). You'll shun the local coffeehouse and drink herbal tea instead.

Scan familiar packages of prepared foods and put them back on the supermarket shelf if they contain preservatives or flavor enhancers like monosodium glutamate. Avoid high-sodium foods and concentrate on high-potassium foods to restore the sodium:potassium ratio. Stop grazing on the convenient antifoods you've been indulging in and start planning your menus carefully. Use food to heal your mind instead of filling up an empty space in your midsection.

Your own nutritional needs during adulthood will vary considerably, depending on whether or not you are female giving birth to children, how much stress you are struggling with, how much physical activity you engage in, and your own unique nutritional/biochemical needs. At the very least, you will need to follow the diet and supplement program listed in the previous chapter for teenagers, supplementing with a high-quality multivitamin and mineral supplement and essential fats. I recommend that you include two to four tablespoons of raw, organic oils in your diet each day. Use fish oil capsules, flaxseed capsules, or add flaxseed oil to a breakfast protein drink, or use raw olive oil on your freshly prepared salad each day.

If you are struggling with mental issues, read the next chapter carefully. There is no substitute for a personal consultation with a nutritionist or a nutritionally educated physician, but as a second-best option, I will in the following chapter take you through a nutritional counseling appointment and help you sort through some of your personal issues. Make full use of the information contained in this chapter, then reference Appendix II in the back of the book.

Conclusion

As we approach the final years of our life, some deterioration in brain function is expected. The brain is susceptible to free-radical damage from oxygen just like other fat-rich substances. The brain can wear out, just like other organs. If we lived in a more healthy world, ate natural food, and encountered less stress, we might grow old more gracefully, with most of our brain cells intact and functional. Our world, though, is loaded with environmental toxins that trick our endocrine systems and disrupt our normal biochemical processes. And possibly most damaging of all is our food culture.

The questions to ask ourselves are: How can we fix it? How can we nourish our brains, to provide the nutrition they need to ease depression and stimulate cognitive ability? The answers lie not so much in drugs and therapy but in our kitchens. In our pantries. In the foods we raise to our mouths.

7

A Case for Optimism

There is reason for optimism. The human body has a remarkable ability to compensate, even in the face of such poor nutrition. While we honestly don't know if we can completely reverse the damage caused by poor nutrition throughout our lives, there is good clinical evidence that good nutrition can make a huge difference in our mental capabilities, whether we are babies, young children, teenagers, or adults. Our bodies *want* to be well, and to encourage us to eat more nutritiously, the body (and the brain) responds rapidly.

Jake was twenty-two years old when he finally came to see me. He was fresh out of jail, having served his term, and was struggling to get back into a productive life. I asked him what his goals were in seeking nutrition counseling. He responded that he wanted to feel calmer, more in control of his anger and his life. He wanted to shut off his mind in the evening so he could sleep soundly. He wanted to feel contented for the first time in his life.

I started him out on a carefully chosen supplement program, designed to reduce his anxiety (magnesium, B complex), and recommended dietary changes. I selected fairly high doses of zinc to help reduce his anger and aggression. I recommended essential fatty acids and a well-balanced multivitamin and mineral supplement. Most of the supplements were to be taken in the morning for energy; others were to be taken in the evening to help him sleep.

Jake also completed a "Profile of Mood States" (POMS) questionnaire so we would have an objective means of assessing his progress. I asked him to fill out an intake form and a food diary, and made an appointment to see him in two weeks.

RESULTS OF JAKE'S "PROFILE OF MOOD STATES" QUESTIONNAIRE

	May 13	*July 1*	*July 26*
Tension-Anxiety	30	14	5
Depression-Dejection	31	17	5
Anger-Hostility	42	12	17
Vigor	29	25	29
Fatigue	19	11	3
Confusion-Bewilderment	17	4	4
Total Score	110	36	5

*Because "vigor" is a positive mood, it is a negative number. The "vigor" score is subtracted from the total of the other scores. In this particular test, except for "vigor," lower scores are better.

At the initial meeting, prior to starting on his nutritional program, his total score was nearly at the top of the charts.

At our appointment four weeks later, I asked how he was feeling. "Better," he said. "I don't feel as angry, as stressed. The other day I had a really good reason for being angry and just couldn't get very worked up about it." I asked him to redo the "Profile of Mood States" questionnaire. (The results of subsequent testing is listed in the table above.) As the nutrition began to affect his brain chemistry, he felt more in control of his emotions and his life. He may have to learn some new life skills, i.e., he may need to learn how to avoid situations that have stimulated poor choices in the past. He may need to work on anger management or life skills with a counselor, but Jake is, for the first time in his life, in control of his brain and his emotions.

Over time, Jake made commitments about changing his eating habits, and even though he is a single guy, he is getting his "nutritional house in order." As he puts each step into place and learns new eating habits, his body and brain are responding positively. Instead of tracking downward in antisocial, criminal behaviors, Jake is working, paying his own bills, and is becoming a happy, productive citizen. He is also, for the first time in his life, bonding with his adoptive parents, and they are enjoying his company.

Cassie was brought to me for nutrition counseling when she was ten, when she first displayed her depression and her suicide ideation. In addition to her depression, Cassie suffered from severe mood swings, phobias and panic attacks, aggressiveness and hostility, and attention deficit problems. Even though she was an extremely bright child, she was nearly at the bottom of her class and had little motivation to improve.

We put her on a program that restricted her allergic foods, and we simultaneously increased her minerals, her essential fatty acids, and her vitamins. Slowly her depressive attitude began to turn around and we saw her personality emerge. She proved to be a quick-witted, creative, funny, delightful child who initiated games with her little sisters.

When she turned fourteen, however, things took a downward turn. Her hormones were out of control; her family went through a period of severe stress that affected her deeply. She went out of the country on a two-month mission assignment.

During the trip, Cassie abandoned her supplement program and the quality of the food she was given to eat was extremely poor. Cassie tumbled down rapidly. In response to the stress and her fragile mental state, she began self-mutilating and came back with words carved deeply into her skin. She was smoking, drinking, and defiant. In the next few months, she tumbled even further into destructive behaviors, including experimenting with drugs and occultism, and she finally ran away from home.

Her parents admitted her into a residential juvenile facility where she would be safe, and put her back on her nutrition program. Within a few days, her head started to clear. Her defiance and anger dissipated, and she settled into her new home and into her new school. Her grades improved and she was able to stay on task. She was forced by the program to stop smoking, drinking, and drugs, but over time her desire for these substances disappeared. She expressed happiness that she had not felt in a long time, and she started planning her future.

Both Cassie and Jake will need to watch their diets for the rest of their lives. They will have to pay special attention to sugars, artificial ingredients, and allergic foods, and they will need to supplement with magnesium, zinc, the B complex, fatty acids, and other nutrients to correct their biochemistry. They will need to shun the American food culture and eat real food. But if they do, they will lead a normal, happy life. Their brains will work well.

CAN YOU DO IT?

Jake and Cassie were able to improve both mood and cognition through improved nutrition. With a little coaching you, too, can take control of your emotional life and your cognitive abilities.

While it is best to do nutrition counseling in one-on-one sessions in my office, I will, in the next few pages, take you through the protocol I use for my clients.

STEP ONE: Arriving to see me for a counseling appointment, your first task would be to fill out an extensive intake form and take the POMS test. In lieu of the POMS test, which can only be administered by a professional, take the Mental Health Inventory on page 218–19, an informal quiz to help you track your mental and emotional progress over the next few months.

In lieu of filling out the intake form, take out a notebook and explore your own medical history. You will need to ask yourself the following questions:

1. Does hypothyroidism run in my family? Have I been diagnosed with hypothyroidism? Do I have the symptoms of hypothyroidism? Symptoms of hypothyroidism:

- Fatigue
- Cold hands and feet, or low body temperature
- Weight gain

- Constipation
- Menstrual irregularities
- Muscle cramps
- Cool, rough, dry skin
- Puffy face and hands
- Hoarse, husky voice
- Slow reflexes
- Yellowish color of the skin
- Low blood pressure
- Anemia
- Muscle weakness
- Inability to concentrate
- Poor memory
- Depression or extreme agitation
- Other intellectual impairment with a gradual change in personality, including psychosis
- Dull facial expression
- Drooping eyelids
- Sparse, coarse, dry hair
- In children: retarded growth and evidence of mental retardation
- In adolescents: precocious puberty, short stature

If you are experiencing several of these symptoms, please see your physician for a diagnosis and treatment of possible hypothyroidism.

2. Do alcoholism, obesity, or blood sugar disorders (diabetes or hypoglycemia) run in my family? Do I have a problem with any of these conditions?

Symptoms of blood sugar disorders include the following:

- Mental confusion with impaired abstract and concrete thought processes
- Bizarre antagonistic behaviors
- Rapid heartbeat
- Palpitations of the heart
- Sweating and tremulousness

- Nausea, hunger
- Headaches
- Anxiety
- Food cravings
- Chronic fatigue
- Irritability
- Mood swings
- Impaired coordination
- Increased thirst
- Sudden weight gain or loss
- Lack of mental clarity
- Vision problems
- Depression, anxiety
- Symptoms similar to a panic attack

If you are experiencing several of these symptoms, please consult with a nutritionist or a nutritionally trained physician for treatment.

3. Do food or environmental allergies run in my family? Have I been diagnosed with allergies, or do I suspect that allergies could be contributing to my symptom profile?

Pinpointing allergies or food intolerance can be difficult because sensitivities can present with any type of symptom to virtually any part of the body. Symptoms may also appear up to seven days after exposure. Some of the typical symptoms of allergy may including the following:

- Hay fever (congested nose or eyes, itchy mouth or ears, sneezing, etc.)

- Itchy, red eyes; swollen eyes; bags under the eyes or a swelling in the upper cheekbone area; wrinkles under the eyes just below the lower eyelids

- Stuffy, runny, drippy nose

- Asthma; allergic coughing

- Hives

- Eczema or atopic dermatitis

- Bad breath, belching, intestinal gas

- Irritable bowel, Crohn's disease, ulcers, mucous colitis, ulcerative colitis, abdominal discomfort, pain or cramps, diarrhea, constipation, nausea, vomiting

- Headaches, nose or chest complaints, fatigue, hyperactivity, depression, agitation, muscle aches, skin rashes, joint tightness, heart irregularities, problems with memory or cognition

According to Dr. Philpott, author of *Brain Allergies,* the following symptoms are typical of a cerebral or brain allergy:

- Acute localized physical effects (rhinitis, bronchitis, asthma, eczema, gastrointestinal, and other symptoms)

- Headache, fatigue, myalgia, arthralgia, neuralgia, and other generalized physical syndromes

- Acute mental effects (confusion, depression, delusions, hallucinations, and other advanced cerebral and behavioral abnormalities)

Remember that allergic symptoms can appear up to seven days after exposure. If you suspect that food allergies may be causing symptoms, please consult with a nutritionist or a nutritionally trained physician for assistance.

4. Am I taking any medications? (Side effects of many medications can include mental and emotional symptoms. If you are taking any medications or have taken any medications in the past, check the package insert or ask your pharmacist if your symptoms could be caused by the medication. *Do not discontinue the medication without consulting with your physician.*)

5. Have I been exposed to environmental toxins or heavy metals? Toxic metals such as lead, cadmium, mercury, aluminum, and others typically cause mental or emotional symptoms. Exposure can come from many sources and you may not even remember if exposure has occurred. Check with your nutritionally trained physician for testing for possible contamination with environmental toxins, and for treatment.

STEP TWO: Examine your nutritional history. This may be the most time-consuming portion of your journey. First, go through the following nutrient-deficiency charts and check off the symptoms that pertain to you. See if you can find clusters of symptoms in certain charts. If so, you may want to focus special attention to meeting those needs. I will explain how to do that later.

Second, follow the week-by-week instructions in changing your eating habits. Do not proceed through this list quickly. Allow each step to become part of your lifestyle before proceeding on to the next step, to increase the opportunity for these habits to become a permanent part of your lifestyle.

Are your nutritional needs being met? Although every nutrient is potentially essential to brain function, some nutrients seem to be specifically related to the nervous system. Many of the deficiency symptoms are mental or emotional in nature. Some of the more common "brain nutrients" include many of the vitamin B complex, vitamin C, magnesium, zinc, manganese, and chromium. Other nutrients seem to play a lesser or less visible role in the functionality of the brain. Of the macronutrients (essential fatty acids, proteins, and carbohydrates), all are of equal importance, and must be adequately provided on a daily basis.

The following nutrient-deficiency lists are not inclusive but will give you a general indication of your own nutritional status.

List of vitamin B complex deficiency symptoms:

- Headaches
- Insomnia
- Heaviness and weakness in legs
- Rapid, irregular heartbeat
- Apathy
- Loss of memory
- Confusion

- Inability to concentrate
- Anorexia
- Loss of weight and strength
- Emotional instability
- Irrational fears
- Depression
- Changes in the eyes (increased light sensitivity, tearing, burning and itching, eye fatigue, decrease in the sharpness of vision)
- Tiny lesions in the mouth or cracks in the corners of the mouth
- Flaking of skin around the nose, eyebrows, chin, cheeks, earlobes, and hairline
- Moodiness, nervousness, irritability
- Apprehension
- Psychosis
- Sleeping difficulties
- Fatigue

While many of these symptoms could be symptomatic of other conditions, they may also signal a vitamin deficiency. See the diet recommendations that follow for correcting these possible deficiencies.

Symptoms of Magnesium Deficiency

The following symptoms are often characteristic of a deficiency in magnesium, a mineral that is essential to brain function:

- Short-term memory loss
- Emotional ups and downs
- Irrational fears
- Panic attacks, anxiety disorders
- Depression
- Easy anger
- Insomnia (early-morning awakening)
- Fatigue
- Muscle twitches and tremors

- Muscle cramps
- Constipation
- Cravings for chocolate and/or other sweets
- Unusual sensitivity to loud noises and sounds
- Hyperactivity
- Hyperirritability
- Excessive perspiration
- Unpleasant body odor
- Diastolic high blood pressure
- Increased frequency of urination

Notice that many of the symptoms of magnesium deficiency are mental or emotional in nature. See the diet recommendations that follow for correcting these possible deficiencies.

Symptoms of Iron Deficiency

Iron is very important to the functionality of the brain. Iron overload can be a serious problem, however. If you suspect that you may be deficient in this mineral, please consult with your nutritionally trained physician before using iron supplements.

- Attention difficulty
- Fatigue
- Pale skin
- Hyperactivity
- Brittle, ridged fingernails, or fingernails that are spoon-shaped
- Chronic dull headaches
- Inflammation of the tongue
- The urge to eat nonfood substances (sand, paint, dirt, etc.)

Symptoms of Zinc Deficiency

Zinc is another critical "brain nutrient," and is commonly undersupplied in the American diet. The following symptoms are typical of zinc deficiency:

- Poor sense of taste and smell
- Poor wound healing
- Scaly, inflamed skin
- Loss of appetite
- Dislike of protein foods
- Cravings for breads or other carbohydrates
- Poor nail growth
- White spots on the fingernails
- Frequent, frontal headaches
- Tendency toward allergies
- Poor immune function (frequent colds and flu)
- Acne or other skin eruptions
- Dry, flaky, inflamed skin
- Severe depression, to the point of suicide ideation
- Poor cognitive abilities
- Poor digestion
- Poor fingernail growth

If you are experiencing several of these symptoms, you may be deficient in zinc. See the diet recommendations that follow for correcting these possible deficiencies.

Now that you have an idea of what nutrients you may need, you can begin to correct the possible deficiencies by *manipulating* the diet and by *supplementing* your diet. It is difficult to make huge changes in your diet all at once. I counsel my clients to make gradual, incremental changes to their nutritional habits, and find that if they incorporate small changes at a time, long-term success is more likely to occur.

Supplemental nutrition can also provide immediate benefit, both in reducing mental symptoms and making it easier to correct the diet. Use the following guide when planning your supplement program:

Regardless of how you did in the above deficiency quiz, everyone needs to take a daily multivitamin that provides an adequate amount of all essential micronutrients. Consult your local nutritionist for recommendations on a supplement that will be appropriate for you. It should contain more than just RDA levels of nutrients, and it should provide for nutrients that are not covered in the RDA/RDI.

If you checked many of the symptoms in the above lists, you should consider providing a little more of these individual nutrients. As a nutritionist, I generally write a supplement recommendation based on individual needs, but in this setting, I can make the following generalized recommendations, in addition to the daily multivitamin:

- Vitamin B complex: up to 100 mg/mcg per day
- Vitamin C: up to 1,000 mg per day
- Vitamin E: 400 IU per day
- Salmon oil: 3–5 grams per day
- Flax oil: 1–3 grams per day
- DHA: 100 mg per day
- Phosphatidylserine: 300 mg per day– for premature senility or memory loss
- Phosphatidylcholine: 500 mg per day– for premature senility or memory loss
- Magnesium citrate or magnesium chelate: up to 500 mg per day (less if diarrhea occurs)
- Zinc picolinate or zinc chelate: up to 50 mg per day (less if nausea occurs)
- Manganese chelate: 3 mg per day (only if recommended by your nutritionally trained physician or nutritionist)

Maximize Your Diet

1. Add one large salad with an olive oil–based dressing to your lunch and dinner. Follow the salad recipe in Chapter 8 of this book to make sure you include a variety of vegetables in the blend. Salad is much more than iceberg lettuce coated in thick dressings. Salad should be a lightly seasoned blend of many colors, textures, and flavors to delight your palate.

When you take the salad for lunch, do not add the dressing until just before you toss and serve so that it does not turn limp and soggy.

2. Gradually reduce the amount of nonwater beverages you consume each day, so that within two weeks you are drinking only eight to ten large glasses of water per day. Addictive symptoms are decreased if you progress slowly. You may also enjoy hot or warm herbal teas for variety, or you may squeeze a fresh lemon or lime into the cool water for added flavor. Serve water with your meals. Sip water throughout the day to keep your body hydrated.

3. Go through the recipes and menus in this book and follow our menu plan carefully for the next few weeks. Plan to include several servings of freshly prepared vegetables with your lunch and dinner meals. Get your family used to the taste of well-prepared vegetables. Plan to prepare one protein food with each dinner meal, especially seafood. Fish is brain food.

4. Reduce the amount of sugar you are using. Stop purchasing all cookies, candies, cakes, and ice creams, and start making your own. You can easily reduce the amount of sugar in a cookie recipe by one-half and you will notice little difference. Cakes and other confections cannot be altered as easily, so you will wish to purchase a cookbook that has already done this work for you. See the back of this book for a listing of some of my favorite cookbooks.

5. Go through your pantry and remove all processed foods and snack items. Replace them with healthy snacks and healthy foods. The only canned foods I use occasionally are beans, tomatoes, and tuna fish. I do not customarily purchase frozen vegetables and fruits; I enjoy preparing fresh,

---

The diet should also supply adequate amounts of high-quality protein. (If you have chosen a vegetarian lifestyle, please consult with a nutritionist or nutritionally trained physician for counsel on balancing your essential amino acids and making up for other possible deficiencies.)

The average woman requires from forty-five to eighty-five grams of protein per day. She may require slightly more if she is physically very active or if she has been under a considerable amount of stress.

The average man requires from fifty-five to ninety-five grams of protein per day. He may require slightly more if he is physically very active or if he has been under a considerable amount of stress.

The average child requires less protein (based on body size), but the quality of the protein should be very high.

Animal protein provides about nine grams of protein per ounce, and provides all essential amino acids.

seasonal vegetables. Yes, it takes a little more time and thought, but the wonderful flavors and the good health we enjoy make it worth the extra trouble.

6. The last step: Congratulate yourself! You have accomplished the difficult task of turning your back on the destructive American food culture, exchanging it for natural foods that heal your body and brain. You know how difficult it was. You did not accomplish it overnight. How do you now feel? It is time to take another mental health inventory.

Mental Health Inventory

You may wish to take this simple test before you begin your program, and then every four weeks. While this test has no scientific validity, it will help you to take inventory of how you are feeling mentally and emotionally. You will be able to track your progress.

Scoring:
0 = Never
1 = A little or occasionally
2 = Moderately
3 = Quite a bit or frequently
4 = Extremely

Unable to concentrate on my work	0	1	2	3	4
Poor short-term memory	0	1	2	3	4
Angry	0	1	2	3	4
Fatigued	0	1	2	3	4
Discontented	0	1	2	3	4
Emotionally exhausted	0	1	2	3	4
Fearful	0	1	2	3	4
Anxious	0	1	2	3	4
Panic attacks	0	1	2	3	4
Ill-tempered	0	1	2	3	4
Rebellious	0	1	2	3	4
Guilty	0	1	2	3	4
Unhappy	0	1	2	3	4
Shaky	0	1	2	3	4
Gloomy	0	1	2	3	4
Confused	0	1	2	3	4

(continued on next page)

Unable to make and carry out plans	0	1	2	3	4
Inefficient	0	1	2	3	4
Worthless	0	1	2	3	4
Hopeless	0	1	2	3	4
How would you describe your overall mood?					
Depressed?	0	1	2	3	4
Happy?	0	1	2	3	4
How would you describe your mental energy?					
Tired?	0	1	2	3	4
Vigorous?	0	1	2	3	4
Do you feel confident about your future?					
Yes	0	1	2	3	4
No	0	1	2	3	4
Do you take pleasure in your life?	0	1	2	3	4
Are you able to handle your life?	0	1	2	3	4
Are you able to perform your tasks efficiently?	0	1	2	3	4
Do you feel a sense of satisfaction at the end of your day?	0	1	2	3	4

You may also wish to have a family member or close friend evaluate your mental state. It may be difficult for you to be objective; a friend or family member can often provide valuable insight. Don't be afraid to ask for help.

Nature has provided wonderful tools to help us deal with depression and other mental disorders. St. John's wort has been shown to relieve mild to moderate depression, using just 900 milligrams daily. The form should preferably contain .3% hypericin, considered to be the active ingredient. Kava kava is particularly helpful in relieving anxiety, especially when combined with California poppy. Other calming herbs are valerian, hops, and chamomile. The herb ginkgo biloba is an ancient herb that stimulates the flow of blood into the brain, improving memory and cognitive functions, particularly in the elderly. Gotu kola is another herb that is good for memory and reducing age-related cognitive decline.

The amino acid GABA (gamma aminobutyric acid) is a calming amino acid that greatly reduces anxiety. GABA's sister amino acid, L-glutamine, is also calming and helps reduce addictive cravings (nicotine, caffeine, alcohol, sugar, and other drugs).

L-tryptophan (in the form of 5-hydroxytryptophan, or 5-HTP) is converted in the body to serotonin, a calming neurotransmitter. The amino acid tyrosine is converted in the body to thyroid hormone and the neurotransmitter dopamine, exerting a calming effect on the brain, helping to relieve depression and addictions.

One of the vitamins in the B complex, choline, has been shown to improve learning and memory in experimental animals and humans.

None of these agents is a substitute for good nutrition, however. Don't be tempted to think that taking a pill is a shortcut to good mental health. As a clinical nutritionist, I often recommend using herbs or nutrients to help relieve symptoms more rapidly while we are altering nutritional biochemistry through the diet. If you are interested in exploring the use of these products further, I recommend that you consult with your nutritionist or nutritionally trained physician.

FINAL STEP: Check back over these steps and make sure you have followed instructions carefully. Continue to work on your diet. Make little improvements each day. Encourage your family to walk with you. Do not purchase or prepare separate foods for the rest of the family. If the food is good for you, it is good for them also. Don't be discouraged if you fail occasionally; we all do. Just begin again, and before you know it, you'll be eating healthy, delicious meals nearly all the time.

Best of all, you'll feel wonderful nearly all the time!

This journey is best taken with a coach, a companion. I urge you to seek the counsel of a nutritionist or a nutritionally trained physician and work closely with them. (See Appendix I in the back of this book for referral information.) It is likely that your insurance will not pay for nutritional therapy, but do not let that deter you. There are some things worth paying for—and your mental health is at the top of the list!

WHAT TO EXPECT FROM THIS PROGRAM

Jake began to feel better after just four weeks. Cassie didn't notice much difference for six months or longer. People respond to good nutrition in different ways. Some people respond slowly, making tiny incremental steps forward. They respond so slowly they don't even notice that they feel better, that they think better. They are relieved when they take a diagnostic test like the POMS test that gives them an objective measure of their progress and find that the issues they complained about originally are greatly improved. Sometimes they forget just how bad they used to feel and are surprised when they are reminded of their original complaints. Other people respond rapidly and dramatically.

Sometimes poor psychological behaviors have become deeply embedded in our personalities during our seasons of malnutrition, and after the nutritional therapy has worked to correct the biochemistry, counseling needs to be initiated to relearn behaviors and patterns of thinking. Nutrition is not a magic bullet. Nutrition works at a deep level to restore the underlying biochemical imbalances in the blood and brain. When key fatty acids are used to correct hyperactivity or learning disorders, sometimes the positive effects are noticed quickly as the fatty acids become part of the active neurotransmitters. At other times it may take months for benefits to be noticed as the fatty acids embed themselves into the nerve tissue and help rebuild the cell membrane.

Currently, there are few diagnostic tests to determine just how nutrition is improving brain structure or function. We have to rely on subjective measures.

If you feel that you are not making the significant progress you would like to see, I recommend that you seek the counsel of a heath care practitioner who can guide you. This is not a journey you should be taking alone.

Conclusion

You may be feeling a mixture of emotions: relief, fear, and anxiety about how to proceed or what to eat. You are determined to work with a nutritionist or a physician and improve your mental and emotional health with nutrition. You're going to take the steps outlined in this chapter and you're going to start today.

What will you do next? The answer to that question may decide your mental health for the rest of your life. The next logical step may be figuring out what to make for dinner, what to feed your family. If you can't load up on junk food, what will you eat?

The next chapter provides the practical solution: recipes and menus. While this isn't an exhaustive treatment of everything you need to know about healthy cooking, it is a primer. A guide to get you started. Inspiration to excite your own creativity in the kitchen. Make full use of these ideas, then expand to include your own. You'll find a new pleasure in indulging yourself in new taste sensations, and your brain will benefit from it.

8

A Recipe and Menu Primer

A rtificial foods pale in sensory richness when compared to real aromas and tastes. Food and the preparation of it is a valuable part of our shared family experiences, bringing us together, nourishing our spirits as well as our bodies and our brains. Remember walking through the back door of your house in the late afternoon, to be greeted by the fragrance of vegetable soup simmering on the back burner?

This section of the book is by no means an exhaustive treatment of all brain-nourishing foods. The recipes and menus that follow are designed to whet your appetite and get you started on the road to brain health. Each recipe is followed by a brief nutritional breakdown so you can see how this food nourishes the brain.

Most of the recipes are simple enough that your own children can assist in meal preparation. As they are gaining necessary cooking skills by serving as your assistant, they'll be feeding their brains and nervous systems. They'll learn what *Really Good Food* tastes like, how to read nutrition labels, how to say "no" to the American food culture. It may be the most valuable education they ever receive.

RECIPES FOR THE MOTHER-TO-BE

The time to start good nutrition for your child is before you become pregnant. Hopefully, by the time you've discovered you are expecting a child, you will have been indulging your palate with fresh seafoods, fresh vegetables and fruits, and whole grains and you've avoided as many food chemicals as possible. During your pregnancy, use the following "milk shake" each day, along with a good-quality vitamin and mineral supplement that provides superoptimal levels of all essential nutrients.

Pregnancy Milk Shake

This is a modified version of a breakfast drink recipe given to me by my midwife when I was carrying my third child. My third child is now a prepubertal, healthy, extremely bright, and beautiful young lady.

Sip this shake in small amounts throughout the day, starting with breakfast. It can take the place of breakfast, if you wish. Struggling with morning sickness? It feels particularly comforting on an unsettled stomach.

1 scoop rice protein powder or whey-based protein powder
¼ cup noninstant, organic powdered milk
1 tablespoon blackstrap molasses
1 medium banana or any other fruit
2 tablespoons flaxseed oil
½ teaspoon vanilla extract
16 ounces ice-cold water

Combine all ingredients in a blender and whiz for a few seconds until it is well blended. Store unused portion in the refrigerator and rewhiz each time you pour off a portion.

Calories: 1,010; Protein: 60.53 g; Carbohydrates: 103.4 g; Fat: 40.28 g; Thiamin: .160 mg; Riboflavin: .529 mg; Niacin: 1.713 mg; Sodium: 211.4 mg; Potassium: 1608 mg; Iron: 7.094 mg; Calcium: 623.8 mg; Magnesium: 119.5 mg; Zinc: 1.64 mg.

More nutritional tips for the pregnant mother:

When choosing a dietary supplement for pregnancy and the lactation period, it is imperative that the nutrients known to serve as cofactors in brain enzymes, or as part of the physical structure of the brain or its chemicals, are particularly well supplied. Make sure your prenatal vitamin is complete, and that it provides much more than the nutrients listed in the RDA/RDI.

The prenatal supplement augments careful choices of food. Of particular importance are the following nutrients:

- folic acid (more than 800 mcg per day)
- magnesium (around 500 mg per day)
- the entire B complex (around 100 mg/mcg or so per day of each one)
- zinc (around 30 mg per day)
- iron (around 15 mg per day) as ferrous fumerate, ferrous amino acid chelate, or iron mixed with yellow dock for added absorption. You will want to avoid ferrous sulfate, a poorly absorbed source of iron that constipates.

For further recommendations about dietary requirements during pregnancy and lactation, please consult with your midwife or your obstetrician. While no government agency has yet devised an RDA (Recommended Dietary Allowance) or RDI (Recommended Daily Intake) of essential fatty acids, specific amino acids, or many of the minerals, prudence suggests that foods rich in these nutrients be part of your daily diet.

Read through the information in the preceding chapter. If you have further questions about the quality of your diet, please consult with a midwife, a nutritionist, or a nutritionally trained physician. The pregnant or breast-feeding mother should enjoy several servings of organic seafood or other meats per day. Seafoods like wild-raised salmon, halibut, and tuna are rich in Omega-3 fatty acids that form brain tissue. The proteins in animal protein are well suited to laying down the protein structures of the brain and nervous system, and supply the amino acids used to synthesize hormones and neurotransmitters. Minerals activate enzymes, along with vitamins. A good source of minerals is organic vegetables; organic fruits provide a rich source of vitamins.

I strongly recommend buying organic foods whenever possible. Most of the beef, chicken, and other meats on the market today are laced with estrogens that can disrupt the delicate endocrine system of your growing child.

RECIPES FOR THE SMALLEST FAMILY MEMBER

There is no reason to purchase baby foods in a jar. If you are preparing healthy foods for your family, your baby will enjoy the flavors and nutrition as well. That being said, if you need to occasionally supplement your home-prepared meals with the prepared variety, choose only organic baby foods to reduce your baby's exposure to harmful chemicals. (See Appendix I in the back of this book for recommendations.)

Mom, while you are preparing meals for the rest of the family, let these baby foods simmer on the back burner. Preparation is simple. When they are finished cooking, let them cool slightly, puree them in the blender or food processor, and divide into serving sizes. They can be frozen for several days or weeks, and defrosted just before serving. I recommend that you defrost and heat the foods in a hot-water bath on the stove, not the microwave. Concerns have been raised about the molecular structure of microwaved foods, and just to be on the safe side, take the few extra minutes and heat baby's food the conventional way.

Baby's Chicken Stew

This meal involves a couple of steps, but the extra work means extra flavor. This recipe makes a large portion. Simply scoop off baby's portion and blend it in the food processor or blender, and serve the family's portion as is.

2 tablespoons olive oil (divided)
2 tablespoons butter (divided)
3 lb chicken legs
½ lb chicken livers
1 medium onion, diced
2 celery stalks with leaves, diced
2 carrots, scrubbed and diced
3 cloves garlic, minced
½ cup raw brown rice or barley
1 teaspoon parsley
1 teaspoon basil
10 cups water

Melt 1 tablespoon butter in a soup kettle over medium heat and add 1 tablespoon olive oil. Rinse the chicken legs carefully, remove any excess fat, and dry them thoroughly. Brown the chicken pieces in the oil on all sides. Pour off the fat. Add the water, cover, and bring to a slow boil. Lower the heat and set the lid of the kettle slightly ajar to let the steam escape. Let the chicken simmer for one hour, then remove the pieces carefully to a plate, and let them cool. Remove the meat from the bones and cut into small pieces. Strain the broth and return to the pot. Add the rice and the chicken livers to the broth and cook for 20 minutes.

Melt the remaining butter in a skillet and add the remaining olive oil. Sauté the vegetables in the oil slowly until they are lightly browned. Set aside. Add the vegetables to the broth mixture, bring back up to a simmer, and cook for about 20 minutes or until the vegetables and rice are soft.

For the family portion of the "soup," dice the chicken livers and return them to the soup. Serve immediately, or freeze for a quick meal later in the week.

For the baby's portion of the soup: Let the soup cool so that it can safely be pureed in the blender or the food processor. Puree the soup thoroughly, then store in meal serving sizes. Should be used within 2 days if stored in the refrigerator. Can be frozen up to 2 weeks.

Calories: 92.68; Protein: 7.056 g; Carbohydrates: 4.709 g; Fat: 5.027 g; Thiamin: .040 mg; Riboflavin: .160 mg; Niacin: 1.985 mg; Sodium: 44.07 mg; Potassium: 114 mg; Iron: 1.002 mg; Calcium: 15.74 mg; Magnesium: 13.39 mg; Zinc: .812 mg.

Baby's Salmon Rice Mousse

Why not feed your child salmon or halibut? The oils in the deep-sea fish will feed his brain, and he'll learn to enjoy the flavors of the sea at an early age. This tastes like a delicate salmon mousse.

3 ounces fresh salmon (or halibut)
8 ounces vegetable broth (without MSG or salt)
¼ cup brown rice

Heat the broth to a slow boil and add the rice. Lower the heat, cover tightly, and let it cook for 30 minutes or until it is almost done. Wash the salmon thoroughly and remove all bones carefully. Add the salmon to the rice, cover, and let it poach for 10 minutes or until done all the way through. Allow the salmon and rice to cool enough that it can be pureed safely in the blender or food processor. If it is too thick, add just enough water to obtain the consistency you want. Serve with a pureed vegetable.

Calories: 62.40; Protein: 5.843 g; Carbohydrates: 7.548 g; Fat: .963 g; Thiamin: .059 mg; Riboflavin: .025 mg; Niacin: 4.119 mg; Sodium: 34.20 mg; Potassium: 108 mg; Iron: .551 mg; Calcium: 1199 mg; Magnesium: 17.94 mg; Zinc: .300 mg.

Baby's Peas and Carrots

2 large carrots, scraped and cut into 1" pieces
Enough water to cover
1 cup fresh or frozen baby peas
A little pat of butter

Bring the carrots to a boil in the water, reduce the heat, and simmer for about 10 minutes or until the carrots are tender. Add the peas, return to a boil, and let the mixture cook for about 3 minutes or until the peas are thoroughly heated. Put the mixture into the blender and whiz for a few seconds until all the chunks are pureed. Add the butter and serve.

Calories: 83; Protein: 3.134 g; Carbohydrates: 15.66 g; Fat: 1.265 g; Thiamin: .134 mg; Riboflavin: .110 mg; Niacin: 1.262 mg; Sodium: 70.70 mg; Potassium: 312.8 mg; Iron: 1.176 mg; Calcium: 38.91 mg; Magnesium: 27.33 mg; Zinc: .745 mg.

Baby's Winter Squash

So simple to prepare, and so much more delicious than the store-bought kind.

1 acorn or butternut squash
2 teaspoons butter

Preheat the oven to 375 degrees. Cut the squash in halves and remove the seeds. Top each half with the butter. Bake the squash for 45 minutes or until soft when pierced with a fork. Puree baby's portion, and serve the rest to the family.

Calories: 57.5; Protein: .94 g; Carbohydrates: 10.75 g; Fat: 1.974 g; Thiamin: .074 mg; Riboflavin: .018 mg; Niacin: .996 mg; Sodium: 23.24 mg; Potassium: 291.6 mg; Iron: .619 mg; Calcium: 42.55 mg; Magnesium: 29.80 mg; Zinc: .135 mg.

MENUS AND RECIPES FOR THE WHOLE FAMILY

The secret to meal preparation is PLANNING. When you leave a menu decision to the last minute, your creativity flees and you put the easiest thing on the table—usually packaged junk food. Spend one hour each week planning a seven-day menu, including breakfast, lunch, and dinner. Make out your grocery list at the same time, then do the shopping. Prepare as much as you can in advance, before you put the groceries into the refrigerator, then work your meal plan.

Here is a typical seven-day meal planner, especially designed with foods to feed your brain. Recipes follow the menus. Some bonus recipes have been included for your pleasure.

DAY ONE:
Breakfast: Granola with Fruit and Nuts, with a sprinkle of organic milk, or rice or almond milk

Lunch: Chicken Stew (see recipe in Baby's Section), Salad with an olive oil and balsamic vinegar dressing

Dinner: Oven-Roasted Glazed Salmon

Braised Celery

Large Salad

Brown Rice in Vegetable Broth

Quick Meal Tip: While you are preparing dinner, make the split pea soup for dinner tomorrow night.

DAY TWO:

Breakfast: Breakfast Parfait

Lunch: Leftover Oven-Roasted Glazed Salmon on a salad

Dinner: Savory Split Pea Soup

Baked potato with a dab of butter

Cornbread

Quick Meal Tip: While the cornbread is baking or while you are tidying the kitchen after dinner, prepare Angelo's Heirloom Chicken and Olives. Leave it slightly undercooked so you can finish it up within 20 minutes tomorrow.

DAY THREE:

Breakfast: A Date with Oatmeal

Lunch: Leftover Savory Split Pea Soup and a salad

Dinner: Angelo's Heirloom Chicken and Olives

Stir-Fry Broccoli and Peppers

Salad with olive oil and balsamic vinegar dressing

Quick Meal Tip: Bake the Dill Casserole Bread, remove from the casserole dish, and let it cool. When thoroughly cool, wrap tightly, and set aside for dinner tomorrow night. While it is baking, prepare the vegetable soup. The soup can easily be prepared several days in advance so you may wish to prepare it on your day off to enjoy later in the week.

DAY FOUR:

Breakfast: Breakfast Crepes with fresh fruit or Cheesy Nutty Crepe Filling

Lunch: Left-over Angelo's Heirloom Chicken and Olives

Dinner: Heartwarming Vegetable Soup

Dill Casserole Bread

DAY FIVE:

Breakfast: Breakfast Burritos

Lunch: Leftover Heart-warming Vegetable Soup and Dill Casserole Bread

Dinner: Rice and Chicken Casserole

Baked Winter Squash

Quick Meal Tip: Prepare and bake the pie crusts for the quiche tomorrow night. The recipe makes two crusts. If you have time, go ahead and make two quiches. One can be refrigerated for two or three days for an even quicker meal then.

DAY SIX:

Breakfast: Bean Muffins (and granola, if you wish)

Lunch: Leftover Rice and Chicken Casserole

Leftover Stir-Fry Broccoli and Peppers in Olive Oil

Dinner: Spinach and Mushroom Quiche

Large Salad

Quick Meal Tip: Make the Vegetable Rice Pilaf for tomorrow's dinner while the quiche is baking.

DAY SEVEN:

Breakfast: Frosty Fruit Shake

Lunch: Leftover Spinach and Mushroom Quiche

Dinner: Florentine Sole

Vegetable Rice Pilaf

Other vegetable of choice

RECIPES

Granola with Fruit and Nuts

This crunchy, slightly sweet breakfast granola is wonderful as a topping for creamy yogurt, or enjoyed as breakfast or a midafternoon snack topped with organic milk, rice milk, or almond milk.

Store tightly sealed in a food storage bag in the refrigerator so the oils do not become rancid.

4 cups rolled oats

2 cups oat bran

1 cup raw sesame seeds
2 cups raw sunflower seeds
1 cup unsweetened coconut flakes
1 cup almonds, chopped
1 cup walnuts, chopped
1 cup raisins
1 cup dried apricots, diced
1 cup dried papaya or figs, diced
½ cup olive oil
¼ cup honey

In a large roasting pan, mix together the oats and oat bran, seeds, flakes, and nuts. Over a low flame, heat the oil and honey together until the mixture is very thin and easily poured. Drizzle the oil and honey mixture over the dry ingredients, mixing constantly, until all the pieces are coated evenly. In a 325-degree oven, bake the granola, stirring thoroughly every 15 minutes or so, until lightly browned. Takes about 45 to 60 minutes.

Meanwhile, prepare the fruit. When the granola is baked and cooled slightly, mix the fruit with the granola and stir thoroughly to mix. After the granola has cooled completely, store in food storage bags or plastic containers in the refrigerator.

Calories: 537.5; Protein: 15.86 g; Carbohydrates: 43.29 g; Fat: 34.24 g; Thiamin: .832 mg; Riboflavin: .222 mg; Niacin: 2.287 mg; Sodium: 6.104 mg; Potassium: 559.9 mg; Iron: 5.569 mg; Calcium: 184.1 mg; Magnesium: 190.8 mg; Zinc: 3.156 mg.

Breakfast Parfait

Arrange the elements of this breakfast treat in a brandy snifter or a tall wineglass. The balance of protein, carbohydrates, and fats will steady your blood sugar for hours, but what I enjoy most is the contrast of textures: the crunch of the granola, the smoothness of the yogurt, and the soft sweetness of the fruit. Use seasonal fruits for variety and added nutrition.

½ cup Granola with Fruit and Nuts
8 oz vanilla yogurt (no added sugars)
1 cup fresh fruit, cut into bite-sized pieces (can substitute unsweet-
*   ened frozen fruit)*

In parfait style, alternate layers of granola, yogurt, and fruit, starting
with granola at the bottom of the glass and ending with fresh fruit on the
top. If you are feeling especially festive, add a sprig of mint as garnish.

Calories: 449.3; Protein: 22.07 g; Carbohydrates: 53.85 g; Fat: 17.78 g; Thiamin: .573 mg; Riboflavin: .817 mg; Niacin: 2.255 mg; Sodium: 163.1 mg; Potassium: 1057 mg; Iron: 3.486 mg; Calcium: 369.1 mg; Magnesium: 161 mg; Zinc: 4.346 mg.

Raisin Rice Pudding

SERVES 6

Believe it or not, this is a terrific breakfast, but it can also serve as
dessert! Easily prepared the night before and served room temperature before school or work.

3 beaten organic eggs
1½ cups organic milk, scalded
⅓ cup date sugar
1 teaspoon vanilla
1 cup cooked brown rice
½ cup raisins
A sprinkle of nutmeg

Preheat the oven to 325 degrees. Combine the eggs, sugar, and vanilla
in a custard-baking dish. Stir until thoroughly blended. Stir in the milk,
then add the rice and raisins. Sprinkle the nutmeg on top.'

Place the custard dish into a pan with 1" of water in the bottom of the
pan. Insert both the pan and dish (carefully!) into the oven. Bake for 50 to
60 minutes or until a knife inserted in the middle comes out clean. Serve
either warm or cool.

Calories: 175.7; Protein: 5.561 g; Carbohydrates: 27.02 g; Fat: 5.108 g; Thiamin: .098 mg; Riboflavin: .255 mg; Niacin: .86 mg; Sodium: 64.36 mg; Potassium: 287.1 mg; Iron: .823 mg; Calcium: 97.44 mg; Magnesium: 31.99 mg; Zinc: .758 mg.

Bean Muffins

You read it correctly. These muffins are sure to keep your kids regular! But the real treat is in the taste—moist and rich, like a brownie. Just don't tell your kids the secret ingredient.

> *1½ cups cooked pinto beans*
> *1½ cups bean juice or water*
> *½ cup molasses or maple syrup*
> *1 egg*
> *1 teaspoon vanilla*
> *2 teaspoons non-aluminum baking powder*
> *1½ cups whole-wheat flour*
> *⅓ cup cocoa powder*
> *½ teaspoon cinnamon*
> *Pinch of nutmeg*

Blend the beans, juice, molasses (or maple syrup), egg, and vanilla in a blender or food processor. Add dry ingredients to the blender and mix just until smooth. Fill oiled muffin tins ⅔ full. Bake at 350 degrees for 25 minutes or until done.

Calories: 105.4; Protein: 3.792 g; Carbohydrates: 21.03 g; Fat: 1.025 g; Thiamin: .102 mg; Riboflavin: .089 mg; Niacin: 1.011 mg; Sodium: 95.57 mg; Potassium: 551.8 mg; Iron: 3.293 mg; Calcium: 133.5 mg; Magnesium: 26.43 mg; Zinc: .592 mg.

Frosty Fruit Shake

Make sure all the fruits you use in this drink have not been sugared. Feel free to experiment with the combination of fruits in this drink—mix and match different fruits to enjoy your favorite flavors.

2 cups frozen banana chunks
2 cups orange juice
1 cup fresh or frozen strawberries
1 tablespoon honey
1 tablespoon flaxseed oil
1 scoop rice or whey protein powder

Combine all the ingredients in a blender and whiz for a few seconds until thoroughly blended. Pour into tall glasses and serve immediately.

Calories: 407.4; Protein: 27.45 g; Carbohydrates: 56.25 g; Fat: 8.776 g; Thiamin: .015 mg; Riboflavin: .054 mg; Niacin: .222 mg; Sodium: 69.75 mg; Potassium: 439 mg; Iron: 2.193 mg; Calcium: 121 mg; Magnesium: 7.765 mg; Zinc: .107 mg.

Oatmeal and Fruit for a Cool Morning

The secret to good oatmeal is stir it only once—when you add the oatmeal to the boiling water. If you stir it during the cooking process, it will have the consistency of wallpaper paste, and no one likes that! When it is finished cooking, the individual oat flakes should still be visible.

2¼ cups water
1 cup extra-thick rolled oats (from your health food store, preferably)
A sprinkle of salt
1 cup fresh or frozen fruit
1 teaspoon butter

Bring the water to a boil in a saucepan and add the oatmeal and salt, stirring just once briefly. Turn the heat down to a low simmer and let it cook for about 7 minutes. It should still be a little soupy, but the flakes should be tender. Remove from heat and stir in the fruit and butter. The fruit will cool it slightly. Better served without milk, but if your children want milk, use almond milk or rice milk.

Calories: 274.7; Protein: 6.23 g; Carbohydrates: 54.55 g; Fat: 5.465 g; Thiamin: .203 mg; Riboflavin: .152 mg; Niacin: .636 mg; Sodium: 188.3 mg; Potassium: 607.2 mg; Iron: 2.179 mg; Calcium: 14.29 mg; Magnesium: 36.40 mg; Zinc: .257 mg.

A Date with Oatmeal

See above recipe for tips on preparing oatmeal that doesn't stick to the roof of your kid's mouth. And forget what oatmeal was like when we were kids! This tastes delicious and provides several hours of brain fuel for your schoolchildren. Date sugar is expensive, but a little bit lends a lovely sweetness and the flavor of dates to their cereal.

2¼ cups water
1 cup extra-thick rolled oats (from your health food store, preferably)
A sprinkle of salt
2 tablespoons date sugar
1 teaspoon butter

Bring the water to a boil in a saucepan and add the oatmeal and salt, stirring just once briefly. Turn the heat down to a low simmer and let it cook for about 7 minutes. It should still be a little soupy, but the flakes should be tender. Remove from heat and stir in the date sugar and butter. Better served without milk, but if your children want milk, use almond or rice milk.

Calories: 166.7; Protein: 5.020 g; Carbohydrates: 27 g; Fat: 4.90 g; Thiamin: .150 mg; Riboflavin: 0.35 mg; Niacin: .001 mg; Sodium: 187.1 mg; Potassium: 141.7 mg; Iron: 1.815 mg; Calcium: 7.235 mg; Magnesium: 2.297 mg; Zinc: .069 mg.

Breakfast Crepes with Blueberries

These delicate, lacy crepes are best served on a morning when you can take your time over breakfast. And do yourself a favor: Purchase a non-stick crepe pan. Turning the crepes will be a lot easier.

1½ cups organic milk
½ cup oat flour

¼ cup rice flour
2 eggs
2 tablespoons melted butter

In a bowl combine the milk, flour, eggs, and butter. Beat with a hand beater until well mixed. Let the mixture stand for about 15 minutes to blend. Heat the crepe pan over medium heat. Spoon about 2 tablespoons of the batter into the crepe pan, then lift and tilt the pan to distribute the batter evenly and thinly over the bottom of the pan. Brown on one side (about 2 minutes), then lift carefully with a spatula and turn it over to brown the other side (about 30 seconds). Remove the crepe by tipping the pan upside down over a plate. Spoon 2 tablespoons of the following filling or fruit-only jam in the center of the crepe and spread out to the edges. Roll the crepe quickly and gently with your fingers like a rug and serve immediately.

Cheesy Nutty Blueberry Filling

8 tablespoons low-fat ricotta cheese, whipped in a blender or food processor
4 tablespoons walnuts, very finely chopped
1 cup fresh blueberries

Mix all ingredients together. Spread over the hot crepe and roll up. Serve immediately.

Calories: 594.2; Protein: 28.79 g; Carbohydrates: 45.46 g; Fat: 34.61 g; Thiamin: .322 mg; Riboflavin: .740 mg; Niacin: 1.963 mg; Sodium: 450.2 mg; Potassium: 673.3 mg; Iron: 2.310 mg; Calcium: 559.1 mg; Magnesium: 101.3 mg; Zinc: 2.641 mg.

Breakfast Burritos

8 corn tortillas
6 eggs, well beaten
1 tablespoon butter

1 scallion, chopped very fine
4 tablespoons diced red bell pepper
1 cup refried beans, heated
1 diced tomato
1 cup shredded dark-green lettuce
¼ cup salsa of your choice
Cooking oil

Heat a skillet over medium heat and add 2 tablespoons of cooking oil. When it is hot, add one tortilla and cook just until heated through but still soft (about 2 minutes). Carefully turn it over and heat on the other side about 1 minute. Remove from the oil and place on an absorbent paper towel to absorb the excess oil. Keep frying the tortillas until they are all cooked, placing a paper towel between each one. Keep warm.

In another skillet, melt the butter and add the scallion and red pepper. Cook for a few minutes until the vegetables are slightly soft. Add the beaten eggs and stir constantly until they are done but still moist.

Spread each tortilla with the refried beans.

Place about two tablespoons of the egg mixture in each tortilla and fold in half. Top with the tomato and lettuce, and a spoonful of the salsa.

Calories: 333.6; Protein: 17.08 g; Carbohydrates: 39.54 g; Fat: 12.40 g; Thiamin: .175 mg; Riboflavin: .430 mg; Niacin: 1.701 mg; Sodium: 811.7 mg; Potassium: 621.3 mg; Iron: 3.517 mg; Calcium: 179.8 mg; Magnesium: 76.02 mg; Zinc: 2.329 mg.

Brain-Friendly Dinners and Lunches

You will recognize most of these entrées as traditional family fare: soups, casseroles, and the like. These are not low-fat versions of the dishes your mother prepared when you were a child. These contain natural fats for the Omega-3 and Omega-6 fatty acids and other fats that have been so deficient in our diets. They also use vegetables to provide minerals to fuel the enzymes and neurotransmitters of your brain.

Most of these meals can be prepared ahead of time and reheated for a quick meal-on-the-run. You may wish to spend a few hours in the kitchen on your day off preparing several meals at once. Having two or three meals waiting in the refrigerator takes a great deal of stress off your mind—and you'll only dirty the kitchen once.

Rich Brown Chicken Broth

Most commercially prepared chicken or beef canned broths are flavored with MSG. I do not purchase any prepared products with MSG, and I urge you to avoid these products as well. Broth without MSG is available in some supermarkets, but if you wish, you can make your own. Because the entire process takes several hours, I put the broth on to cook while I'm working around the house or preparing dinner. Can be frozen up to several weeks.

This preparation of chicken broth requires a couple more steps but is well worth the effort, because it produces a lovely, rich broth that works well in vegetable soups and in casseroles.

If you need beef broth, simply substitute the stewing hen with beef shanks. Browning the meat in the oil before adding the water intensifies the flavor.

1 medium-sized stewing hen
1 cup chopped onions
1 cup chopped celery
1 cup chopped carrots
8–10 cloves garlic, peeled and chopped
3–4 small bay leaves
1 tsp basil (or one large fresh stalk)
1 tsp thyme (or 3 tsp. fresh thyme)
Any other seasonings you enjoy
Olive oil

Heat the olive oil in a large soup pot (preferably a heavy pot) to a medium heat. Remove the giblets from the chicken and set aside for another use. Cut up the fryer into manageable pieces and brown on both sides in the oil. Make sure it doesn't burn, but sauté until the chicken is a nice brown color. As the pieces brown, remove them and continue to add chicken pieces until they have all been browned.

Add the vegetables to the same oil and stir until they are lightly browned. Add the chicken and the herbs. Add 3 quarts hot water to the soup pot, stir gently, and cover loosely, to let a little of the steam evaporate as it cooks.

Bring the broth to a boil, then turn the stove down so it barely simmers. Let it cook for 3 to 4 hours, or until it is the strength you desire. Remove foam as it floats to the top.

Remove the chicken pieces from the broth and use in another recipe. Strain the broth, pressing the juice out of the vegetables. Defat the broth. You now have about two quarts of chicken broth to use for soups, gravies, or casseroles.

Rice and Chicken Casserole

This is one of those comfort foods that your family will request often. It is so simple to prepare, but the flavors from the homemade chicken broth add a delightful nuance to an otherwise simple dish.

1 cup raw brown rice
2 cups water
2 tablespoons butter
2 tablespoons flour
3 cups homemade chicken broth, warmed
½ red pepper, diced
½ medium white onion, diced
1 celery stalk, diced
1 cup frozen baby peas
1–2 cups cooked chicken, diced
½ cup Italian-style bread crumbs (optional)

Bring two cups of water to a light simmer and add the brown rice, stirring once or twice. Add salt to taste. Do not cover. Turn down the heat so that it simmers slowly. Cook for about 40 minutes or until tender.

Meanwhile, in a saucepan, melt the butter. When it is bubbly, add the red pepper, onion, and celery and let them cook for a few minutes until they have started to wilt. Add the flour and stir until it browns slightly, then stir in the warmed chicken broth. Stir continuously with a wire whisk until the sauce thickens, then shut off the heat. Add the baby peas and let them defrost in the sauce while the rice is finished cooking.

When the rice is done, assemble the casserole: In a casserole dish, combine the rice, the chicken, and the sauce. Stir gently just until the rice is moistened and the chicken is evenly distributed. Sprinkle the bread crumbs on top. Place in a preheated oven at 350 degrees for 20 minutes or until thoroughly heated.

Serve immediately with a tossed green salad and a green vegetable.

Calories: 486.4; Protein: 32.35 g; Carbohydrates: 61.60 g; Fat: 13.66 g; Thiamin: .290 mg; Riboflavin: .231 mg; Niacin: 10.79 mg; Sodium: 385.4 mg; Potassium: 515.1 mg; Iron: 3.413 mg; Calcium: 105.6 mg; Magnesium: 39.13 mg; Zinc: 1.252 mg.

Savory Split Pea Soup

The first step to making this pea soup recipe is to prepare a flavorful broth. You won't believe the difference it makes in your finished soup.

The Broth

2 packages of ham hocks
4 quarts water
4 tablespoons olive oil or butter (or a combination of both)
2 carrots, peeled and chopped fine
1 large onion, chopped fine
2 celery stalks with leaves, chopped fine
3 bay leaves
1 teaspoon each of thyme, parsley, basil, or other herbs of your choice

In a large soup pot, melt the butter and add the vegetables. Let them brown slowly, stirring frequently. Add the water, ham hocks, and herbs. Cover and bring to a simmer, set the lid slightly ajar, and let it simmer for 3 to 4 hours. Remove the ham hocks and set on a plate to drain. Strain the broth into a large container, pressing the juice out of the vegetables into the broth.

The Soup

4 tablespoons butter
2 stalks of celery, chopped fine
1 medium onion, chopped fine
1 medium rutabaga, peeled and chopped fine
1 medium turnip, peeled and chopped fine
2 carrots, chopped fine
4 tablespoons flour
2 quarts of the ham stock, heated
1½ cups dried green peas

Melt the butter in a large soup pot, add the celery, onion, turnip, rutabaga, and carrots, and let them sauté until they are slightly browned, stirring frequently. Add the flour and blend into the vegetables. Let the mixture cook for a couple minutes or so, then add the ham broth and split peas. Cover, bring to a simmer, and let the soup cook for 45 minutes or until the peas are done. Using a potato masher, mash some of the soup for a creamier texture. Cut the meat off the ham bone, chop into fine pieces, and add to the soup.

If the soup is too thick, you may add more ham stock or water, to taste.

Can be frozen for a quick meal on the run.

Calories: 222.6; Protein: 12.42 g; Carbohydrates: 28.17 g; Fat: 7.978 g; Thiamin: .364 mg; Riboflavin: .209 mg; Niacin: 2.602 mg; Sodium: 484.1 mg; Potassium: 767.4 mg; Iron: 2.457 mg; Calcium: 92.95 mg; Magnesium: 53.73 mg; Zinc: 1.548 mg.

Heartwarming Vegetable Soup

This soup is warming to the soul and body on a cool evening. But don't deprive your baby of the wonderful flavors and nutrition! Skim off some of the vegetables and broth and puree for your baby to enjoy as well.

2 tablespoons butter
2 cups chopped leeks or white onion
6 cloves garlic, minced
1 28-ounce can of tomatoes (without added salt), diced
2 large carrots, peeled and chopped
2 celery stalks, chopped
1 turnip or rutabaga, peeled and chopped
¼ cup brown rice or barley
8 cups chicken broth (unsalted, no MSG) or homemade
¼ head shredded cabbage
¼ pound green beans cut into 1" pieces
1 tablespoon herbs (oregano, basil, parsley, or your favorite herbs)
2 tablespoons olive oil

In a large soup pot, heat the butter and cook the leeks or onion until wilted (about 5 to 10 minutes). Add the garlic; cook for 1 minute, then add the tomatoes, carrots, celery, turnips, rice, and the broth. Simmer for 30 minutes. Add the cabbage, beans, and herbs. Cook for about 10 minutes or until the cabbage and beans are tender.

Calories: 146.2; Protein: 5.158 g; Carbohydrates: 20.42 g; Fat: 6.063 g; Thiamin: .131 mg; Riboflavin: .110 mg; Niacin: 1.576 mg; Sodium: 165.2 mg; Potassium: 589.4 mg; Iron: 2.216 mg; Calcium: 111.1 mg; Magnesium: 436 mg; Zinc: .603 mg.

Angelo's Heirloom Chicken and Olives

This recipe comes from our family's traditional cookbook. You don't have to be Italian to enjoy the flavors. But this recipe is best served on brown rice to let the rich gravy moisten the rice.

4 boneless chicken breasts, skin and excess fat removed
4 tablespoons olive oil
2 tablespoons flour
2 medium onions, chopped
3–4 cloves garlic, minced
¾ cup chicken broth (unsalted, no MSG)
½ cup white wine
½ cup each of black and green olives, pitted and diced
½ teaspoon sage
½ teaspoon parsley
2 bay leaves

Heat the olive oil in a skillet, add the chicken breasts, and brown on both sides. Remove to a platter. Add the onions and garlic to the oil in the skillet and cook until they are wilted but not browned. Stir in the flour and let it cook for 2 minutes, then add the broth and wine, the olives, and the herbs. Lay the chicken breasts over the mixture, cover loosely to let a little steam escape, and let it simmer for 30 minutes or until the chicken breasts are tender.

If the broth has not thickened enough, raise the heat and reduce until it is the consistency of gravy.

Serve over Brown Rice in Vegetable Broth.

Calories: 637.4; Protein: 39.02 g; Carbohydrates: 36.88 g; Fat: 39.50 g; Thiamin: .249 mg; Riboflavin: .373 mg; Niacin: 15.29 mg; Sodium: 282.1 mg; Potassium: 568.7 mg; Iron: 2.875 mg; Calcium: 80.57 mg; Magnesium: 61.40 mg; Zinc: 3.441 mg.

Oven-Roasted Glazed Salmon

Even people who don't enjoy salmon think this salmon dish is wonderful. Enjoy it frequently! Remember that salmon is brain food.

2 pounds fresh salmon fillet
2 tablespoons fruit-only apricot (or peach) jam
1 tablespoon soy sauce
¼ teaspoon garlic powder

Using a pair of pliers, pluck the tiny bones out of the salmon filet. (You can feel the bones more easily if you press firmly with your fingers.) Wash the fillet carefully and dry with a paper towel.

Preheat your stovetop grill, and lay the salmon fillet skin-side down on the grill. When the skin is quite brown, turn it carefully with a spatula and brown it slightly on the other side. It takes about 5 minutes on each side. Be careful that the oils don't burst into flame as it cooks.

(If you do not have a grill, use the broiler instead, broiling on the skin side first until lightly browned, then turning it carefully to lightly brown the other side.)

Remove the fillet from the grill and place it into a lightly oiled baking dish. Mix the jam, soy sauce, and garlic powder together in a small bowl, then spread the mixture evenly over the salmon fillet.

Place into a preheated 375-degree oven, uncovered. Let it finish cooking in the oven (about 10 to 15 minutes). The fillet is done when the inside has lost the shiny, raw look and the color is consistent throughout. Do not overcook or the fillet will be dry.

Serve immediately.

Calories: 459.4; Protein: 39.46 g; Carbohydrates: 14.17 g; Fat: 26.14 g; Thiamin: .324 mg; Riboflavin: .381 mg; Niacin: 4.836 mg; Sodium: 258.3 mg; Potassium: 19.04 mg; Iron: .196 mg; Calcium: 2.89 mg; Magnesium: 2.155 mg; Zinc: .028 mg.

Spinach and Mushroom Quiche

OIL PASTRY SHELL:

I find this pie pastry a lot simpler to make, but I love the texture, too. The olive oil is good for the brain and the heart. I usually prebake the bottom layer before adding the filling, especially when making a dinner pie. The crust turns out crispy, tender, and a little flaky.

Don't be tempted to use a store-purchased pie shell. Yes, it is easier, but those pie crusts are loaded with artery-clogging fats and taste terrible. Make your own and you'll see the difference. For added flavor, sprinkle the bottom layer with toasted sesame seeds and press them into the shell before baking, or add ¼ cup of grated Parmesan cheese or minced herbs to the flour mixture.

> *2 ¼ cups flour*
> *¼ teaspoon salt (omit if using Parmesan cheese)*
> *½ cup olive oil*
> *⅓ cup cold organic milk*

In a mixing bowl, stir together the flour and salt. Pour the oil and milk into a bowl and add all at once to the flour. Stir with a fork until blended, then press into 2 balls.

Between waxed paper, roll out the balls with a rolling pin to the size of the pie pan. Fit into the pie pan, trim the edges, and crimp the sides of the pastry. Make sure there are no holes in the crust.

Bake the crust at 400 degrees for 10 minutes, then remove and fill with the following filling:

> FILLING:
> *1 ½ cups organic milk*
> *4 organic eggs, beaten*
> *2 cups raw, chopped spinach, washed and dried thoroughly*
> *¼ pound mushrooms, washed and sliced thin*
> *½ red bell pepper, seeded and sliced thin*
> *1 scallion, minced*
> *2 tablespoons butter*
> *1 cup shredded light Jarlsberg or Swiss cheese*
> *¼ teaspoon ground black pepper*

Prepare the pastry crust.

Preheat oven to 400 degrees. Heat the olive oil in a skillet and add the mushrooms, red pepper, and scallions. Let them cook for a few minutes until barely soft. In a large bowl, stir the mushroom mixture, spinach, eggs, milk, cheese, and pepper until well blended.

Pour the vegetable mixture into the quiche shell, spreading evenly.

Bake the quiche for 55 to 60 minutes until the filling and the crust are golden and a knife inserted in the center comes out clean.

Cool quiche slightly on wire rack. Serve warm. Can be frozen for a few days.

Calories: 550.5; Protein: 15.82 g; Carbohydrates: 44.11 g; Fat: 35.08 g; Thiamin: .372 mg; Riboflavin: .435 mg; Niacin: 3.616 mg; Sodium: 169.5 mg; Potassium: 367.1 mg; Iron: 3.959 mg; Calcium: 388.7 mg; Magnesium: 75.06 mg; Zinc: 1.763 mg.

Salmon Salad

The flavors of these vegetables in this salad blend beautifully with the richness of the salmon. Feel free to experiment: Use halibut instead of salmon or even grilled chicken breast. They are all satisfying.

1 clove garlic, crushed
1 package prepared salad mix (not iceberg lettuce)
Olive oil
Balsamic vinegar
6–8 ounces Oven-Roasted Glazed Salmon
  (or seafood/chicken of your choice)

Rub the bottom and sides of the serving bowls with the crushed garlic and either discard it or put it with the greens. Place the salad mix in a large mixing bowl and lavishly sprinkle olive oil over the greens. Mix thoroughly to coat each piece with the oil, but don't drench it. Sprinkle just enough vinegar over the greens to lightly flavor them. Divide the salad between two serving bowls. Divide the salmon into 2 pieces and set gently on top of the salad. Serve immediately.

Calories: 317; Protein: 26.98 g; Carbohydrates: 4.031 g; Fat: 21.01 g; Thiamin: .50 mg; Riboflavin: .266 mg; Niacin: 9.707 mg; Sodium: 79.16 mg; Potassium: 770.9 mg; Iron: 1.806 mg; Calcium: 43.13 mg; Magnesium: 42.75 mg; Zinc: .795 mg.

Florentine Sole

1 bundle of fresh spinach, washed and chopped
1 cup yogurt
1½ tablespoons flour
¼ cup raw green onions
½ teaspoon lemon juice
¼ teaspoon salt
1 lb. sole fillets (or another mild-flavored white fish)
1 tablespoon butter

Cook spinach and drain well. Blend the yogurt with the flour, onions, lemon juice, and salt. Combine half with the spinach and spread over bottom of a 10" × 15" baking dish. Arrange the sole over the spinach, overlapping the pieces. Dot with butter. Spread remaining yogurt mixture evenly over the sole. Sprinkle with paprika, if desired. Bake at 375 degrees for 25 minutes.

Calories: 205.1; Protein: 31.50 g; Carbohydrates: 7.492 g; Fat: 4.734 g; Thiamin: .139 mg; Riboflavin: .334 mg; Niacin: 2.801 mg; Sodium: 327.5 mg; Potassium: 677.9 mg; Iron: .867 mg; Calcium: 170 mg; Magnesium: 99.01 mg; Zinc: 1.328 mg.

SIDE DISHES:

Brown Rice in Vegetable Broth

2 cups vegetable broth (without MSG or added sodium)
1 cup brown rice

Bring the vegetable broth to a light simmer and add the brown rice. Stir once, lower the heat, and cover. Simmer for 45 minutes or just until the rice is done.

Calories: 108; Protein: 2.52 g; Carbohydrates: 22.40 g; Fat: .880 g; Thiamin: .094 mg; Riboflavin: .025 mg; Niacin: 1.490 mg; Sodium: 4.5 mg; Potassium: 41.50 mg; Iron: .410 mg; Calcium: 10 mg; Magnesium: 41.50 mg; Zinc: .615 mg.

Vegetable Rice Pilaf

2 tablespoons butter or olive oil
1 carrot, peeled and diced very small
1 celery stalk, strings removed and diced very small
3 or more cloves of garlic, minced
¼ onion, diced very small
2 cups chicken stock (without monosodium glutamate), or
  homemade, heated to a simmer
1 cup brown rice
¼ cup Parmesan cheese, freshly grated

In a medium saucepan, heat the butter and olive oil. Add the vegetables and let them slowly cook until slightly browned. Add the hot chicken stock and the rice. Stir once or twice, then cover and let rice simmer until done (about 40 minutes).

Just before serving, grate the Parmesan cheese over the rice and stir thoroughly. Serve immediately.

Calories: 218.7; Protein: 6.878 g; Carbohydrates: 25.14 g; Fat: 10.72 g; Thiamin: .114 mg; Riboflavin: .134 mg; Niacin: 3.628 mg; Sodium: 259.5 mg; Potassium: 438.6 mg; Iron: 1.178 mg; Calcium: 142.9 mg; Magnesium: 45.01 mg; Zinc: .898 mg.

Stir-Fry Broccoli and Peppers

Even George Bush could enjoy this broccoli dish! It is colorful, flavorful, and easily prepared.

1 bunch of broccoli, trimmed, cut into bite-sized pieces
4–6 garlic cloves, diced
1 red pepper, cored, seeded, and sliced into ½-inch slices
¼ white onion, sliced
2 tablespoons olive oil
1 tablespoon soy sauce

Heat the olive oil in a wok or skillet. Add the garlic and let it cook for a few minutes (don't let it get brown), and add the rest of the vegetables. Stir them constantly while cooking about 4 to 5 minutes or until the broccoli is still crunchy but done. Add the soy sauce, stir to coat the vegetables thoroughly, and serve.

Calories: 81.89; Protein: 1.344 g; Carbohydrates: 4.592 g; Fat: 6.859 g; Thiamin: .049 mg; Riboflavin: .034 mg; Niacin: .370 mg; Sodium: 117.3 mg; Potassium: 137.9 mg; Iron: .377 mg; Calcium: 17.98 mg; Magnesium: 8.974 mg; Zinc: .166 mg.

Braised Celery

Celery is a wonderful vegetable, with natural potassium and sodium to increase energy. I especially enjoy this preparation of celery as a side dish. Your children will as well.

> *1 full "head" of celery, washed and cut into 1-inch pieces (including*
> *some leaves)*
> *2 tablespoon butter or olive oil*
> *1 cup chicken broth (no MSG)*

Sauté the celery pieces in the butter for a few minutes until they are starting to brown lightly. Add the chicken broth, cover, and let it simmer slowly for about 10 to 15 minutes or until the celery is tender. Remove the cover and reduce the liquid by half.

Calories: 85.40; Protein: 1.410 g; Carbohydrates: 4.090 g; Fat: 7.555 g; Thiamin: .045 mg; Riboflavin: .060 mg; Niacin: .1423 mg; Sodium: 110.1 mg; Potassium: 325 mg; Iron: .504 mg; Calcium: 40.01 mg; Magnesium: 11 mg; Zinc: .135 mg.

The Basic Salad

Does it seem silly to include a recipe for a basic salad? I've discovered that many people don't realize that a salad is more than iceberg lettuce smothered in Thousand Island dressing! A version of this salad recipe was included in my book *Your Fat Is Not Your Fault* and is so important as a source of brain-friendly minerals that I needed to include it here. Make this salad a part of your evening meal several times per week.

> *1 clove garlic*
> *1½ cups broccoli*
> *¾ cup scallions*
> *½-bunches salad greens or one package prepared salad mix*
>   *(not iceberg lettuce!)*
> *1 whole zucchini*
> *1 stalk celery*
> *2 carrots*
> *½ jicama*
> *1 cucumber*
> *1 whole beet, raw*
> *¾ cup cauliflower*
> *2 tablespoons extra-virgin olive oil*
> *Juice of one lemon or 2 tablespoons balsamic vinegar*

It is a good idea to prepare all salad ingredients when you bring them home from the grocery store. Wash the greens carefully, dry them, and seal them in storage bags in the refrigerator. Wash and peel the other vegetables, then seal them in food storage bags and store in the refrigerator until needed. They will keep well for several days.

At mealtime, mash the garlic clove with a fork and rub the inside of the salad bowl with it. Either leave it in the bowl or discard it, as you wish. Prepare all salad ingredients and place them in the salad bowl. Toss gently.

If you are planning to enjoy the entire salad immediately, add the dressing to the whole salad. If you plan to save part of it for another meal, remove that portion and store in the refrigerator in a tightly covered container without dressing.

Lightly sprinkle the salad with the olive oil and toss gently but thoroughly to coat all the pieces with the oil. Rub the lemon firmly around on the table to break up the tissues inside, then cut it in half. Squeeze the juice over the salad with as much juice as you like. Toss again briefly to distribute the lemon juice, and serve immediately.

If you are using balsamic vinegar instead of the lemon, sprinkle the vinegar over the salad and serve immediately.

You may add any other herbs to the oil that you wish to add more flavor or variety. You may also use other vegetables, but be sure to include at least eight different types of brightly colored vegetables. Learn to be creative with your salad and it will become one of your favorite parts of the meal.

Calories: 156.6; Protein: 5.661 g; Carbohydrates: 25.94 g; Fat: 5.173 g; Thiamin: .209 mg; Riboflavin: .198 mg; Niacin: 2.140 mg; Sodium: 109.2 mg; Potassium: 923.7 mg; Iron: 2.479 mg; Calcium: 85.94 mg; Magnesium: 57.68 mg; Zinc: .957 mg.

Mom's Pineapple Coleslaw

My mother used to make this coleslaw every summer from huge heads of cabbage and young carrots, harvested daily from her garden. I loved to push the dirt away from the tops of the carrots to see if they were ready to pluck from the ground. I washed the dirt off under the faucet outside the house and munched their juicy sweetness. This salad brings back those memories.

¼ head cabbage, shredded and chopped into tiny pieces
1 large carrot, peeled and grated
⅛ head red cabbage, shredded and chopped into tiny pieces
1 can unsweetened crushed pineapple, well drained (reserve the juice)
½ cup mayonnaise

Combine the cabbage and carrots in a large mixing bowl. Add the crushed pineapple. Mix together the mayonnaise and just enough of the reserved pineapple juice to make a fairly thin dressing. Pour over the salad and mix thoroughly.

Calories: 138.7; Protein: 1.341 g; Carbohydrates: 9.123 g; Fat: 12.21 g; Thiamin: .093 mg; Riboflavin: .048 mg; Niacin: .613 mg; Sodium: 92.60 mg; Potassium: 284 mg; Iron: .516 mg; Calcium: 40.46 mg; Magnesium: 19.98 mg; Zinc: .204 mg.

Dill Casserole

You'll never eat Wonder Bread again. As it bakes, the aroma will draw the neighborhood kids to your back door. Not only is this bread incredibly soft and delicious, but the cottage cheese gives it a higher protein content than ordinary bread.

1 envelope yeast
¼ cup lukewarm water
1 cup lukewarm organic, low-fat, low-sodium cottage cheese
2 tablespoons date sugar or honey
1 tablespoon chopped onion
1 tablespoon butter
2 tablespoons dill seed
¼ teaspoon baking soda
1 organic egg
2¼ cups flour
Butter
Salt

Melt the yeast in the lukewarm water in a large mixing bowl and let it set until it is foamy. Meanwhile, soften the onion in the butter over a low flame. Stir in the cottage cheese, sugar, onion, dill seed, salt, baking soda, and egg. Stir in the flour gently to form a stiff dough. Set the bowl in a pan of warm water, cover with a towel, and let the dough rise until it has doubled in size (60 minutes or so). Stir down, then spoon into a greased casserole dish. Let rise again until double (30 to 40 minutes). Bake at 350 degrees for about 45 minutes until golden brown. Brush with soft butter and sprinkle with a little salt.

Carefully remove it from the casserole dish with a flexible knife and serve immediately, while still hot.

Calories: 195; Protein: 8.367 g; Carbohydrates: 33.38 g; Fat: 2.885 g; Thiamin: .183 mg; Riboflavin: .208 mg; Niacin: 1.774 mg; Sodium: 83.12 mg; Potassium: 79.18 mg; Iron: 1.846 mg; Calcium: 48.8 mg; Magnesium: 13.61 mg; Zinc: .633 mg.

Brain-Friendly Desserts

These desserts were not included in the menus above because you may enjoy them whenever you wish. These after-meal treats are so delicious that your family will never suspect they are healthy. Take a tip from a mom: Unless your children have become accustomed to using tofu, don't tell them that tofu provides the base in the pudding. They won't know the difference, but you'll feel comfortable giving them such a healthy dessert.

Deep, Dark, Delicious Chocolate Pudding

Sandra Woodruff generously donated this recipe from her book, *Secret of Cooking for Long Life*. It is so wonderful, I couldn't resist including it here for your pleasure.

2 packages (12.3 ounces each) light, silken extra-firm tofu
¾ cup plus 2 tablespoons dark brown sugar
⅓ cup plus 1 tablespoon Dutch processed cocoa powder
2 teaspoons vanilla extract
2 tablespoons coffee liqueur

Place all the ingredients in a food processor, and, scraping down the sides as needed, process for about 3 minutes or until the mixture is smooth and creamy.

Divide the pudding among five 8-ounce serving dishes or wineglasses, cover with plastic wrap, and chill for at least 2 hours before serving.

Calories: 249; Protein: 14.30 g; Carbohydrates: 43.14 g; Fat: 2.845 g; Thiamin: .069 mg; Riboflavin: .064 mg; Niacin: .467 mg; Sodium: 191.4 mg; Potassium: 585 mg; Iron: 4.571 mg; Calcium: 122.4 mg; Magnesium: 66.38 mg; Zinc: .999 mg.

Jungle Bars

These delicious snack bars are chock full of minerals and fiber. Great for a quick breakfast on the run, or for dessert.

2 ripe medium bananas, peeled
½ pound dried figs
½ pound dried apricots
½ pound pitted dates
½ pound raisins
2 cups granola
½ pound almonds, toasted, chopped
1 cup unsweetened flaked coconut

Process the bananas, figs, apricots, dates, raisins, and granola in a food processor. Stir in almonds. Press mixture into a buttered 13" × 9" inch baking dish. Sprinkle with coconut. Cover and refrigerate 24 hours to allow the flavors to blend. Cut into squares.

Calories: 581.9; Protein: 14.45 g; Carbohydrates: 87.95 g; Fat: 24.38 g; Thiamin: .322 mg; Riboflavin: .624 mg; Niacin: 2.119 mg; Sodium: 23.45 mg; Potassium: 1161 mg; Iron: 4.844 mg; Calcium: 201.8 mg; Magnesium: 201.7 mg; Zinc: 2.701 mg.

Almond Butter Cookies

These cookies are some of my absolute favorites. Make a double batch, because they'll go fast, especially with kids in the house. Notice that the sugar is reduced. They won't notice the difference.

¼ cup brown sugar
¼ cup granulated sugar
½ cup butter, unsalted
1 organic egg
1 cup almond butter

½ teaspoon vanilla
½ teaspoon baking soda
1½ cups oat flour

Beat the sugars and the butter together until fluffy. Beat in the egg, almond butter, vanilla, and soda, then gradually add the flour and mix until thoroughly blended.

Roll the dough into walnut-sized balls, place on a greased baking sheet, and press them flat with a floured fork, crisscross fashion.

Bake in a 375-degree oven for about 12 to 15 minutes, or until a little brown around the edges.

Calories: 141.7; Protein: 3.573 g; Carbohydrates: 10.46 g; Fat: 10.31 g; Thiamin: .043 mg; Riboflavin: .124 mg; Niacin: .272 mg; Sodium: 33.54 mg; Potassium: 30.53 mg; Iron: .713 mg; Calcium: 27.95 mg; Magnesium: 1.005 mg; Zinc: .031 mg.

Cream Puffs with Fresh Fruit Filling

These cream puffs are incredibly delicious and low in sugar. Your kids will beg you to make them frequently. Use a variety of seasonal berries when possible. In the winter when fresh fruit is not available, you may use frozen fruit without added sugar. Defrost them just until they are still firm, but not so cold they freeze your teeth!

½ cup butter
1 cup water
1 cup all-purpose flour
4 organic eggs

In a medium saucepan, combine the butter and water. Bring to a boil. Add the flour and stir vigorously, letting it cook until the mixture forms a ball that doesn't separate. Remove from the heat and allow to cool for 10 minutes. Add the eggs, one at a time, beating vigorously with a wooden spoon after each addition until smooth.

Drop batter by heaping tablespoons onto a greased baking sheet and bake in a 400-degree oven for 30 to 35 minutes or until lightly browned. Turn oven off. Remove the pan from the oven and, with a sharp knife, cut a slit in each puff sideways about 1 to 2 inches long. Place back in the oven for about 5 minutes to let the center dry out slightly.

Place on a wire rack and allow them to cool completely.

FILLING:
2 cups whipping cream (ice cold)
2 teaspoons sugar
1 teaspoon vanilla (not vanillin)
1 cup (or more) fresh fruit

Make sure your mixing bowl is ice cold and very clean. Beat the whipping cream with an electric mixer until it stands in soft peaks. Add the sugar and vanilla and whip briefly to blend and stiffen the cream slightly. Fold the fruit into the whipped cream.

Carefully open each cream puff (you will have to slice it a little) and stuff with the whipped cream mixture.

For a decorative touch, pile the filled cream puffs on a plate in a pyramid, then lightly sprinkle *a little* powdered sugar over top (just for garnish—no more).

Serve immediately.

Calories: 407.7; Protein: 6.208 g; Carbohydrates: 16.47 g; Fat: 35.72 g; Thiamin: .102 mg; Riboflavin: .241 mg; Niacin: .768 mg; Sodium: 94.46 mg; Potassium: 130.7 mg; Iron: 1.094 mg; Calcium: 61.13 mg; Magnesium: 12.56 mg; Zinc: .566 mg.

School Lunches

I am preparing this section separately because the problem of school lunches for your children is very real. Kids can be very picky. Not only do lunches have to taste and look good; they have to be similar (or identical) to what their friends are eating or they feel that their social life is in jeopardy.

Following are some brown-bag lunch ideas that I think your children will enjoy, but I encourage you to let your children help design healthy lunch menus. Mutual consent encourages compliance! Serve fresh fruit with a homemade low-sugar cookie for dessert each day.

BROWN BAG LUNCH #1: Deviled eggs, carrot sticks, Bean Muffins, potato chips (no MSG)

BROWN BAG LUNCH #2: Chili on tortilla chips (prepare your favorite chili recipe, preheat, and send to school in a thermos). Grate some cheese and place in a separate baggie. Include a paper plate in his/her lunch box. Your child will spread the tortilla chips on the plate, spoon the chili over the chips, and top with grated cheese. Yum!

BROWN BAG LUNCH #3: Heartwarming Vegetable Soup (or other homemade soup) with tortilla chips on the side

BROWN BAG LUNCH #4: Healthy nut mix from your local health food store, carrot and celery sticks with ranch dressing (check for MSG!)

BROWN BAG LUNCH #5: Corn chips with organic bean dip

BROWN BAG LUNCH #6: Nancy's or Alta Dena (or other low-sugar) yogurt

BROWN BAG LUNCH #7: Cottage cheese with fruit

BROWN BAG LUNCH #8: Veggies dipped into favorite dressing, with ham or turkey cubes

BROWN BAG LUNCH #9: Chili in a pot (your favorite chili in a thermos) with tortilla chips

BROWN BAG LUNCH #10: Beans and franks (purchase nitrite-free franks from your health food store, cut into chunks, stir into low-sugar baked beans, and send to school in a thermos, with catsup on the side)

Notes

Introduction
  1. Michael Jacobson, "Liquid Candy," *Nutrition Action Newsletter,* 25, no. 9, 8.
  2. L. Kathleen Mahan and Marian Arlin, *Food, Nutrition & Diet Therapy* (Philadelphia: W. B. Saunders Company, 1992), 268.
  3. Candace B. Pert, Ph.D., *Molecules of Emotion* (NY: Scribner, 1997), 28.

Chapter One
  1. Joseph F. Borzelleca, "Foods of the Future: What Will We Be Eating in the Next Century?" in *Practical Handbook of Nutrition in Clinical Practice* (CRC Press, 1994). As cited in *Clinical Pearls 1995,* 216.
  2. General Mills Public Relations Department, "The Story of Betty Crocker."
  3. Barbara Griggs, *The Food Factor* (NY: Viking, 1986): 89.
  4. Joseph D. Beasley, M.D., and Jerry J. Swift, M.A., *The Kellogg Report: The Impact of Nutrition, Environment & Lifestyle on the Health of Americans* (Annandale-on-Hudson, NY: The Institute of Health Policy and Practice, 1989), 131.
  5. Bonnie Liebman, "Sugar: The Sweetening of the American Diet," *Nutrition Action Healthletter* 25, no. 9, 5.
  6. Beasley, 1989, 144.
  7. Griggs, 1986, 87.
  8. Griggs, 1986, 115.
  9. Griggs, 1889, 221–22.
  10. Beasley, 1989, 128–29.
  11. Liebman, 8.
  12. "Major depression: Assessing the role of new antidepressants," *American Family Physician,* January 1997.
  13. "Self-reported frequent mental distress among adults—United States, 1993–1996 (from the Centers for Disease Control and Pre-

vention), *The Journal of the American Medical Association* 279, no. 22 (June 10, 1998): 1772(2).

14. "Obsessive-compulsive disorder," *Cosmopolitan, MDX Health Digest,* December 1995.

15. Anne Brown, "Mood disorders in children and adolescents," *NARSAD Research Newsletter,* winter 1996.

16. Barbara Strauch, "Use of antidepression medicine for young patients has soared; to bolster market, makers seek F.D.A. sanction," *New York Times* 196, no. 50 (August 10, 1997): 880, 1.

17. Martha Glazer, "Annual Rx Survey," *Drug Topics,* April 8, 1996, 97.

18. Barbara Strauch, "Prozac-type drugs being given to kids," *Seattle Times,* August 10, 1997.

19. Skye Weintraub, N.D., *Natural Treatments for ADD and Hyperactivity* (Pleasant Grove, UT: Woodland Publishing, 1997): 13–14.

20. L. S. Goldman, M. Genel, R. J. Bezman, et al., "Diagnosis and treatment of attention-deficit/hyperactivity disorder in children and adolescents," *The Journal of the American Medical Association* 279, no. 14 (April 8, 1998): 1100–7.

21. Marcia Byalick, "More pupils taking prescribed drugs to relieve distress," *The New York Times on the Web,* May 3, 1998.

22. Mike Huckabee, "Youth violence: By the numbers," *Register-Guard,* November 23, 1998.

23. Linda Dusenbury, Mathea Falco, Antonia Lake, et al., "Nine critical elements of promising violence prevention programs," *Journal of School Health,* December 1997.

24. Centers for Disease Control, "Rates of homicide, suicide, and firearm-related death among children—26 industrialized countries," *The Journal of the American Medical Association* 277, no. 9 (March 5, 1997): 704(2).

25. "Suicide among black youths—United States, 1980–1995." From the Centers for Disease Control, *JAMA, The Journal of the American Medical Association* 279, no. 18 (May 13, 1998): 1431(1).

26. Ronald W. Manderscheid, Ph.D., and Mary Anne Sonnenschein,

M.A., *Mental Health, United States, 1992* (Rockville, MD), U.S. Department of Health and Human Services.

27. "Suicide among children, adolescents, and young adults—United States, 1980–1992," *The Journal of the American Medical Association* 275, no. 6 (August 9, 1995): 451(2).

28. Laura Kann, Steven Kinchen, Barbara Williams, et al., "Youth Risk Behavior Surveillance—United States, 1997," August 14, 1998/ 47(SS-3): 1–89. *Morbidity & Mortality Weekly Report CDC Surveillance Summary,* August 14, 1998; 47(3): 1–89.

29. "Big increase in booze for young," *The Dominion,* November 12, 1998.

30. Janet Greenblatt, "Year-End Preliminary Estimates from the 1996 Drug Abuse Warning Network" (Rockville, MD: SAMHSA, Office of Applied Studies), November 1997.

31. J. B. Hewitt, "Violence in the workplace," *Annual Review of Nursing Research,* 1997; 15:81–99. Also: T. Hales, P. J. Seligman, S. C. Newman, et al., "Occupational injuries due to violence," *Journal of Occupational Medicine* 30, no. 6 (June 30, 1988): 483–87.

32. L. J. Warshaw and J. Messite, "Workplace violence: preventive and interventive strategies," *Journal of Occupational and Environmental Medicine* 38, no. 10 (October 1996): 993–1006.

33. R. Bachman, "Epidemiology of violence and theft in the workplace," *Occupational Medicine* 11, no. 2 1996 April–June; 11(2): 237–41.

34. John J. Ratey, M.D., and Catherine Johnson, Ph.D, *Shadow Syndromes* (NY: Bantam Books, 1998).

35. H. G. Westenberg, "The nature of social anxiety disorder," *Journal of Clinical Psychiatry* 59 (1998) Suppl. 17:20–26.

36. Barent W. Walsh, and Paul M. Rosen, *Self-Mutilation: Theory, Research, & Treatment* (NY: Guilford Press), 11–12.

37. Walsh, 1988, 14.

38. E. Katherine Battle and Kelly D. Brownell, "Confronting a rising tide of eating disorders and obesity: Treatment vs. prevention and policy," *Addictive Behaviors* 21, no. 6 (1996), 755–765. Also: John P.

Foreyt, S. Walker, Carlos Poston, II, and G. Ken Goodrick, "Future directions in obesity and eating disorders," *Addictive Behaviors* 21, no. 6 (1996), 767–78, 1996.

39. Beasley, 1989, 444.

40. *Statistical Abstract of the United States, 1995,* U.S. Department of Commerce, Table 271.

41. David Hoff, "Panel assails assessment calculations," *Teacher Magazine on the Web,* September 30, 1998.

42. Mark Walsh, "Colo. officials couldn't be happier with low scores," *Teacher Magazine on the Web,* November 26, 1997.

43. Debra Viadero, "U.S. seniors near bottom in world test," *Teacher Magazine,* March 4, 1998.

44. Jane M. Healy, Ph.D., *Endangered Minds: Why Children Don't Think and What We Can Do About It* (NY: Touchstone, 1990), 28.

Chapter Two

1. William H. Philpott, M.D., and Dwight K. Kalita, Ph.D, *Brain Allergies: The Psychonutrient Connection* (New Canaan, CT: Keats Publishing Inc., 1980), Foreword.

2. Ruth L. Pike and Myrtle L. Brown, *Nutrition: An Integrated Approach* (NY: Macmillan Publishing Company, 1984), 662.

3. Candace B. Pert, Ph.D, *Molecules of Emotion* (NY: Scribner, 1997), 224.

4. Gerald M. Edelman, *Bright Air, Brilliant Fire: On the Matter of the Mind* (NY: Basic Books, 1992), 17.

5. "The critical role of nutrition on brain development," *Current Problems in Pediatrics* (May/June 1992): 228–29. As cited in *Clinical Pearls 1992,* 352.

6. W. Allan Walker, M.D., and John B. Watkins, M.D., *Nutrition in Pediatrics: Basic Science and Clinical Application* (Boston/Toronto: Little, Brown and Company, 1985), 235. According to one researcher, the "critical window" of opportunity for optimal brain development occurs in the first few weeks of life (postnatal life), and if malnutrition or undernutrition occurs then, the result is lifelong de-

ficiency in mental capacity. A letter in *The Lancet* stated the following: ". . . that early malnutrition led to poor mental development . . . Whether this finding is due to changes in the central
nervous system, in child activity, or in maternal responsiveness is,
however, unclear. The 'programming' hypothesis, in which a stimulus or insult operating at a critical period of development (but
harmless at any other time) leads to long-term effects on structure
and function of an organism, was invoked to account for such effects: Dr. Alan Lucas . . . suggested that this critical 'window' in
time occurred (though not exclusively) in the first few weeks of life.
His data from an ongoing long-term prospective study on preterm
infants randomly assigned to various diets (breast milk, standard
term formula, or preterm formula) show that a 1-month postnatal
dietary manipulation has serious consequences for motor and mental development . . . ages 9 and 18 months and 5 and 7–8 years . . ."
Pia Pini, "We are what we eat," *The Lancet* 337 (June 29, 1991):
1596–97. Also: A. Lucas, R. Morley, and T. J. Cole, "Randomised
trial of early diet in preterm babies and later intelligence quotient,"
BMJ 317, no. 7171 (November 28, 1998): 1481–87. P. Willatts, J. S.
Forsyth, M. K. DiModugno, et al., "Effect of long-chain polyunsaturated fatty acids in infant formula on problem solving at 10
months of age," *The Lancet* 352, no. 9129 (August 29, 1998): 688–91.
7. Sheila M. Innis, P.h.D., "Essential fatty acids in growth and development," *Progress in Lipid Research* 30, no. 1 (1991): 58.
8. Innis, 1991, 69.
9. Innis, 1991, 55.
10. Gerard J. Tortora and Sandra Reynolds Grabowski, *Principles of
Anatomy and Physiology* (NY: Harper College, 1993), 349–52.
11. Innis, 1991, 30–103.
12. Alan Parkinson, J., et al., "Elevated concentrations of plasma
Omega-3 polyunsaturated fatty acids among Alaskan Eskimos,"
American Journal of Clinical Nutrition 59 (1994): 384–8. As cited in
Clinical Pearls 1994, 249.
13. Weston Price, D.D.S., *Nutrition and Physical Degeneration* (Price-

Pottenger Nutrition Foundation, 1945; reprint, New Canaan, CT: Keats Publishing, Inc., 1989), 261.

14. Price, 1989, 6–14.

15. Price, 1989, 275.

16. Nancy R. Raper, M.S., R.D., et al., "Omega-3 fatty acid content of the U.S. food supply," *Journal of the American College of Nutrition* 11, no. 3 (1992): 304–308.

17. Artemis P. Simopoulous et al., "Omega-3 fatty acids in health and disease and in growth and development," *American Journal of Clinical Nutrition* 191, no. 54: 438–63. As cited in *Clinical Pearls 1991,* 379. Also: Pierre Guesry, M.D., "The role of nutrition in brain development," *Preventive Medicine* 27 (1998): 189–194. As cited in *Clinical Pearls 1998,* 117. In his book, Dr. Siguel wrote, "Some studies have shown that eating the Omega-3 fats in vegetable oils will produce effects similar to those of fish oils when eaten for at least 15–20 weeks. For immediate effects (within a few days), fish oils act far more quickly than vegetable oils because they almost immediately increase EPA . . . Eating linolenic acid . . . from vegetable oils takes many weeks before it is converted to EPA . . . However, there are great individual variations and more research is needed to understand the clinical differences between the w3s (Omega-3s) in vegetable and fish oils." (Edward N. Siguel, M.D., Ph.D., *Essential Fatty Acids in Health and Disease* [Brookline, MA: Nutrek Press, 1994], 229).

18. D. F. Hebeisen, F. Hoeflin, H. P. Reusch, et al., "Increased concentrations of omega-3 fatty acids in milk and platelet rich plasma of grass-fed cows," *International Journal of Vitamin Nutrition Research* 63, no. 3, 229–233.

19. Michael A. Schmidt, N. D. Telephone interview by Carol Simontacchi, Vancouver, Washington, March 10, 1999.

20. Charlotte Gallagher-Allred, "Managing common adolescent nutritional problems," *Family Practice Recertification,* July 1995; 17(7):21–34. As cited in *Clinical Pearls 1995,* 222. Also: "U.S. scores 64% in new healthy eating index," *Nutrition Week* 25, no. 28 (July

28, 1995): 2. As cited in *Clinical Pearls 1995,* 225. F. Ferandez-Banares, et al., "Suboptimal Vitamin Status Widespread," *International Journal of Vitamin and Nutrition Research* 63 (1994): 68–74. As cited in *Clinical Pearls 1994,* p. 254.

Chapter Three

1. Patricia Stuart-Macadam and Katherine A. Dettwyler, *Breastfeeding: Biocultural Perspectives* (NY: Aldine DeGruyter, 1995), 149.

2. Stuart-Macadam, 1995, 168.

3. *Journal of the American Medical Association* 95, no. 22 (November 22, 1930): 1699.

4. *Journal of the American Medical Association* 95, no. 19 (November 8, 1930): 1505.
Journal of the American Medical Association 96, no. 24 (June 13, 1931): 2037.

5. *Journal of the American Medical Association* 96, no. 1 (January 3, 1931): 42.

6. *Journal of the American Medical Association* 95, no. 5 (January 31, 1931): 385.

7. Web site: http://www.oneworld.org/vso/campaign/baby.htm.

8. Web site: http://www.oneworld.org/unicef/igbm.htm.

9. A. S. Ryan, "The resurgence of breastfeeding in the United States," *Pediatrics* 99, no. 4 (April 1997): E12.

10. Rachael Hamlet, Web site for Breastfeeding Advocacy.

11. Web site: http://www.carnationbaby.com/home/special.html.

12. "Infant formula boycott," *Nutrition Week* 27, no. 12 (March 28, 1997): 7/*New York Times,* March 3, 1997. As cited in *Clinical Pearls 1997,* 211.

13. Carol L. Wagner, M.D., and Diane M. Anderson, Ph.D., R.D., William B. Pittard, III, M.D., "Special properties of human milk," *Clinical Pediatrics,* June 1996, 285–86.

14. Karen Pryor, *Nursing Your Baby* (NY: Harper & Row Publishers, 1973), 47–48.

15. J. Lehtonen, M. Kononen, M. Purhonen, et al., "The effect of nurs-

ing on the brain activity of the newborn," *Journal of Pediatrics* 132, no. 4 (April 1998): 646–51.

16. K. Paul, J. Dittrichova, and H. Papousek, "Infant feeding behavior: Development in patterns and motivation," *Developmental Psychobiology* 29, no. 7 (November 1996): 563–76.

17. Jean A. T. Pemington, *Food Values of Portions Commonly Used* (NY: Harper & Row Publishers, 1989), 151.

18. Udo Erasmus, *Fats and Oils: The Complete Guide to Fats and Oils in Health and Nutrition* (Vancouver, Canada: Alive Books, 1986), 218.

19. James Woods, "Is docosahexaenoic acid necessary in infant formula? Evaluation of high linolenate diets in the neonatal rat," *Pediatric Research,* 40, no. 5 (1996): 687–693. As cited in *Clinical Pearls 1997,* 210.

20. Innis, 1991, 66–67.

21. Odutuga, "Long-term deficiency of essential fatty acids in rats and its effect on brain recovery," *Clinical and Experimental Pharmacology and Physiology* 6, no. 4 (July–August): 361–66.

22. R. A. Gibson and M. Makrides, "The role of long chain polyunsaturated fatty acids (LCPUFA) in neonatal nutrition," *Acta Paediatr* 87, no. 10 (October 1998): 1017–22.

23. Sheila Innis, Ph.D, "Plasma and red blood cell fatty acid values as indexes of essential fatty acids in the developing organs of infants fed with milk or formulas," *Journal of Pediatrics,* 120, no. 4, part 2 (April 1992): S78–S86.

24. James L. Groff, Sareen S. Gropper, and Sara M. Hunt, *Advanced Nutrition and Human Metabolism* (Minneapolis/St. Paul: West Publishing Company, 1995), 490.

25. Groff, 1995, 490–91.

26. Some research seems to indicate that formula feeding may result in higher rates of schizophrenia. In one study published in Scotland, researchers noted that "schizophrenia may in some cases be a neurodevelopmental disorder. Breast milk is important to the developing brain . . . patients who had not been breast-fed had more

schizoid and schizotypal personality traits in childhood and a poorer social adjustment than their siblings; breast-fed patients did not differ from their siblings. Fewer schizophrenic patients than normal were breast-fed. Lack of breast milk may be a risk factor in the neurodevelopmental form of schizophrenia." (R. G. McCreadie, "The Nithsdale Schizophrenia Surveys. Breast-feeding and schizophrenia: preliminary results and hypotheses," *British Journal of Psychiatry* 170 (April 1997): 334–37. The problem may not be so much in the quantity of fatty acids in the formulas but in the way the body processes those fatty acids. Schizophrenics lack an enzyme that processes fatty acids, leading to a fatty acid metabolism disorder. (S. P. Mahadik, N. S. Shendarkar, R. E. Scheffer, et al., "Utilization precursor essential fatty acids in culture by skin fibroblasts from schizophrenic patients and normal controls," *Prostaglandins Leukotrienes, Essential Fatty Acids* 55, nos. 1–2, 65–70.

27. G. Dorner, G. Bewer, and H. Lubs, "Changes of the plasma tryptophan to neutral amino acids ratio in formula-fed infants: possible effects on brain development," *Experiments in Clinical Endocrinology* 82, no. 3 (November 1983): 368–71.

28. M. W. Yogman, S. H. Zeisel, "Diet and sleep patterns in newborn infants," *New England Journal of Medicine* 309, no. 19 (November 10, 1983): 1147–49. Also: M. W. Yogman, S. H. Zeisel, "Nutrients, neurotransmitters and infant behavior," *American Journal of Clinical Nutrition* 42, no. 2 (August 1985): 352–60. L. A. Steinberg, N. C. O'Connell, T. F. Hatch, M. F. Picciano, and L. L. Birch, "Tryptophan intake influences infants' sleep latency," *Journal of Nutrition* 122, no. 9 (September 1992): 1781–91. See also article by Burgos I. Gonzalez-Burgos, et al., "Tryptophan restriction causes long-term plastic changes in corticofrontal pyramidal neurons," *International Journal of Developmental Neuroscience* 14, no. 5 (August 14, 1996): 673–79.

29. Wagner, 1996, 283–284.

30. D. L. Sparks and J. C. Hunsaker, III, "Sudden infant death syn-

drome: altered aminergic-cholinergic synaptic markers in hypothal-amus," *Journal of Childhood Neurology* 6, no. 4 (October 1991): 335–39.

31. L. J. Horwood and D. M. Fergusson, "Breastfeeding and later cog-nitive and academic outcomes," *Pediatrics* 101, no. 1 (January 1998): E9. Also: J. Golding, I. S. Rogers, P. M. Emmett, "Association be-tween breast feeding, child development and behaviour," *Early Hu-man Development* 49 (October 29, 1997) Suppl: S175–84.

32. G. Faldela, M. Govoni, R. Alessandroni, et al., "Visual evoked potentials and dietary long chain polyunsaturated fatty acids in preterm infants," *Archives of Disease in Childhood, Fetal, Neonatal Ed* 75, no. 2 (September 1996): F108–12. Also: Sheila M. Innis, "Es-sential fatty acids in growth and development," *Progress in Lipid Re-search* 30, no. 1 (1991): 82. J. Woods, G. Ward, and N. J. Salem, "Is docosahexaenoic acid necessary in infant formula? Evaluation of high lenolenate diets in the neonatal rat," *Pediatric Research,* 40 no. 5 (1996): 687–94. As cited in *Clinical Pearls 1997*, 210. V. P. Carnielli, D. J. Wattimena, I. H. Luijendijk, et al., "The very low birth weight premature infant is capable of synthesizing arachidonic and docosa-hexaenoic acids from linoleic and linolenic acids," *Pediatric Research* 40, no. 1 (1996): 169–74. C. L. Jensen, H. Chen, J. K. Fraley, et al., "Biochemical effects of dietary linoleic/alpha-linolenic acid ratio in term infants," *Lipids* 31, no. 1 (1996): 107–13. K. K. Carroll, "Up-per limits of nutrients in infant formulas: polyunsaturated fatty acids and trans fatty acids," *Journal of Nutrition* 199, no. 12S (1989): 1810–13.

33. D. L. Johnson, P. R. Swank, V. M. Howie, et al., "Breast feeding and children's intelligence," *Psychology Report* 79, no. 3, part 2 (Decem-ber 1996): 1179–85.

34. M. Morrow-Tlucak, R. H. Haude, and C. B. Ernhart, "Breastfeed-ing and cognitive development in the first 2 years of life," *Social Science Medicine* 26, no. 6 (1988); 26(6): 635–39. Also: N. Gor-don, "Nutrition and cognitive function," *Brain Development* 1997

Apr;19(3): 165–70. Ricardo Uauy and Isidora e Andraca, "Human milk and breast feeding for optimal mental development," *Journal of Nutrition* 125 (8 Suppl.) (August 1995): 2278S–2280S.

35. Margit Hamosh, "Should infant formulas be supplemented with bioactive components and conditionally essential nutrients present in human milk," *Journal of Nutrition* 127 (5 Suppl.) (May 1997): 971S–974S.

36. Jean Golding, Imogen S. Rogers, and Pauline M. Emmett, "Association between breast feeding, child development and behavior," *Early Human Development* 49 (October 29, 1997): S175–S184. Also: Nancy Auestad, Michael B. Montalto, Robert T. Hall, et al., "Visual acuity, erythrocyte fatty acid composition, and growth in term infants fed formulas with long chain polyunsaturated fatty acids for one year," *Pediatric Research* 41, no. 1, (1997): A8081.

37. "Unresolved issues in the composition of infant formulas; Nutrition for Healthy Term Infants." Statement of the Joint Working Group: Canadian Paediatric Society, Dietitians of Canada, Health Canada, n.d.

38. Scientists have been looking at this issue of formula vs. breast-feeding since 1929. Although scores of studies have been done, scientists can't quite agree on what the results mean. Out of twenty-six publications, from 1929 through 1998, nineteen supported the position that breast-feeding improves cognitive function, but authors complained about the methodology used in the studies. The authors concluded, "Although pediatricians should encourage and support breastfeeding, we should also reassure mothers who formula feed that no convincing evidence indicates they are harming their child's intelligence." A. Jain, J. Concto, and J. M. Leventhal, "How Good is the evidence linking breastfeeding and intelligence?" *APA Abstracts,* no. 369, 135. (See also: A. A. Odutuga, "Long-term deficiency of essential fatty acids in rats and its effect on brain recovery," *Clinical and Experimental Pharmacology and Physiology* 1979 Jul–Aug; 6(4): 361–6.

39. W. V. Welshons, Ph.D. Telephone interview June 8, 1999, with Carol Simontacchi at Vancouver, WA.

40. W. V. Welshons, Ph.D. Telephone interview June 8, 1999, by Carol Simontacchi at Vancouver, WA.

41. H. G. Irvine, M. G. Fitzpatrick and S. L. Alexander, "Phytoestrogens in soy-based infant foods: concentrations, daily intake, and possible biological effects," *Proceedings of the Society of Experimental Biology and Medicine* 217 (1998): 250.

42. Sally Fallon, Telephone interview with Carol Simontacchi, February 11, 1999, Vancouver, WA.

43. Irvine, 1998, 247–53.

44. Dr. Welshons is more concerned about the effects of artificial estrogens (xenoestrogens) than plant estrogens (phytoestrogens). Artificial estrogens (found in many plastics, for example) have only been around for forty years, and we have not developed protection against them. Artificial estrogens are ubiquitous in the environment and have similar effects on the body as our own estrogens. (W. V. Welshons, Ph.D. Telephone interview with Carol Simontacchi, June 8, 1999, Vancouver, WA.)

45. "Baby Alert: New findings about plastics," from the Consumer Reports Website, 4/23/99.

46. Mike Fitzpatrick and Sue Dibb, "Soya infant formula: the health concerns and addendum. A food commission briefing paper," October, 1998. Unpublished in the private collection of Dr. Mike Fitzpatrick, New Zealand.

47. Ann Louise Gittleman, *Why Am I Always So Tired?* (San Francisco: HarperCollins, 1999): 56–57.

48. Fallon, 1999, Vancouver, WA.

49. A. Odutuga, "Effects of low-zinc status and essential fatty acid deficiency on growth and lipid composition of rat brain," *Clin Exp Pharmacol Physiol* 9, no. 2 (May–April 1982): 213–21. Also: E. Wasantwisut, "Nutrition and development: other micronutrients' effect on growth and cognition," *Southeast Asian Journal of Tropical Medicine Public Health* 28, Suppl. 2 (1997): 78–82.

50. *Journal of the American Medical Association,* 95, no. 21 (November 22, 1930): 1616.

51. Elizabeth Williams, M.D., M.P.H., and Lawrence W. Hammer M.D., "breast feeding attitudes and knowledge of pediatricians-in-training," *American Journal of Preventive Medicine* 11, no. 1 (1995): 11(1)26–33. As cited in *Clinical Pearls 1995,* 45.

52. S. M. Virtanen et al., "Diet, cow's milk protein antibodies and the risk of IDDM in Finnish children," *Diabetologia* 37 (1994): 381–87. As cited in *Clinical Pearls 1994,* 144. Also: Woodrow C. Monte, Ph.D., R. D., et al., "Bovine serum albumin detected in infant formula as a possible trigger for insulin-dependent diabetes mellitus," *Journal of the American Dietetic Association* 94, no. 3 (March 1994): 34–316. As cited in *Clinical Pearls 1994,* 143. David J. Pettitt, et al., "Breastfeeding and incidence of non-insulin-dependent diabetes mellitus in Pima Indians," *The Lancet* 350 (July 19, 1997): 166–68. As cited in *Clinical Pearls 1997,* 131.

53. "American Academy of Pediatrics committee on nutrition: The use of whole cow's milk in infancy," *Pediatrics* 89, no. 6, part 1 (June 1992): 1105–9.

54. M. A. Crawford, "The role of essential fatty acids in neural development: Implications for perinatal nutrition," *American Journal of Clinical Nutrition* 57 (5 Suppl); (May 1993): 703S–709S; discussion 709S–710S.

55. Jill B. Becker, S. Marc Breedlove, and David Crews, *Behavioral Endocrinology* (Cambridge, MA: A Bradford Book, 1993), 242.

56. Berthold Koletzko, "Trans fatty acids and the human infant," *World Review in Nutrition and Diet* 75 (1994): 82–85. As cited in *Clinical Pearls 1995,* 217. Also Susan E. Carlson, et al., "Trans fatty acids: infant and fetal development," *American Journal of Clinical Nutrition* 66, no. 3 (September 1997).

57. Sally Fallon, *Nourishing Traditions* (San Diego, CA: ProMotion Publishing, 1995), 559–62.

Chapter Four

1. Nancy Appleton, Ph.D., *Lick the Sugar Habit* (Garden City Park, NY: Avery Publishing Group, 1996), 149–150.
2. L. Kathleen Mahan and Marian Arlin, *Krause's Food, Nutrition & Diet Therapy* (Philadelphia: W. B. Saunders Company, 1992), 275.
3. Environmental Working Group, press release issued January 29, 1998.
4. "Group Finds Low Levels of Pesticides in Baby Food," *Nutrition Week* 25, no. 3 (July 28, 1995): 3. As cited in *Clinical Pearls 1996*, 212.
5. Herman Delvo and Biing-Hwan Lin, "AREI./Production Inputs," USDA Web site, 104.
6. Information from the Environmental Working Group Web site.
7. "Infant risks from pesticides," in Environmental Working Group home page.
8. Gerard Tortora and Sandra Reynolds Grabowski, *Principles of Anatomy and Physiology* (NY: HarperCollins College Publishers, 1993), 418.
9. HVP (hydrolyzed vegetable protein) contains large amounts of MSG. Dr. Blaylock writes, ". . . this substance is even more dangerous than MSG . . . and there is evidence that excitotoxins are still added to baby foods today. Usually these are in the form of caseinate, beef or chicken broth, or flavoring." Russell L. Blaylock, M.D., *Excitotoxins: The Taste That Kills* (Santa Fe, NM: Health Press, 1997), xix.
10. Russell Blaylock, M.D., interview by Carol Simontacchi, telephone interview, March 1, 1999, Vancouver, WA.
11. "Food allergies rare but risky," *FDA Consumer*, May 1994.
12. Blaylock, 1997, 66.
13. Russell L. Blaylock, M.D. Private correspondence with the author, March 8, 1999.
14. Betsy Bates, "Rich or poor, children aren't eating right," *Family Practice News*, July 1, 1995: 19. As cited in *Clinical Pearls 1995*, 213.
15. Ernest Pollitt, Santiago Cueto, and Enrique R. Jacoby, "Fasting and cognition in well- and undernourished schoolchildren: A review of

three experimental studies," *The American Journal of Clinical Nutrition* 1198, no. 67 (Suppl.): 779S–84S.

16. Anna Maria Siega-Riz, Barry M. Popkin, and Terri Carson, "Trends in breakfast consumption for children in the United States from 1965 to 1991," *The American Journal of Clinical Nutrition* 67 (Suppl.) (1998): 748S–756S.

17. Ernesto Pollitt and Rebecca Mathews, "Breakfast and cognition: An integrative summary," *The American Journal of Clinical Nutrition* 67 (Suppl.) (1998): 804S–13S. Also: Eileen Kennedy and Carol Davis, "US Department of Agriculture school breakfast program," *The American Journal of Clinical Nutrition* 67 (Suppl.) (1998): 798S–803S.

18. "How breakfast foods were invented" Kelloggs.com Web site.

19. B. A. Dennison, et al., "Fruit and vegetable intake in young children," *Journal of the American College of Nutrition* 17, no. 4 (1998): 371–78. As cited in *Clinical Pearls 1998*, 284.

20. The source of nutrition information for this chart is taken from the Nutritionist IV database. The nutritional information provided to the database by the manufacturers has not been verified by independent assay.

21. Jay Wade White and Mark Wolraich, "Effect of sugar on behavior and mental performance," *American Journal of Clinical Nutrition* 62 (Suppl.) (1995): 242S–9S. As cited in *Clinical Pearls 1995*, 105. Mark L. Wolraich, M.D., et al., "The effect of sugar on behavior or cognition in children: A meta-analysis," *Journal of the American Medical Association* 274, no. 20 (November 22/29, 1995): 1617–1622. As cited in *Clinical Pearls, 1996*, 46.

22. G. Borok, "Is butter bad for you?" *South African Medical Journal* 72 (August 1, 1987): 227. As cited in *Clinical Pearls 1996*, 182.

23. Melvyn R. Werbach, M.D., *Nutritional Influences on Mental Illness: A Sourcebook of Clinical Research* (Tarzana, CA: Third Line Press, Inc., 1991).

24. K. H. Hofle, "Magnesium in psychotherapy," *Magnesium Research* 1, no. 1/2 (1988): 99. As cited in *Clinical Pearls 1990*, 378.

25. Sherry Rogers, M.D., "Chemical sensitivity: Breaking the paralyzing paradigm: How knowledge of chemical sensitivity enhances the treatment of chronic disease," *Internal Medicine World Report* 1992:7(8):13–41. As cited in *Clinical Pearls 1992*, 173.

26. Alvin N. Eden, M.D., and Mohammad A. Mir, M.D., "Iron Deficiency in 1- to 3-Year Old Children: A Pediatric Failure?" *Archives of Pediatric and Adolescent Medicine* 151 (October 1997): 986–988. As cited in *Clinical Pearls 1998*, 251.

27. "The use of whole cow's milk in infancy: Committee on nutrition," *Pediatrics* 89, no. 6 (June 1991): 1105–1107. As cited in *Clinical Pearls 1992*, 354.

28. B. Lozoff and G. M. Brittenham, "Behavioral alterations in iron deficiency," *Hematological Oncology Clinic of North America* 1, no. 3 (September 1987): 449–64.

29. Melvyn R. Werbach, M.D., *Nutritional Influences on Mental Illness: A Sourcebook of Clinical Research* (Tarzana, CA: Third Line Press, Inc., 1991).

30. Harold H. Sandstead, M.D., "Is Zinc deficiency a public health problem," *Nutrition* 11 (1995): 87–92. As cited in *Clinical Pearls 1995*, 279. Also: Ananda S. Prasad, M.D., Ph.D. "Zinc: An Overview," *Nutrition* 11 (1995): 93–99. As cited in *Clinical Pearls 1995*, 280.

31. Mari S. Golub, Peter T. Takeuchi, Carl L. Keen, et al., "Activity and attention in zinc-deprived adolescent monkeys," *The American Journal of Clinical Nutrition* 64 (1996): 908–15.

32. David L. Watts, *Elemental and Other Essential Nutrients* (First Writer's B-L-O-C-K, 1995), 162.

33. Bryan Lask, M.D., et al., "Zinc deficiency and child-onset anorexia nervosa," *Journal of Clinical Psychiatry* 54, no. 2 (February 1993): 63–66. As cited in *Clinical Pearls 1993*, 23. Also: "Anorexia nervosa, vegetarianism and zinc supply, absorption are reduced," *Nutrition and the M.D.* (June 1993): 3. As cited in *Clinical Pearls 1993*, 23.

34. Information taken from the FDA Web site.

35. Audrey H. Ensminger, M. E. Ensminger, James E. Konlande, and

John R. K. Robson, *Foods & Nutrition Encyclopedia,* 2nd edition (Boca Raton, FL: CRC Press), 17.

36. E. Hollander, M. R. Liebowitz, J. M. Gorman, B. Cohen, A. Fyer, and D. F. Klein, "Cortisol and sodium lactate-induced panic," *Archives of General Psychiatry* 46, no. 2 (February 1989): 135–40.

37. M. R. Liebowitz, J. M. Gorman, A. Fyer, et al., "Possible mechanisms for lactate's induction of panic," *American Journal of Psychiatry* 143, no. 4 (April 1986): 495–502.

38. K. E. Binkley and S. Kutcher, "Panic response to sodium lactate infusion in patients with multiple chemical sensitivity syndrome," *Journal of Allergy and Clinical Immunology* 99, no. 4 (April 1997): 570–74. Also: E. Hollander et al., "Cortisol and sodium lactate-induced panic," *Archives of Geneneral Psychiatry* 46, no. 2 (February 1989): 135–40; M. R. Liebowitz, "Possible mechanisms for lactate's induction of panic," *American Journal of Psychiatry* 143, no. 4 (April 1986): 495–502; E. R. Peskind et al., "Sodium lactate and hypertonic sodium chloride induce equivalent panic incidence, panic symptoms, and hypernatremia in panic disorder," *Biological Psychiatry* 44, no. 10 (November 15, 1998): 1007–16.

39. W. A. Nish, B. A. Whisman, D. W. Goetz, D. A. Ramirez, "Anaphylaxis to annatto dye: A case report," *Annals of Allergy* 66, no. 2 (February 1991): 129–31.

40. K. S. Rowe and K. J. Rowe, "Synthetic food coloring and behavior: a dose response effect in a double-blind, placebo-controlled, repeated-measures study," *Journal of Pediatrics* 125, no. 5, part 1 (November 1994): 691–98.

41. C. M. Carter, M. Uranowicz, and R. Hemsley, "Effects of a few food additives in attention deficit disorder," *Archive of Diseases of Childbirth, Fetal, Neonatal* 69, no. 5 (November 1993): 564–68. Also: Z. E. Koslowska, "Evaluation of mental status of children with malabsorption syndrome after long-term treatment with gluten-free diet," *Psychiatria Polska* 25, no. 2 (March–April 1991): 130–34. S. H. Zeisel, "Dietary influences on neurotransmission," *Adv Pediatr* 33 (1986): 23–47.

42. H. M. Anthony, et al., "Food Intolerance," *The Lancet,* July 9, 1994: 344: 136–37. As cited in *Clinical Pearls 1994,* 21.

43. Miriam E. Tucker, "Reaction to food not necessarily an allergy," *Family Practice News,* April 15, 1998, 38. As cited in *Clinical Pearls 1998,* 75.

44. Philpott, 1987, 16, 17. Also: C. Peter Bennett, Leonard M. McEwen, Helen C. McEwen, and Eunice Rose, "The Shipley Project: Treating food allergy to prevent criminal behaviour in community settings," *Journal of Nutritional & Environmental Medicine* 8 (1998): 77–83.

45. T. Gilat, "Lactase Deficiency: The World Pattern Today," *Israel Journal of Medical Science* (1979), 15: 369.

46. Price-Pottenger Nutrition Foundation, Fall/Winter '98 Resource Catalog, 9–11.

47. Campaign for Food Safety, 860 Hwy 61, Little Marais, MN 55614, in the Campaign for Food Safety Web site.

Chapter Five

1. Irene Alleger, "Murderous Children: Morality or Pathology?" *Townsend Letter for Doctors & Patients,* June 1998, 123.

2. George J. Siegel, Bernard W. Agranoff, R. Wayne Alberts, and Perry B. Molinoff, *Basic Neurochemistry.* (NY: Raven Press, 1994), 127.

3. "Young adults have worse eating habits, study says," *Nutrition Week,* April 1996: 2. As cited in *Clinical Pearls 1996,* 141.

4. Susan M. Krebs-Smith, Ph.D., et al., "Fruit and vegetable intakes of children and adolescents in the United States," *Archives of Pediatric and Adolescent Medicine,* 1996;150: 81–86. As cited in *Clinical Pearls 1996,* 213.

5. L. Kathleen Mahan and Marian Arlin, *Krause's Food, Nutrition & Diet Therapy* (Philadelphia: W. B. Saunders Company, 1992), 278.

6. G. I. Feunekes, C. de Graaf, S. Meyboom, and W. A. van Staveren, "Food choice and fat intake of adolescents and adults: associations of intakes within social networks," *Preventive Medicine* 27, no. 5, part 1 (September–October): 645–56.

7. D. Neumark-Sztainer, M. Story, M.D., Resnick, and R. W. Blum, "Lessons learned about adolescent nutrition from the Minnesota Adolescent Health Survey," *Journal of the American Dietetic Association* 98, no. 12 (December 1998): 1449–56.

8. "Share of F/S biz jumps to 14.8% in 1997," *Food Service Director,* July 15, 1998, 1S–2S.

9. Jeff Hirshfield, "School vending: Healthy foods vs. profits," *Food Service Director,* July 15, 1998, 8S.

10. *The Little Big Fact Book,* American School Food Service Association pamphlet, 3.

11. Shelley Morrison, "Borrowing from the best," *School Foodservice & Nutrition,* May 1998, 19.

12. Penny McLaren, "School foodservice gets value from vending," *School Food Service & Nutrition,* May 1998, 29.

13. Penny McLaren, "Dealing with the devil?" *School Foodservice & Nutrition,* May 1998, 30.

14. Advertisement, *School Foodservice & Nutrition,* February 1990, 75.

15. M. Siega-Riz, B. M. Popkin, and T. Carson, "Trends in breakfast consumption for children in the United States from 1965–1991," *American Journal of Clinical Nutrition* 67, no. 4 (April 1998): 748S–756S.

16. J. A. Pennington, "Intakes of minerals from diets and foods: Is there a need for concern?" *Journal of Nutrition* 126 (9 Suppl.) (September 1996): 2305S–2308S. Also: Charlotte Gallagher-Allred, Ph.D., "Managing common adolescent nutritional problems," *Family Practice Recertification* 17, no. 7 (July 1995): 21–34. As cited in *Clinical Pearls 1996,* 212.

17. J. A. Pennington and S. A. Schoen, "Total diet study: Estimated dietary intakes of nutritional elements, 1982–1991," *International Journal of Vitamin Nutrition Research* 66, no. 4 (1996): 350–62.

18. D. I. Evans, "Cerebral function in iron deficiency: A review," *Child Care Health Developments* 11, no. 3 (May–June 1985): 105–12. Also: I. de Andraca, M. Castillo, and T. Walter, "Psychomotor development and behavior in iron-deficient anemic infants," *Nutrition Review* 55, no. 4 (April 1997): 125–32.

19. O. B. Oloyede, A. T. Folayan, and A. A. Odutuga, "Effects of low-iron status and deficiency of essential fatty acids on some biochemical constituents of rat brain," *Biochemistry International* 27, no. 5 (August 1992): 913–22.

20. Y. A. Parks and B. A. Wharton, "Iron deficiency and the brain," *Acta Paediatrics Scandandavia Suppl* 361 (1989): 71–7. See also: T. Walter, "Infancy: mental and motor development," *American Journal of Clinical Nutrition* 50 (3 Suppl.) (September 1989): 655–61.

21. P. W. Landfield and G. A. Morgan, "Chronically elevating plasma Mg2+ improves hippocampal frequency potentiation and reversal learning in aged and young rats," *Brain Research* 322, no. 1 (November 1984): 167–71.

22. Groff, 1995, 370–72.

23. Y. H. Ahn, Y. H. Kim, S. H. Hong, and J. Y. Kohn, "Depletion of intracellular zinc induces protein synthesis-dependent neuronal apoptosis in mouse cortical culture," *Experimental Neurology* 154, no. 1 (November 198): 47–56. Also: D. W. Choi and J. Y. Kohn, "Zinc and brain injury," *Annual Review of Neuroscience* 21 (1998): 347–75.

24. M. M. Black, "Zinc deficiency and child development," *American Journal of Clinical Nutrition* 68 (2 Suppl.) (August 1998): 464S–69S.

25. Kristin E. Weaver, R.N., M.S., and Lola D. McBean, M.S., R.D., "Zinc Deficiency and the Risk of Infection," *Special Report: Zinc*, December 20, 1993, 15–20. As cited in *Clinical Pearls 1994*, 197.

26. Watts, 1995, 84. Also: Gittleman, 1999, 58–59.

27. Wayne Colwell, Ph.D. Personal interview with Carol Simontacchi, January, 1999, Vancouver, WA.

28. James Dobson, Ph.D., "Who's at fault when kids go bad?" *Dr. James Dobson's Bulletin,* March, 1999.

29. Stephen J. Schoenthaler, Ph.D., and Ian D. Bier, N.D., Ph.D. (candidate) "Vitamin-mineral intake and intelligence: A macrolevel analysis of randomized controlled trials," *The Journal of Alternative and Complementary Medicine* 5, no. 2 (April 1999): 125–134.

30. J. B. Tu, H. Shafey, and C. VanDewetering, "Iron deficiency in two

adolescents with conduct, dysthymic and movement disorders," *Canadian Journal of Psychiatry* 39, no. 6 (August 1994).

31. "New studies show strong links between diet, behavior," *Crime Times,* 4, no. 1 (1998): 1–4.

32. J. R. Hibbeln, J. C. Umhau, M. Linnoila, et al., "A replication study of violent and nonviolent subjects: cerebrospinal fluid metabolites of serotonin and dopamine are predicted by plasma essential fatty acids," *Biological Psychiatry* 44, no. 4 (August 15, 1998): 243–49. Also: M. F. Virkkunen, D. F. Horrobin, D. K. Jenkins, M. S. Manku, "Plasma phospholipid essential fatty acids and prostaglandins in alcoholic, habitually violent, and impulsive offenders," *Biological Psychiatry* 22, no. 9 (September 1987): 1087–96.

33. Stephen Schoenthaler, Ph.D., Stephen Amos, Ph.D., Walter Doraz, Ph.D., et al., "The effect of randomized vitamin-mineral supplementation on violent and non-violent antisocial behavior among incarcerated juveniles," *Journal of Nutritional and Environmental Medicine* 7 (1997): 343–52.

34. Peter W. Bennett, B.A., M.A., M.B.A.; Leonard M. McEwen, M.A., B.M., B.C.; Helen C. McEwen, M.B., B.S.; and Eunice L. Rose, "The Shipley Project: Treating food allergy to prevent criminal behaviour in community settings," *Journal of Nutritional and Environmental Medicine* 8 (1998): 77–83.

35. Joy G. Dryfoos, *Adolescents at Risk: Prevalence and Prevention* (NY: Oxford University Press, 1990), 96.

36. "Brains and vitamins," *The Lancet* 337, no. 8741 (March 9, 1991): 587(2).

37. William Walsh, Ph.D. Telephone interview with Carol Simontacchi, June 8, 1999, Vancouver, WA.

38. Ian Bier, N.D., Ph.D. Telephone interview with Carol Simontacchi, June 8, 1999, Vancouver, WA.

Chapter Six

1. Deepak Chopra, M.D., *Quantum Healing: Exploring the Frontiers of Mind/Body Medicine* (NY: Bantam Books, 1990), 48–49.

2. Daniel H. Lowenstein and Jack M. Parent, "Enhanced: Brain, heal thyself," *Science* 283, no. 5405 (February 19, 1999): 1126–27.

3. Jill B. Becker, S. Marc Breedlove, and David Crews, *Behavioral Endocrinology* (Cambridge, MA: A Bradford Book, 1993), 295.

4. Becker, 1993, 353.

5. Michael Jacobson, Ph.D, "Liquid candy: How soft drinks are harming Americans' health," *CSPI newsletter.*

6. B. E. Garrett and R. R. Griffiths, "The role of dopamine in the behavioral effects of caffeine in animals and humans," *Pharmacology, Biochemistry, and Behavior* 57, no. 3 (July 1997): 533–41. Also: S. J. Heishman and J. E. Henningfield, "Stimulus functions of caffeine in humans: Relation to dependence potential," *Neuroscience Biobehavioral Review* 16, no. 3 (Fall 1992): 273–87. Also: A. Nehlig, A. "Are we dependent upon coffee and caffeine? A review on human and animal data," *Neuroscience and Biobehavioral Review,* 23, no. 4 (March 1999): 563–76.

7. J. W. Daly, J. Holmen, and B. B. Fredholm, "Is caffeine addictive? The most widely used psychoactive substance in the world affects same parts of the brain as cocaine," *Lakartidningen* 95, nos. 51–52 (December 16, 1998): 5878–83.

8. Becker 1993, 114.

9. Becker 1993, 326.

10. A. Nehlig, J. L. Daval, and G. Debry, "Caffeine and the central nervous system: Mechanisms of action, biochemical, metabolic and psychostimulant effects," *Brain Research Review* 17, no. 2 (May–August 1992): 139–70.

11. If you think coffee isn't driving you crazy, think about the effects it is having on your unborn child. Heavy caffeine consumption (four hundred milligrams per day) during pregnancy increases the risk of SIDS (Sudden Infant Death Syndrome). Mice and rat studies show that when pregnant females drink coffee, their offspring show greater tendency toward hyperactive behavior, were more likely to pick fights with others, felt more threatened in social situations, were more likely to bite, and showed anger more quickly. They also

spent less time grooming themselves and staying amused with interesting objects. (J. S. Ajarem and M. Ahmad, "Behavioral and biochemical consequences of perinatal exposure of mice to instant coffee: A correlative evaluation," *Pharmacol Biochem Behav* 40, no. 4 (December 1991): 847–52. Also: J. S. Ajarem and M. Ahmad, "Teratopharmacological and behavioral effects of coffee in mice," *Acta Physiologica Pharmacologica Bulgaria* 22, no. 2 (1996): 51–61.) Are the problems associated with effects on the fetus confined to caffeine beverages? Unfortunately, no. Decaffeinated coffee produced the same types of behavioral changes in the offspring of coffee drinkers. Those effects may come from one of the other two hundred ninety-nine chemicals in the brew. While these studies focused on rats and mice, human studies confirm that fetal exposure to relatively high levels of coffee, cigarettes, or alcohol predisposes both boys and girls (but, more commonly, boys) to obsessive-compulsive disorders mixed with Tourette's syndrome.

12. Jack E. James, Ph.D., "Caffeine withdrawal and cardiovascular risk. Is habitual caffeine use a preventable cardiovascular risk factor?" Interview cited in *Clinical Pearls 1997*, 283–84.

13. Lois E. Krahn, M.D., "Use of caffeine in medically refractory seizure patients," *Neuropsychiatry, Neuropsychology and Behavioral Neurology* 7, no. 2 (1994): 136. As cited in *Clinical Pearls 1994*, 290.

14. M. Gary Hadfield, "Caffeine and the olfactory bulb," *Molecular Neurobiology* 15 (1997): 15: 31–39. As cited in *Clinical Pearls 1998*, 121.

15. Eric C. Strain, M.D., et al., "Caffeine Dependence Syndrome: Evidence from case histories and experimental evaluations," *Journal of the American Medical Association* 272, no. 13 (October 5, 1994): 1043–1048. As cited in *Clinical Pearls 1994*, 66.

16. "Supermarket Shopping Basket," *The Wall Street Journal Almanac*, 1998.

17. "Caffeine Abuse," COHIS Web site, March 31, 1999.

18. Ted R. Lingle, "Avenues for growth: A 20-year review of the U.S. specialty coffee market," Prepared for the Specialty Coffee Association of America, January 1993.

19. "The Story of NutraSweet," Monsanto Web site, April 13, 1999.

20. Groff, 1995, 499.

21. "Report on all adverse reactions in the adverse reaction monitoring system," Department of Health and Human Services, February 25 and 28, 1994. As cited by the Aspartame Consumer Safety Network.

22. Eric R. Braverman, M.D., and Carl C. Pfeiffer, M.D., Ph.D, *The Healing Nutrients Within* (New Canaan, CT: Keats Publishing Company, 1987): 220.

23. Groff, 1995, 499.

24. "Aspartame is, by far, the most dangerous substance on the market that is added to foods," Aspartame Consumer Safety Network monograph.

25. Mary Nash Stoddard and George Leighton. "Aspartame & flying: The incredible untold story," Aspartame Consumer Safety Network monograph.

26. Monsanto.com Web site information, April 13, 1999.

27. Deborah Halber, "Study reaffirms safety of aspartame," *Tech Talk*, MIT News Office at the Massachusetts Institute of Technology, Cambridge, Mass. From the Monsanto Web site, April 12, 1999.

28. Colleen Dermody and Penny Miller, "Saccharin review corrupted by industry influence, charges CSPI," from the CSPI Web site, December 17, 1998.

29. Steven Farber, "The Price of Sweetness," *Technology Review* (January 1990): 46–53.

30. Francis S. Greenspan and John D. Baxter, *Basic & Clinical Endocrinology* (Norwalk, CT: Appleton & Lange, 1994), 335.

31. M. L. Budd, "Hypoglycemia and Personality," *Complementary Therapies in Medicine* 2 (1994): 142–46. As cited in *Clinical Pearls 1994*, 190.

32. "Over 7,000 aspartame complaints since '81, FDA says; controversy remains," *Nutrition Week* 25, no. 20 (May 26, 1995): 1–2. As cited in *Clinical Pearls 1995*, 8.

33. Nathan Pritikin, *The Pritikin Promise* (NY: Pocket Books, 1983), 29.

34. John A. McDougall, M.D., *The McDougall Program: 12 Days to Dynamic Health* (NY: Penguin Books, 1990), 40, 41.

35. John A. McDougall and Mary A. McDougall, *The McDougall Plan* (NY: New Win Publishing, Inc., 1983), 76, 77.

36. McDougall, 1983, 89.

37. Joseph R. Hibbeln and Norman Salem, Jr., "Dietary polyunsaturated fatty acids and depression: When cholesterol does not satisfy," *American Journal of Clinical Nutrition* 62 (1995): 1–9.

38. Ross E. Morgan, et al., "Plasma cholesterol and depressive symptoms in older men," *The Lancet* 341 (January 9, 1993): 75–79. As cited in *Clinical Pearls 1993*, 129.

39. Barbara Ploeckinger, et al., "Rapid decrease of serum cholesterol concentration and postpartum depression," *British Medical Journal*, September 14, 1996; 313: 664. As cited in *Clinical Pearls 1997*, 128.

40. M. Y. Agargun et al., "Low cholesterol level in patients with panic disorder: The association with major depression," *Journal of Affective Disorders*, 1998: 59L28032. As cited in *Clinical Pearls 1998*, 162.

41. John E. Morley, M. B., "Nutritional modulation of behavior and immunocompetence," *Nutrition Reviews* 52, no. 8 (August 1994): S6–S8. Also: Andrew L. Stoll, M.D.; W. Emanual Severus, M.D., Ph.D.; Marlene P. Freeman, M.D.; et al., "Omega-3 fatty acids in bipolar disorder," *Archive of General Psychiatry* 56 (May 1999): 407–12. R. Edwards, M. Peet, J. Shay, and D. Horrobin, "Omega-3 polyunsaturated fatty acids levels in the diet and in red blood cell membranes of depressed patients," *Journal of Affective Disorder* 48, nos. 2–3 (March 1998): 149–55. M. Maes, A. Christophe, J. Delanghe, et al., "Lowered omega-3 polyunsaturated fatty acids in serum phospholipids and cholesteryl esters of depressed patients," *Psychiatry Res* 85, no. 3 (March 22, 1999): 275–91.

42. Rodolfo R. Llinas, *The Biology of the Brain from Neurons to Networks* (NY: W. H. Freeman and Company, 1988), 5–6.

43. J. C. Ayus, D. L. Armstrong, A. I. Arieff, "Effects of hypernatraemia in the central nervous system and its therapy in rats and rabbits,"

Journal of Physiology (Lond) 492, part 1: 243–55 Also: A. Soupart, R. Penninckx, B. Namias, et al., "Brain myelinolysis following hypernatremia in rats," *Journal of Neuropathology and Experimentive Neurology* 55, no. 1 (January 1996): 106–13.

44. E. R. Peskind, C. F. Jensen, M. Pascualy, et al., "Sodium lactate and hypertonic sodium chloride induce equivalent panic incidence, panic symptoms, and hypernatremia in panic disorder," *Biological Psychiatry* 4410: 1007–16 1998 Nov. 15.

45. Tom Brody, *Nutritional Biochemistry* (San Diego: Academic Press, 1994), 512–13.

46. R. Mocharla, S. M. Schexnayder, and C. M. Glasier, "Fatal cerebral edema and intracranial hemorrhage associated with hypernatremic dehydration," *Pediatr Radiol* 27, no. 10 (October 1997): 785–87. Also: K. Dunn and W. Butt, "Extreme sodium derangement in a paediatric inpatient population," *Journal of Paediatrics and Child Health* 33, no. 1 (February 1997): 26–30.

Appendix I

RESOURCES

Research Project Results

For a formal presentation of the Breakfast Drink research project at Vancouver Christian High School, request an e-mail copy from Carol, or send a SASE to Carol Simontacchi, PO Box 5025, Vancouver, WA 98668. (CSimontacchi@cs.com)

Carol Simontacchi's favorite cookbooks include the following:

Feuer, Janice. *Fruit-Sweet and Sugar Free.* Rochester, VT: Healing Arts Press, 1993.

Child, Julia. *The Way to Cook.* NY: Alfred A. Knopf, 1989.

Woodruff, Sandra. *Secrets of Cooking for Long Life.* NY: Avery Publishing Group, 1999.

Kinderlehrer, Jane. *Smart Cookies.* NY: Newmarket Press, 1985.

Compestine, Ving Chang. *Secrets of Fat-Free Chinese Cooking.* NY: Avery Publishing Group, 1999.

Abrams, Joanne, and Marie Caratozzolo. *The No-Time-to-Cook Cookbook.* NY: Avery Publishing Group, 1999.

You can also obtain many healthy, fresh-food recipes from *Cuisine, Gourmet,* and *Bon Appetit* magazines, available at your local newsstand.

Organic Foods

Your best source of nutritional products and organic foods is your local health food store like Whole Foods, Wild Oats, and the independent natural food stores. Most stores carry excellent lines of baby foods, home meal replacements, and snack foods, like Barbara's Bakery, The Well-Fed Baby, Earth Meals Organic, Cool Fruits, Shiloh Farms, Ener-G Foods (for hypoallergenic baking products),

Pamela's Products, Newman's Own Organics, Santa Cruz Fine Foods, and Annie's Naturals.

Shelton's Poultry provides excellent organic poultry. Shelton's also provides an excellent MSG-free line of broths, as does Pacific Naturals. Coleman's provides organic beef. Organic seafoods are also available from various providers, and browsing the aisles of your local health food store you will find other high-quality, organic food lines.

Appendix II

NUTRITIONIST REFERRALS

For a referral for a nutritionist or a nutritionally trained physician in your area:

International and American Associations of Clinical Nutritionists
1-972-407-9089

American College of Nutrition
1-212-777-1037

American Association of Naturopathic Physicians
1-206-298-0126

American Preventive Medical Association
1-800-230-2762

Pfeiffer Treatment Center
1-630-505-0300
Web site: HRIPTC.org

Society of Certified Nutritionists
1-800-342-8037
Web site: www.certifiednutritionist.com

Vitalcast provides an online information service for complementary medicine, and will provide a list of nutritionally trained physicians in your area, at 813-349-1055.

Index

Acetylcholinesterase, 95

ADD/ADHD, 26

Adenosine triphosphate (ATP), 49, 151–152, 198

Adolescence, 175. *See also* Teenagers

Adrenal glands, 109, 177–178

Adults

  and aspartame, 183–191

  and caffeine, 179–183

  damage to brain cells, 176–177

  and home meal replacements, 196–200

  low blood sugar and aspartame/ sugar combo, 189–191

  and low-fat diet, 191–193

    affect on cognition, 194–196

  nutrition for, 201–202

  responsibilities and tasks of, 175

  stress and cortisol, 177–179

Agricultural changes, 17–18

Ajinomoto Company, 96

Alcohol, 20

  abuse, 28

Aldosterone, 199

Allergens, 120–126

Almond Butter Cookies, 257–258

Alpha-linolenic acid, 48

American Academy of Pediatrics, 61

American food culture, 15–24, 146, 207, 218

American Journal of Clinical Nutrition, 150

American Medical Association, 17, 57–59, 188

American School Food Service Association, 147

Amino acids, 3, 49, 63, 140–141, 161, 185–186, 227

  in infant formula, 67–71

Androgens, 72

Anemia, 151

Angelo's Heirloom Chicken and Olives, 245–246

Annals of Allergy, 119

Annatto, 119

Anorexia, 31–32, 116

Antidepressants, 26

Antinutrition, 177

Arachidonic acid (AA), 43, 71

Artificial ingredients, list, 118. *See also* Food additives

Artificial sweeteners, 3. *See also* Aspartame

Aspartame, 84, 96, 170

  combined with sugar, and low blood pressure, 189–191

  controversy over, 183–189

Aspartame Consumer Safety Network, 187

Aspartic acid, 186–187

Athletic water bottle, 167

Autolyzed yeast, 97

Axons, 40–41, 90, 98, 140

B complex vitamins, 3, 50, 110

  deficiency symptoms, 155, 212–213

Baby food recipes, 227–231

Basic Salad, 252–254

Bean Muffins, 236

Beasley, Joseph, Dr., 20, 32

Beef, hormone-injected, 3

Bier, Ian, Dr., 164

Blaylock, Russell, Dr., 97–99

Blood sugar, 108–110
  disorders, 209–210

Blood-brain barrier, 67, 194

Bonding instinct, 81

Bovine serum albumin (BSA), 78

Boys, effect of soy milk on develop-
    ment, 71–76

Brain
  and aspartame, 183–191
  capacity for regeneration, 176–
    177
  chemistry of and food, 2, 5, 34–35,
    108, 197–200
  and cortisol, 178
  critical growth period in, 16, 39–40,
    42–44
  development
    adolescent, 139–141
    children, 89–91
    infants, 39–52, 79–80
  effect of low-fat diet on cognition,
    194–196
  effect of nutrient deficiencies on,
    150–157
  enzyme activity in, 111–112, 115
  health, 3
    and minerals, 110–117
  new foods and thinking, 15
  nutrients for, 212
  structure, 40–42

Brain Allergies (Philpott), 123, 211

Braised Celery, 252

Bran, 17

Branched-chain amino acids (BCAAs),
    67–68

Breakfast, 150
  drink study, 12–15
  effects of missing, 103–104
  healthy, ideas for, 131–132

Breakfast Burritos, 239–240

Breakfast cereal, 21
  nutrient table, 107–108
  sugar content, 107

Breakfast Crepes with Blueberries,
    238–239

Breakfast Parfait, 234–235

Breast milk composition, 62–65

Breast-feeding, 55–56

Broccoli and Peppers, Stir-Fry, 251–252

Brown Rice in Vegetable Broth, 250

Bulimia, 32, 116

Burritos, Breakfast, 239–240

Caffeine, 180–183

Calcium, 49, 76, 113, 181

Campaign for Food Safety, 92

Campbell's Soup, 199, 201

Cancer, 193

Carbamate, 95

Carbohydrate sensitivity, 190

Carson, Rachel, 1

Celery, Braised, 252

Celeste frozen pizza, 199

Center for Science in the Public Inter-
    est, 118, 188–189

Cereal manufacturers, 106

Cerebral allergy, 122, 211
Cheesy Nutty Blueberry Filling, 239
Chicken and Olives, Angelo's Heirloom, 245–246
Chicken Broth, Rich Brown, 241–242
Chicken Casserole, and Rice, 242–243
Chicken Stew, Baby's, 228–229
Childbirth, 175
Children
    additives in food, 117–120
    allergens in diet, 120–126
    brain development of, 89–91
    caloric requirements for, 91
    food diaries, 101–106
    high-sugar, low-nutrient diet,
        106–108
    minerals and brain health, 110–117
    MSG in food, 96–100
    nutrition for, 130–133
    pesticides in food, 91–96
    sugar trail through the body,
        108–110
Chocolate, 121
Chocolate Pudding, Deep, Dark,
    Delicious, 256
Cholesterol, 64–65, 77, 191–192, 196
Choline, 220
Chopra, Deepak, Dr., 176
Church of England, 61
Cofactors, 141
Coffee, 179–182, 200
Cognition
    disorders of, 32–33
    and nutrition, 208
Cola, 180
Coleslaw, Mom's Pineapple, 254–255

Color Additive Amendment, 93
Colostrum, 62
Community milk banks, 56, 61
Cookies, Almond Butter, 257–258
Copper, 76, 154–155
Corn, 120
    oil, 65
Cortisol, 109, 177–178, 190
Cow's milk, 62, 65–66
Crazy, defined, 1
Cream Puffs with Fresh Fruit Filling,
    258–259
Crepes with Blueberries, Breakfast,
    238–239
Critical period, brain development, 16,
    39–40, 42–44

Dairy, 120–121
A Date with Oatmeal, 238
Deep, Dark, Delicious Chocolate
    Pudding, 256
Delaney Clause, 4
Dendrites, 40–41, 90, 98, 140
Denmark, 19
Depression, 24, 162–165, 195–196
Desserts, brain-friendly, 256–259
Destructive behaviors, 157–159, 207
Diabetes, 193
Diet maximization, 216–220
Diet sodas, 201
Dieticians, 147
Dihomogammalinolenic acid
    (DGLA), 64
Dill Casserole, 255–256
Dinner, 104, 133
    brain-friendly recipes, 240–256

DNA, 112, 115
Dobson, James, Dr., 158
Docosahexaenoic acid (DHA), 43,
    48–49, 66, 71, 161
Dopamine, 140, 181, 220

Eating
    disorders, 24–25, 31–32, 116
    habits, 212
Eicosapentaenoic acid (EPA), 43, 48–49
Endangered Minds (Healy), 33
Endocrine system, 5
Environmental Working Group, 93
Enzyme cofactors, 50
Enzymes, 63, 111–112, 115, 141, 194, 200
Equal, 183
Eskimo, 79
Essential fatty acids, 3, 64–66, 79, 85,
    91, 161, 205, 221
    deficiencies in, 44–49, 98–99,
        138–140, 195–196
*Essential Fatty Acids in Growth and
    Development* (Innis), 65
Estrogen, 71–77, 81, 95, 155, 227
Excitotoxins, 96–99

Fallon, Sally, 73, 85
Family meal, 129, 168
Fast-food, 18, 141, 146–150
Fat-free foods, 24
Fats, 42–49, 139–140, 193, 240. *See also*
    Essential fatty acids; Oils;
    individual fats
    and brain development, 44–49,
        64–66, 91, 98–99
    in breast milk, 64–65

FDA, 98, 117, 184–186, 188
Fish, 79, 227
    oil, 202
Fitzpatrick, Mike, Dr., 75–76
Flaxseed oil, 12, 49, 170, 202
Florentine Sole, 250
Food
    additives, 4–5, 117–120
    allergies, 120–126, 207, 210–211
    ancestral, 2, 44–49
    artificial, 15, 52, 101–106
    genetically altered, 123
    historical role of, 15–16
    manufacturing companies, 1–3
    MSG in, 84, 96–100, 241
    pesticides in, 91–96
Food diaries
    of children, 101–106
    of teens, 21–23, 141, 143–145
The Food Factor (Griggs), 16–17, 19
The Food Factor in Disease (Hare), 20
French fries, 106
Frosty Fruit Shake, 236–237
Fruit Shake, Frosty, 236–237
Fruits, 18, 141, 145

Gamma aminobutyric acid (GABA),
    219–220
Gamma-linolenic acid (GLA), 64
Gerber, 93, 97
Ginkgo biloba, 219
Glucose, 41, 109
Gotu kola, 219
Grain allergies, 83
Granola with Fruit and Nuts, 233–234
Griggs, Barbara, 16–17, 19

Growth factors, 64
Gulf War Syndrome, 187

Hamosh, Margit, 70–71
Hare, Francis, Dr., 20
Healy, Jane, Dr., 33
Heart disease, 191–193
Heartwarming Vegetable Soup, 245
Heavy metal exposure, 211–212
Heme iron, 114
Hidden defects, 51–52
High-sugar, low-nutrient diet, 106–108
Hindhede, Mikkel, 19
Hippocampus, 109, 153, 178
Home meal replacements, 110–111, 113,
    129, 196–200
Homicide rates, 27
Hormones, 5, 15, 40, 42, 139–140, 166,
    177–178, 194, 207
Hydrogenated fats, 79
Hypernatremia, 199–200
Hypoglycemia, 190–191
Hypothyroidism, 208–209

Ice cream, 201
IG reaction, 121
Infant brain development, 39–52
Infant formulas, 55
    compared with breast milk, 65–66
    homemade, 77–78
    marketing of, 56–62
    soy, 71–77
    sugars, minerals, and protein in,
        67–71
Infant nutrition, 80–85
    recipes, 227–231

Innis, Sheila, 65
Insulin, 109, 190
International Baby Food Action Net-
    work, 59–60
International Code of Marketing of
    Breastmilk Substitutes, 59
Iron, 114
    deficiency symptoms, 151, 161, 214
Isoflavones, 71

JAMA (Journal of the American Medical
    Association), 57–58, 77, 182
Japanese, 79
Johnson, Catherine, 29–30
Jungle Bars, 257
Junk food, 168
Juvenile obesity, 78
Juvenile-onset diabetes, 78

Kava kava, 219
The Kellogg Report (Beasley), 20, 32
Kellogg's, 106
Kid Cuisine frozen entrées, 197
Kool-Aid, 101–102
Krebs cycle, 49

The Lancet, 121, 163, 196
Legal drug culture, 25–29
L-glutamine, 220
The Little Big Fact Book, 147
Liver, 109
Low blood sugar, 189–191
Low-fat diet
    affect on cognition, 194–196
    as fraud, 191–193
L-tryptophan, 68, 220

Lunch
  brain-friendly recipes, 240–256
  healthy, ideas for, 132–133, 259–260
  school, 4, 104, 128

Magnesium, 49, 76, 112–113
  deficiency symptoms, 81, 151–153,
    213–214
Malnutrition, 43
Margarine, 3
Massachusetts Institute of Technology,
    189
McCarrison, Robert, Dr., 19
McDonald's Nutrition Facts, 20
McDougall, John, Dr., 192–193
Medication side effects, 211
Memory, 178
Mental health, 24–25
Mental Health Inventory, 208, 218–
    219
Mental illness, 24, 29–34
Menus, 231–233
Methanol poisoning, 187
Microwaving, 228
Milk
  cow's, 62, 65–66
  mother's, 62–65
  organic, 123
  pasteurized and homogenized,
    124–126
  soy, 71–77
Milk Shake, Pregnancy, 226
Minerals, 47, 49–50, 141, 205, 227
  and brain health, 110–117
Mixed drinks, 28
Mom's Pineapple Coleslaw, 254–255

Monosodium glutamate (MSG), 84,
    96–100, 241
Monsanto, 123, 184, 188–189
Mood, and nutrition, 208
Mother's diet, 44–49
Mother's milk
  and brain growth, 79–80
  compared with infant formulas,
    65–66
  composition, 62–65
Mother-to-be, recipes for, 225–227
Muffins, Bean, 236
Multivitamins, 205
Myelin sheath, 42, 44, 64, 77, 90,
    140

National Academy of Sciences, 95
Natural remedies, 219
Natural Treatments for ADD and Hy-
    peractivity (Weintraub), 26
Nerve cells, 39–42, 176–177, 198
Nestlé, 60–61, 123
Neurohormones, 5, 16, 42
Neuronal mitochondria, 41
Neurons, 40–41, 90
Neurotransmitters, 16, 40, 42, 161, 165,
    194, 221
New foods, 15
The New York Times, 26
Nonheme iron, 114
Noradrenaline, 181
Nourishing Traditions (Fallon), 73, 85
NutraSweet, 183–184, 188
Nutrition. See also Menus; Recipes
  for adults, 201–202
  for breast-feeding mother, 83–84

for children, 130–133
improving mood and cognition
    with, 208
for infants, 80–83
for teenagers, 166–171
Nutrition Action Healthletter, 20–21
Nutritional history, 212
Nutrition Week, 61, 93

Oatmeal, A Date with, 238
Obesity, 78, 109
Obsessive-compulsive disorder, 24
Oils, 79, 202
Olive oil, 202, 216
Olney, John, Dr., 97
Omega-3 fatty acids, 12, 47–49, 64–66,
    70, 79, 139–140, 195–196, 227,
    240
Omega-6 fatty acids, 12, 48, 64–65, 70,
    79, 139–140, 240
Organic foods, 84, 227
    vegetables, 164–165
Organophosphates, 92–93, 95
Oscar Mayer, 110, 119
    Lunchables, 110, 119, 199
Oven-Roasted Glazed Salmon,
    246–247
Oxygen, 194
Oxytocin, 81

Packaged entrées, 110–111, 113, 129,
    196–200
Pancreas, 109, 190
Parental influence, 145
Parfait, Breakfast, 234–235
Paxil, 26

Peanuts, 121
Peas and Carrots, Baby's, 230
Pert, Candace, 40
Pesticides, 91–96
Phenylalanine (PHE), 185–186
Phenylketonuria (PKU), 184–185
Philpott, William, Dr., 123, 211
Phosphatidylserine, 195
Phytic acid, 76
Phytochemicals, 71
Plasticity, 90
Postpartum depression, 81
Potassium, 49, 115, 150, 156–157,
    197–200
Pottenger, Frances Jr., Dr., 124–
    125
Pregnancy Milk Shake, 226
Prenatal supplement, 226–227
Prepared entrées. *See* Packaged
    entrées
Price, Weston, Dr., 44–47
Pritikin, Nathan, 192
*Proceedings of the Society for Experi-
    mental Biology and Medicine*,
    73
Processed foods, 18
Profile of Mood States (POMS), 13–14,
    205–206, 208
Progesterone, 81
Protein, 44, 49, 63, 193
    adolescent need for, 140
    breakfast drink, 167
    metabolism by zinc, 116
    undigested, 164–165
Prozac, 25
Pseudofood, 2

Quantum Healing (Chopra), 176
Quiche, Spinach and Mushroom,
    247–249

Raisin Rice Pudding, 235–236
Randolph, Theron, Dr., 19
Ratey, John, 29–30
Receptor sites (brain), 5, 40, 99, 194
Recipes
    Almond Butter Cookies, 257–
        258
    Angelo's Heirloom Chicken and
        Olives, 245–246
    for babies, 227–231
    Basic Salad, 252–254
    Bean Muffins, 236
    Braised Celery, 252
    Breakfast Burritos, 239–240
    Breakfast Crepes with Blueberries,
        238–239
    Breakfast Parfait, 234–235
    Brown Rice in Vegetable Broth, 250
    Cream Puffs with Fresh Fruit Fill-
        ing, 258–259
    A Date with Oatmeal, 238
    Deep, Dark, Delicious Chocolate
        Pudding, 256
    Dill Casserole, 255–256
    Florentine Sole, 250
    Frosty Fruit Shake, 236–237
    Granola with Fruit and Nuts,
        233–234
    Heartwarming Vegetable Soup, 245
    Jungle Bars, 257
    Mom's Pineapple Coleslaw, 254–255
    for mother-to-be, 225–227

Oatmeal and Fruit for a Cool
    Morning, 237–238
Oven-Roasted Glazed Salmon,
    246–247
Raisin Rice Pudding, 235–236
Rice and Chicken Casserole,
    242–243
Rich Brown Chicken Broth,
    241–242
Salmon Salad, 249
Savory Split Pea Soup, 243–244
Spinach and Mushroom Quiche,
    247–249
Stir-Fry Broccoli and Peppers,
    251–252
Vegetable Rice Pilaf, 251
Recommended Dietary Allowance, 227
    for children, 92
    for teenagers, 141–142
Refined carbohydrates, 49
Reproduction, 175
Restaurants, 130
Rice and Chicken Casserole, 242–243
Rice Pilaf, Vegetable, 251
Rice Pudding, Raisin, 235–236
Rich Brown Chicken Broth, 241–242
Ritalin, 25–26
RNA, 112, 115
Rolling mill, 16–17
Rosen, Paul, 31
Ross Laboratories, 60, 71

St. John's wort, 219
Salad, 167–168, 216
    Basic, 252–254
    Salmon, 249

INDEX

Salmon
  Oven-Roasted Glazed, 246–247
  Rice Mousse, Baby's, 229–230
  Salad, 249
SAT scores, 32
Savory Split Pea Soup, 243–244
Schoenthaler, Stephen, Dr., 161–
    162
School
  lunch, 4, 128, 146–150
  violence, 11
School Foodservice & Nutrition, 148
Seafood, 227
Secret of Cooking for Long Life
    (Woodruff), 256
Self-mutilation, 30–31, 207
Self-mutilation (Walsh & Rosen), 31
Serotonin, 68–69, 140, 161, 165,
    181
Shadow Syndromes (Ratey & Johnson),
    29–30
Shellfish, 121
Shopping guidelines, 128–130
Silent Spring (Carson), 1
Sleep, 69
Snacks
  healthy, 82, 169, 217
  junk, 168
Social anxiety/phobia, 25, 30
Sodium, 114–115, 150, 156, 197–200
  benzoate, 118–119
  lactate, 119
Sodium-potassium pump, 198
Soft drinks, 3, 18, 20–21, 127, 168, 180,
    200
Soil impoverishment, 17

Sole, Florentine, 250
South Africa, Union of, 61
South African Medical Journal, 108
Soy, 121
  infant formulas, 71–77
Speech, 90
Spinach and Mushroom Quiche,
    247–249
Split Pea Soup, Savory, 243–244
Sports drink, 167
SSRIs, 26
Standard American Diet (SAD), 3
Starbucks, 179–180
Steroid hormones, 140
Stir-Fry Broccoli and Peppers, 251–252
Stone mills, 17
Stouffer's frozen entrées, 199
Stress, 177–179
Sugar, 3, 49. *See also* Aspartame
  in breakfast cereal, 21, 107
  following through body, 108–110
  in home meal replacements, 197
  increase in consumption, 17–18
  in infant formula, 67
  introduction in America, 20
  metabolization and B vitamins,
    50
  reducing in diet, 217
Suicide rates, 27–28
Supplements, 166–167, 205, 207,
    215

Tactile stimulation, 90
Tartrazine, 119
Tea, 180
Teacher Magazine, 33

Teenagers
  brain development, 139–141
  diet, 3–4, 21–23
  effect of nutrient deficiencies on
    brain, 150–157
  food diaries of, 21–23, 141, 143–145
  foods they eat, 141, 143–
    150
  nutrition for, 166–171
  self-destructive behavior, 157–159,
    297
  suicide rates, 27–28
  violent behavior and nutrition,
    160–165
Testosterone, 71–73
Thiamin, 161
Third World countries, 59–61
Thorndike, Edward Lee, 47
Thyroid hormone, 140–141
Tofu, 152
Toxins, 211–212
Trans-fatty acids, 83–84
Tryptophan, 67–70, 141, 161
Tyrosine, 141, 220

University of Minnesota School of
    Public Health, 145
USDA, 94

Vegetable
  Rice Pilaf, 251
  Soup, Heartwarming, 245
Vegetables, 3, 18, 106, 141, 145, 217
Violence and nutrition, 11, 27, 29,
    160–165
Vitamin B$_3$ deficiency, 165
Vitamin C, 114
Vitamins, 47, 141

Walking wounded, 11
Walsh, Barent, 31
Walsh, William, Dr., 164
Water, 20, 42, 84, 200, 216–217
Weintraub, Skye, Dr., 26
Welshons, Wade, Dr., 72
Wheat, 120
  germ, 17
White flour, 16–17
Winter Squash, Baby's, 230–231
Woodruff, Sandra, 256
Workplace violence, 11, 29
World Health Organization, 60–61

Zinc, 49, 76–77, 115–117
  deficiency symptoms, 153–155,
    214–215
Zoloft, 26

About the author

Carol Simontacchi is a certified clinical nutritionist (CCN) with a Master of Science in Social Sciences and is currently pursuing her Ph.D. in Brain Nutrition from the Union Institute.

Carol's Web site, FlywithWings.com, provides additional information on health and nutrition, including a fifty-two-week curriculum on permanent weight management, called *Wings: Weight Success for a Lifetime.*

For more information on brain nutrition, you can also visit TheCrazyMakers.com

The author welcomes letters and inquiries through e-mail at CSimontacchi@cs.com. Her mailing address is PO Box 658, Sanibel, FL 33957.